BeYOND
tHe
aLtaR

Beyond the altar

Women Religious, Patriarchal Power, and the Church

Christine L. M. Gervais

WILFRID LAURIER
UNIVERSITY PRESS

This book has been published with the help of a grant from the Canadian Federation for the Humanities and Social Sciences, through the Awards to Scholarly Publications Program, using funds provided by the Social Sciences and Humanities Research Council of Canada. Wilfrid Laurier University Press acknowledges the support of the Canada Council for the Arts for our publishing program. We acknowledge the financial support of the Government of Canada through the Canada Book Fund for its publishing activities. This work was supported by the Research Support Fund.

Library and Archives Canada Cataloguing in Publication

Gervais, Christine L. M., [date], author
    Beyond the altar: women religious, patriarchal power, and the Church / Christine L.M. Gervais.

Includes bibliographical references and index.
Issued in print and electronic formats.
ISBN 978-1-77112-294-8 (softcover).—ISBN 978-1-77112-296-2 (EPUB).—
ISBN 978-1-77112-295-5 (PDF)

    1. Feminism—Religious aspects—Catholic Church. 2. Feminist theology.
3. Nuns. 4. Women in the Catholic Church. 5. Catholic women. I. Title.

BX1795.F44G47 2018   282.082   C2017-905276-4
                                                       C2017-905277-2

Cover design by Martyn Schmoll. Front-cover image from iStockphoto. Text design by Angela Booth Malleau.

This book is printed on FSC˚ certified paper and is certified Ecologo. It contains post-consumer fibre, is processed chlorine free, and is manufactured using biogas energy.

Printed in Canada

With gratitude to all the women featured herein who modelled courage and grace in the struggle toward gender equality in the Roman Catholic Church.

Your contributions are exemplary and enduring.

With hope to all generations of women who will benefit from their accomplishments and carry them forward both within and beyond the Church.

Adelante!

Contents

Preface

As I look back over the four decades of my life, I have come to realize that while there have been many moments and empowering encounters that have contributed to the conceptualization of this book on women religious,[1] there are probably none more precious and pivotal than the ones that occurred on and around the day I was born. I consider there to have been four inter-related occurrences. First, the fact that I was born female is not insignificant. Apparently, my arrival as a girl came as quite a surprise to my parents – an actuality attributable to inaccurate medical speculation in 1970. Rather than the eight-pound boy that the male doctor had predicted, my mother gave birth to my twin sister and me. Yes, two girls instead of one boy. Patriarchal inter-pretations undoubtedly offered countless jokes about how it took two girls to make up the equivalent of one boy. However, I prefer to adopt a feminist-based perspective of mutualism that honours the presence of both female and male (Lyons 2005). Thus, I take pride in the gendered gifts that I have both received and shared throughout my life.

A statement made by eighty-year-old Sister Theresa pertaining to the unde-niable existence of women religious in the Roman Catholic Church also seems to be a fitting interpretation of the gendered reality of the birth of my sister and I: "I mean we're there. What can they do about it?" What did my parents do about it? Well, beyond the immediate scrambling of "re-preparation" for two babies rather than one, I can honestly say that, with the exception of the occasional paternalistic expression and action on the part of my father, sometimes rooted in biblically based patriarchal interpretations that he found humorous, my parents raised my older sister, my twin sister, and I with the same educational and extracurricular opportunities that were made available to our younger brother – yes, "a boy" eventually arrived two and a half years later.

The second matter related to the day of my birth pertains to the feel-ings that my mother sensed as she was forced to face the fragility of my very existence. As the second and smaller twin, I was precariously underweight and the medical team was very concerned for my survival. The doctor had cautioned my mother: "Don't get your hopes up 'cause she may not make it." But it is my mother's reaction to the doctor's forewarning that is most pertinent here. Despite the medical staff's unpromising prognosis, my mother remembered how she "knew" deep down inside that I would survive and how she responded confidently to the doctor: "She's going to make it." My mother's sharing about her maternal instincts toward, and faith in, my resilience has been comforting and empowering for me as both a young and adult woman. Her recounting of the moments following my birth has engendered within me an ongoing attentiveness to girls' and women's capacities to overcome the obstacles in their lives. While such concern and consideration have propelled me to work primarily with girls and women in Latin America, it has also drawn me toward women religious in Canada, women whose lives have been meaningfully interwoven with mine since the day I was born.

In considering the third birth-related occurrence, I have come to believe that my mother's immediate and profound faith in my resilience, and its connection to this book, is inextricably intertwined with the presence of another significant woman on the day of my arrival into this world. Given my fragile state and the associated worry for my very survival, it was determined that I should be baptized immediately. This decision was based on a long-standing Roman Catholic belief that non-baptized infants are to be buried outside of Church cemeteries and that they would spend their afterlife in purgatory[2] rather than in heaven. Thus, my seemingly imminent death and the potential consequences related to exclusionary burial practices and allegedly restricted admissions to heaven, created a sense of urgency for a baptism. However, a male priest was nowhere to be found and time was apparently of the essence. Thus, as I have been told by my mother, in the absence of a male priest, I was baptized by a nun who happened to be working as a nurse on the maternity ward at the hospital – a hospital that the sister's congregation owned and operated at the time.

The sister, whose identity I have never been able to ascertain, was always presented as the alternative to the priest; although I too was conditioned to believe that, I have always been proud that I was baptized by a woman. I took the opportunity to express that pride on the day that I gave my baptismal certificate to the priest who was presiding over my wedding. As I handed him the document, which was required to confirm that I was baptized in "the" Roman Catholic Church and was therefore worthy of a Roman Catholic wedding, which at the time I thought was important, I felt the need to qualify it. So I proudly informed him that "this is my official certificate, but I was actually baptized twice, first by a nun moments after I was born and then later by my parish priest." Upon hearing my explanation, he frowned, turned various shades of red, and emphatically replied, "I'll pretend I didn't hear that." I distinctively remember how I simultaneously delighted in and took offence to his response. Part of me felt satisfied by how my announcement had visibly unnerved him. Yet, another part of me felt offended by his denial of my first baptism by a nun. While I may not have understood the complexity of it then in my early twenties, I certainly felt that something was amiss. I do vividly recall how in that moment of disregard, I was both stirred by sisters' contributions to my spirituality and concerned for their place within the Roman Catholic Church.

When I was confirming the details of the sister-based circumstances surrounding my birth in preparation for this book, my mother recounted a fourth birth-related occurrence that I had never heard before, but it was one that I feel is especially relevant. While I always knew that I had stayed in the hospital for five weeks after my birth to gain sufficient weight and strength in order to be discharged safely, and that the sister-nurses "competitively" took turns to care for me, I do not recall ever being told what had occurred on Christmas day while I was still hospitalized. Parental visits were limited because my family lived a distance from the hospital and my parents were busy caring for my twin and my one-year-old sister. As the story goes, a nun had called my parents to reassure them that I was doing well on Christmas day. She also delighted in informing my mother that as the sisters celebrated in their residence on the fifth floor of the hospital, they had placed me in the manger as "baby Jesus." When I heard the story, I thought immediately of how, through that loving and amusing act, the sisters had feminized the Christ-child – the so-called "son" of God. Of course, without their input, I cannot speculate about whether or not the sisters' intentions were "feminist," but I cannot help but wonder how they reacted to the gendered implications of their gesture in 1970 – a time when gendered restrictions against women in the Roman Catholic Church were quite pronounced. My mind was drawn instantly to all the sisters' feminist-oriented actions, both at and away from the altars, that I have come to know through interview conversations. I could not help but smile as I realized how, in my time as the baby girl in the manger, I had personally been at the very centre of one of the sisters' numerous efforts to feminize Christian celebrations and spaces. As I think about the story in relation to this book, I am grateful to my mother for having shared such a precious and pertinent moment in my life. While the symbolism is apparent to me now, little did the sisters know back then that the infant girl whom they placed in the manger would someday write about them and their feminist spirituality. Yet I cannot help but ponder the meaningful interconnection and wonder if perhaps they did somehow know, either by faith, formula, or fortitude, that they were sowing such a subversive seed.

While I heartwarmingly relate the conception of this book to events surrounding my birth, there have been other formative moments in my life that have caused me to question women's limited rights and unequal status in the Roman Catholic Church. One of the most defining moments occurred when I was in my early teens. By that time, my twin sister and I had already been altar servers for a few years. While we had originally been asked by the parish priest whom we had known since infancy, we continued to serve at the altar when a new and younger priest replaced him upon his retirement. Although my sister and I were aware that we served at the altar due more to the absence or unwillingness of boys in our small rural parish than to the recognition of girls' rights to hold the position, we felt quite welcomed, respected, and appreciated by both priests. However, one Sunday in the mid-1980s when the new priest was on vacation, the welcome mat was pulled abruptly from under us. As my sister and I entered the sacristy[3] to prepare to serve, we were coldly confronted by the replacement priest who demanded to know what we were doing in the sacristy. We politely informed him that we were the altar servers, and we were there to get ready. His callous response is ingrained in my memory: "There are no girls on my altar." Then he dismissed us immediately. We did not contest. It was obvious that his position was non-negotiable. While I had endured sexist jokes by other males, both young and old, for who the idea of altar girls was still either inconceivable or too new, I had never encountered such an absolute and harsh exclusion. We complied and went to sit in the pews with our parents, who were also puzzled by the rejection. Although I sat through much of the Mass in a cloud of disbelief and resentment, I also recall feeling somewhat redeemed as I watched him fumble through the Mass without help.

While I expressed frustration over the incident with my family, I did not associate it at the time with the sexism deeply embedded within the Church. While this is in part because I was not yet equipped with a feminist lens, it can also be attributed to the fact that the dismissal was temporary. The very next week, we were back within the sanctuary at the altar and welcomed by our parish priest, who was quite upset by his colleague's exclusionary attitude and action.[4] Thus, I perceived it as an individual matter, not a systemic issue. It was years later when I entered into conversation with the sisters featured in this book that I began to realize that countless women, including women religious, have lived through similar experiences of exclusion and alienation not only from the altar but also from parishes and from the Church entirely. While the sisters' experiences were disconcerting, they were also affirming. I realized that I was not alone. In fact, after hearing about my exclusion from the altar, all the sisters I interviewed expressed frustration over my experience, and they all related to it since they had faced parallel circumstances. It was sixty-eight-year-old Sister Adele who shed additional light on the hierarchical dimensions of the matter when she pointed out, in a disapproving tone, the visiting priest's possessive claim over the altar as he used the term "my" to describe it.

It is perhaps my own painfully acute awareness of this entrenched presumption and predominance of the patriarchal possession of Roman Catholic altars that has shaped this book's emphasis, not only on the gendered experiences of exclusion but also, and especially, on the other spaces where women religious have created inclusive and empowering sources of spirituality and support. I have come to realize that an extensive number of religious and spiritual initiatives take place in less visible and less known places. In fact, I would go so far as to say, as I do in this book, that many more meaningful spiritual experiences take place away from "the altar" than on or even near it, and women religious are, arguably, at the forefront of the endeavours that enable such experiences. I conceive of these spaces as "beyond the altar" and in some cases, as their own "alternative altars" that consist not only of the locations where sisters work but also of the relations through which they interact – both of which have become non-hierarchical, inclusive, and women-centred. Whether it is in their retreat centres emphasizing feminine spirituality or through their housing projects supporting single mothers or in their spiritual direction offices counselling abuse survivors or on the streets marching for gender equality or in a shelter helping a human trafficking victim or in their foreign missions protecting females from patriarchal oppression or through their educational endeavours empowering girls or in their social justice offices advocating peace, Canadian women religious are modelling feminist agency and activism (Holtmann 2011b). I have had numerous opportunities to bear witness to so many of these efforts in both Canada and Latin America, and now I have the privilege to write about them.

Beyond the day of my birth, women religious have always been present in my life, either at the schools or in the parishes I attended. I also recall family visits to local convents, as well as captivating presentations that sisters made about their foreign missionary work – presentations that would later influence my own work in international development. As a child, my perceptions of sisters and their lives ranged from fascination to ennui, but I remained intrigued by their mysticism, faithfulness, and charitable service. However, it was only in adulthood that I really became aware of the gendered dimensions of their existence within the Roman Catholic Church. As this book exposes, women religious' gendered reality is a story of obstacles and opportunities, as well as of pain and perseverance. There is no doubt that the sisters have decisively and strategically created life-giving opportunities in order to overcome the Church's odds rooted in patriarchy. In so doing, they have been at the forefront of activism promoting social justice and gender equality. The majority of

Canadian citizens, and arguably even many Canadian female citizens, are not aware of the depth of the sisters' involvement in the empowerment of women. We can no longer stereotypically assume that women religious are submissive servants of the patriarchal Church that has so manifestly marginalized them. We must recognize them as agents and activists who are courageously capable of countering the constraints and of creating change.

I am often asked why I write about women religious – a topic that many people assume falls outside the scope of my official academic discipline of crim-inology. My response is threefold. First, regardless of my academic affiliation, I felt compelled to convey both the plight and potential of women whose voices have been silenced and whose contributions are either unknown or sometimes misunderstood. Second, I approach all of my projects from an interdisciplinary perspective, which is made possible by my training as a sociologist and by years of involvement in education, women's rights, international development, law, and religion. Third, criminology is an interdisciplinary domain in which human rights violations and harms of the powerful are now prioritized, particularly in my department at the University of Ottawa. Thus, the discrimination and victimization, as well as the resilience and resourcefulness of women religious within a context of institutionalized patriarchal oppression are topics which, while they may not be considered criminological content by some readers, are nevertheless welcome and relevant within the purview of critical criminology and especially one that serves "as the threat of a good example" (Wise 1999, 184).

Beyond my own personal and professional connections to this book, it is filling a gap, not only in academic literature but also in the public realm. That void is of particular concern to women religious themselves. The significance of my attempt to fill the void in both awareness and understanding became especially evident as I began to recruit participants for my study. When the women who responded to my invitation confirmed their willingness to be interviewed, they simultaneously communicated how they were pleased that their experiences were to become known anonymously and, therefore, safely. In fact, the opening sentence of the first response to my recruitment request in the fall of 2008, which came only seconds after it was received by Sister Agnes, emphatically expressed gratitude for and endorsement of the project: "Thank you! Thank you! Thank you! How wonderful that you are beginning such a research study!" Similarly, during her interview, Sister Agnes shared that "I've been so aware of the male stuff in the diocese. No recognition of women, you know. In all those years we did all that stuff and now for some of this to come out, I'm so glad!" As I completed the final edits of this book and consulted with Sister Agnes one last time to clarify a particular detail, she again thanked me profusely for having undertaken this study and for having written this book.

Similar messages were shared both initially and in later years as I kept the women informed of the progress of the project:

> Thank you, Christine, for all you are doing to ensure the recognition of the contributions of women religious to the Church and to the world. (Sister Theresa)

> I hope your writings are published. Love and gratitude for your dedication to this all-important work. (Sister Kelly)

> I wish you success with your research. May it serve the purpose for which it is intended. (Sister Shannon)

> I think it's a wonderful project you're doing. And I think it's going to be quite revealing so, it's going to be very difficult to write up. (Sister Mabel)

> Thanks so much for bringing the voice of religious women in Ontario out of hiding. (Sister Sarah)

These few messages among many others are included here to illustrate how the women religious themselves perceive the significance of how this book may help to fill the void in terms of awareness of what they have both endured and accomplished.

This book is intended for a wide audience, not only an academic one, for whom the life experiences of women generally, and of women religious specifically, are of interest and may have particular meanings. I trust that the complexities and nuances ever-present in the current and former sisters' lives to which I have drawn attention provide a better understanding of the lived realities of women religious.

Acknowledgements

This book is inevitably the outcome of shared labour. I extend my most profound gratitude to the women who gave abundantly of their time, trust, and thoughtfulness. Their hospitality was always forthcoming and generous. Their courage and encouragement have been exemplary and will be enduring.

I thank the staff of Wilfrid Laurier University Press, especially Lisa Quinn, director, and Siobhan McMenemy, senior editor, who believed immediately and firmly in this book and have perceptively and professionally seen it through to completion. Thanks also to copy editor Shelagh Plunkett, managing editor Rob Kohlmeier, production coordinator Mike Bechthold, and sales and marketing coordinator Clare Hitchens. I am grateful to the anonymous peer reviewers for their comprehensive and constructive comments.

This project has benefited from a dedicated team of research assistants, including those who helped with transcription early on. I recognize Shenell Monteith for her attentive involvement through the Undergraduate Research Opportunity Program at the University of Ottawa. In the mid to latter years, I have had the opportunity to work with very engaged young women whose analytical and administrative contributions to this endeavour have been impressive and insightful on multiple levels. I am forever indebted to Leslie Guldimann, Shanisse Kleuskens, Marshneil Vaz, and to assistant-turned-coauthor, Amanda Watson.

At the University of Ottawa, I gratefully acknowledge the Centre for Academic Leadership and its ever-thoughtful manager, Françoise Moreau-Johnson for the invaluable support provided via its writing days and retreats. I am also beholden to Claire Turenne Sjolander for her meaningful mentorship. I extend my appreciation to my academic and administrative colleagues in the Department of Criminology in the Faculty of Social Sciences and within the

Interdisciplinary Research Laboratory on the Rights of the Child in the Faculty of Law for their curiosity and care, as well as for the considerate context of critical scholarship.

At Saint Paul University, I thank Susan Roll and Joëlle Morgan for their detailed and timely clarifications regarding Church doctrine and indigenous rights, respectively. At both universities, I acknowledge the very helpful assistance of the libraries' staff for their continual book renewals well beyond the borrowing schedules over the extended duration of this project.

Across academic fields, I sincerely thank Heidi MacDonald, Rosa Bruno-Jofré, Cathy Holtmann, Elizabeth Smyth, Elizabeth McGahan, and Jacqueline Gresko for having welcomed me so considerately into the fold of Canadian scholarship on women religious.

This research was funded by the Faculty of Social Sciences and the former Laboratory on Justice Studies and Research at the University of Ottawa, as well as by two anonymous funders. This book has been published with the help of a grant from the Federation for the Humanities and Social Sciences, through the Awards to Scholarly Publications Program, using funds provided by the Social Sciences and Humanities Research Council of Canada.

This project has also benefited from networks of women seeking to address gender (in)justice including the Feminist History Society, which affirmed the significance of this book within the Canadian context. The members of the Catholic Network for Women's Equality in Ottawa and across Canada have been important models of perseverance.

I thank the volunteers and partners of ACCESO International, as well as all friends and neighbours whose care and interest toward this book have been motivating and meaningful. To all those unnamed here in both personal and professional circles, please trust that your inspiration and support are remembered and appreciated.

My relatives, both immediate and extended, have been sources of strength and pillars of challenge. I am grateful to my in-laws, Gail and Roger Perry, whose sense of inclusivity is both inspiring and comforting. I am appreciative of my parents, Margarit and Vincent Gervais. I have been buoyed by my mother's emotion-filled faith and by my father's critical stance vis-à-vis the institutional Church; I am also thankful for his helpful searches and timely clarifications throughout the preparation of this book.

My two sons have kept me grounded and uplifted. Jordan's joyful outlook on diversity and Joël's profound sense of justice have been heartening beyond measure. Lastly, yet quite outstandingly, I extend my deepest gratitude to my husband, Grant Perry, whose unwavering support on every front (familial, emotional, domestic, editorial) has been vital to the completion of this book and to all of my academic and philanthropic pursuits. He truly lives up to the meaning of his name. While his sense of practicality and humour have always been sustaining, his modelling of gender parity to our sons has been especially exemplary and one that male clerics of the institutional Church ought to emulate.

Introduction

Today Religious, especially women, are much more aware of their right to legitimate autonomy ... and are more inclined to question assumptions of arbitrary power. (Schneiders 2013, 528)

B eyond the altar occupied by male priests – the focal point of the Roman Catholic Church's patriarchal power – there exists an abundance of lesser-known spiritual and societal initiatives led by women religious in a wide range of spaces. In this book, I direct attention away from the altar and toward the diverse spheres in which Catholic sisters' innovations emerge and endure and whereby they overcome male-domination both within and outside the Church.

Women religious have indeed been recognized for their foundational contributions in the fields of education, health care, and social service in Canadian society since the seventeenth century (D'Allaire 1983; Dumont 1995; Smyth 2007).[1] In recent decades, however, their iconic popularity has waned, and their visibility has diminished since their participation in both secular and religious spheres has declined as they cope with an aging and shrinking population (Sullivan 2005). Yet, as they adapt to these changes, their societal involvement remains relatively considerable while having noticeably evolved into the realms of gender equality, social justice, and environmental protection. As remarkable as this evolution may appear, the sisters' journeys toward these current directions have been fraught with challenges, particularly by patriarchal forces within the Roman Catholic Church[2] that still limit women's full participation in Church leadership and ministry, particularly at the altars (Chittister 2014, 2004; Johnson 2002a; Schneiders 2014, 2013, 2004; Wittberg 1994).

As I sought answers to the questions "Where are the sisters?" and "What are they doing in the twenty-first century?" while exploring the transitioning roles of women religious in Canada, I encountered vibrant and passionate women informed about and engaged in contemporary social issues, one of which was a profound concern regarding gender inequality not only in the

Roman Catholic Church but also in society (Ruether 2003). Such frustration was born out of their own experiences of gender-based exclusion and marginalization by Church authorities and policies that have limited their presence and participation at, near, and away from Church altars. Yet, the gender discrimination that Canadian Roman Catholic women, and women religious in particular, have suffered remains relatively unknown (Bonavoglia 2005; Bouclin 2006). This oversight is due in part to the recent scandals involving priest-related sexual abuse in parishes and Church-based maltreatment of children in residential schools and workhouses that have dominated public attention to the Roman Catholic Church (Bonavoglia 2005; Morgan 2017). But it is also a result of the sisters' own intentionally quiet and strategic management of their endeavours, and it is arguably related to the stereotypical assumptions that construct nuns as unwaveringly loyal and obedient servants of their Church (Hunt, 2009; Kristof 2010; Gervais and Turenne Sjolander 2015; Mangion 2008). It is the latter two reasons that I examine critically in this book in order to demonstrate the complexities of Canadian women religious' lives on the margins of the institutional Roman Catholic Church as they relate to their ongoing societal contributions beyond Church altars.

In this light, I explore how simultaneous membership in "the Roman Catholic Church" and progressively minded religious congregations has seemingly placed forward-thinking women religious on a tightrope[3] of patriarchal constraint and seemingly thwarted innovation. On the one hand, women religious face hierarchical barriers and gender discrimination by the institutional Church, yet on the other, although their own forward-looking[4] religious communities enable their efforts to advance gender equality and inclusivity both within and beyond "the Church," they continue to encounter compromises and constraints. This tightrope presents challenges to sisters whose membership in the Roman Catholic Church affords them limited participation, yet whose attempts to transcend "the Church" leave them subject to censure and control by the male clerical hierarchy. In view of that apparent tightrope, this book examines the dilemmas faced, the dissonance discerned, and the divergence developed by women religious attempting to reconcile their own position as members of the Roman Catholic Church with their quests for inclusive innovation. While I illustrate the related tensions, I devote particular attention to the spiritual, societal, and leadership contributions that they have been engendering as they move beyond the constraints. I do so because it is important to recognize that despite patriarchal control, women religious do exercise various degrees of autonomy and they accomplish a great deal while exercising that independence (Case 2016; Mangion 2008).

FOCUS AND PURPOSE OF THE BOOK

[W]e fear to ask the questions that make the real difference to the quality and content of our souls. (Chittister 2004, 9)

If women's stories are not told, the depth of women's souls will not be known. (Carol Christ in Chittister 2004, 172)

This book is not about religion. It is about the gendered lived experiences of a particular group of women within a specific religious institution: sisters within the Roman Catholic Church. Their experiences are not gauged by the extent of their adherence to Roman Catholicism, nor by their obedience to Canon Law, nor their displays of perfectionism. For far too long, women religious' success or failure has far too often been decided by the Church's patriarchal authorities' perception of sisters' canonical conformity (Lux-Sterritt and Mangion 2011, 2). Thus, their gendered experiences are reflected in the depth of their efforts to overcome adversity, especially gender-based discrimination within the institutional Church and at its patriarchal altars, as well as in the profoundness of the spiritual, organizational, and societal growth they have generated elsewhere as a result (Case 2016; Chittister 2004, ix).

This book therefore focuses neither on religious certitudes nor dogmatic precision nor categorical questions but rather on the complexities embraced, the challenges encountered, and the evolving uncertainties considered by the women religious whose accounts of balancing a tightrope are featured herein (Ammerman 2003, 224; Chittister 2004). It highlights sisters' awareness, both spiritual and societal, of the significance of insight and integrity, as well as of inclusivity and integration (Chittister 2014, 2013b, 2004). I explore such matters critically by drawing attention simultaneously to gender-based discrimination, as well as to sisters' innovations in spirituality, governance, and activism in various locations beyond Church altars.

This book provides a medium for women religious' voices and, by extension, their "souls" to become acknowledged and understood. They have compelling stories – their own "her-stories" – to tell. Like others (Bonavoglia 2005; Coco 2013; Dugan and Owens 2009; Kalven 2003; Kaylin 2000; Peddigrew 2008; Reed 2004; Winter, Lummis, and Stokes 1994) who have interviewed or edited the writings of women religious and other laywomen,[5] I heard pain-filled stories of male domination, gender injustice, and disparagement against women and their contributions. I also listened to women religious, both current and former, convey their concerns, and oftentimes their indignation, over the institutional Roman Catholic Church's exclusion of people who are divorced, use contraception, have had abortions, are members of the LGBTQ community, and/or advocate for women's ordination.

Yet, I also gathered statements about current and former sisters courageously moving beyond the patriarchal constraints and rigid Church dogma in order to engender inclusive spiritual, organizational, and societal innovations – some of which I witnessed personally during opportunities of participant-observation. In its entirety, the book explores the sisters' experiences with both patriarchal parameters and feminist innovations. As such, it delves into how the sisters' feminist and feminine orientations are articulated and practised within a religious institution that confines the feminine to inferiority and rejects feminism outright (Chittister 1998, 1995; Monk Kidd 1996, 8). I thus shed light on how women religious' achievements are negotiated within and reconciled with the patriarchal culture of their time (Chittister 1995; Monk Kidd 1996, 9).

DRAWING ATTENTION TO PATRIARCHAL EXCLUSION

> *But without the input of women, humanity sees with only one eye, hears with one ear and thinks with only one half of the human mind.* (Chittister 2013b)

Within the deep-rooted patriarchal structure of the Roman Catholic Church, women have been marginalized, degraded, and oppressed by hierarchical authorities, as well as systemically excluded from leadership, decision-making, and the sacramental system (Leonard 2007, 235; Schneiders 2004, 33). This gendered exclusion has been particularly prominent at and around Church altars. For example, according to canon 813, section 2 in the 1917 Code of Canon Law, women were prohibited from even approaching the altar.[6] As Roll (2015b, 470–1) has duly pointed out, the instruction *Quam plurimum* in *Actae Apostolicae Sedis* of 1949 stated that "all the authors teach unanimously that it is forbidden under pain of mortal sin for women, even nuns, to serve *at the altar*"[7] (italics in original). As per section 70 of the 1975 General Instruction of the Roman Missal, the appointment of women to ministries performed "outside of the sanctuary" as well as the designation of the "suitable place" for women to carry out the duty (e.g., reading) remained at the discretion of male clerics (Hoffman 1991).

Even more recent revisions were not fully inclusive (Morrill and Roll 2007; Roll 2015b). For example, based on an interpretation of canon 230, section 2 of the 1983 Code of Canon Law, Church authorities granted permission to females to serve at the altar in 1994; however, male clerics still retained discretionary power over such approval and the reasons for the local bishops' decisions to allow girls to serve at the altar was expected to be explained "to the faithful" members of the parish (Congregation for Divine Worship 1994). Furthermore, it should not go unnoticed that section 1 of canon 230 still privileges the participation of "lay men" in altar-related liturgical ministries "on a stable [and therefore permanent] basis," whereas section 2 permits "lay persons" (e.g., women) to serve as lectors only by "temporary designation" (Code of Canon Law 1983). Although the increased participation of girls and women in recent years demonstrates that the codified gendered exclusion is not practised regularly in all local parishes, the Code of Canon Law is nevertheless available to male clerics who may opt to exercise their discretion in order to formally enforce such distinctions.

Moreover, although the 2002 version of the General Instruction of the Roman Missal currently in use is more inclusive of both males and females in all forms of service at the altar,[8] one cannot overlook the emphasis on the "noble" tradition of altar service by boys in the 1994 version (Congregation for Divine Worship 1994), as well as in the Vatican's 2004 *Redemptionis Sacramentum* (Congregation for Divine Worship and the Discipline of the Sacraments 2004; Morrill and Roll 2007).

Women religious have by no means been immune to these restrictions and their corresponding strains and quandaries (Schneiders 2013). Yet despite the long-standing existence of gender discrimination, relatively few people, including Roman Catholic Church members and non-members, seem to be aware of the extent of the legal minutiae that continues to reinforce the canonical control against the presence of women at the altar, as well as of its exclusionary consequences for women within that religious institution (Roll 2015b). Far fewer seem to be aware of the distinct repercussions for women religious (Bonavoglia 2005).

Both concern and critique have increased in recent years as the patriarchal domination against women religious has become even more entrenched and has manifested itself in numerous ways in the twenty-first century (Leonard 2007, 235; Schneiders 2013, 530). For example, women's exclusion particularly from Church altars was systematically exacerbated in the Roman Catholic Church when women's ordination was further prohibited in 2008 and then criminalized canonically in 2010.[9]

Of additional import is the Vatican's controversial inquiry into women's religious orders in the United States that was intended to pressure women's orders to realign with the sanctioned practices of the Church (McElwee 2013b; Schneiders 2013; Uebbing 2013). Extending in its entirety from 2008 to 2015, the controversial inquiry was two pronged as it involved both an investigation of the Leadership Conference of Women Religious (LCWR)[10] and an apostolic visitation of religious orders – both of which were authorized by Pope Benedict XVI in order to scrutinize the allegedly feminist orientations and practices of women religious and their leaders who were thought to be disobeying[11] Church dogma (Chittister 2013; Kristof 2012, 2010; Parrish 2015; Schneiders 2011). The women under investigation were women who remained in religious life beyond Vatican II and worked tirelessly toward the mandated renewal but were then being accused, through the twenty-first century investigation, of having taken the renewal too far (Schneiders 2011). In 2013, adding insult to injury, Pope Francis,[12] whom many initially thought to be an unlikely opponent to women's actions, appointed an overseer to undertake the revision of the LCWR's statutes, programs, affiliations, liturgies, and ministries – all of which was intended to undermine women's abilities to lead their own initiatives (Chittister 2014; McElwee 2013a,b; Schneiders 2014, 2013; Uebbing 2013).

Although the conclusion and the reports of those investigations were officially framed relatively positively, and as having been prepared in the spirit of co-operation, the processes associated with them were nevertheless "difficult" and "dark" for the representatives and members of the LCWR and the orders (LCWR 2015b; Braz de Aviz 2014). The sisters under scrutiny were made to feel like they were "under siege" and "'personae non grata' in their own Church" (Schneiders 2011, 22). Moreover, as renowned sister-authors Chittister (2014), Schneiders (2014, 2013), and Schenk (2014) cautioned, one should not naively be deceived by the positive and appreciative tone of the reports given that gender inequality within the Church remains deeply entrenched, and one should not quickly forget that such "an unjustified assault on Religious ... [and a] unilateral invasion" should never have occurred in the first place (Schneiders 2013, 530). Furthermore, the mandates of both reports ultimately obliged the LCWR and the women's religious orders to change their statutes and commit to being more doctrinally compliant with Roman Catholic teaching in various areas including their spiritual and societal practices (LCWR 2015a; Braz de Aviz 2014).[13]

Such separate yet simultaneous assessments reflect the persistence of the Roman Catholic Church hierarchy to control women's innovative contributions within both Church and societal contexts. While Canadian women religious orders have not been subjected to the same systematic investigation and reprimand as their US counterparts, Canadian sisters have been negatively affected by the dual investigations of US women religious and their leaders. Beyond the solidarity-based concern, sadness, frustration, and in many cases outrage that the Canadian women religious whom I interviewed felt for sisters in the United States who were being scrutinized for their feminist orientations, the investigations also made them more fearful of potential reprisal. Their apprehension was certainly warranted given the extent to which they have been controlled and criticized by male clerics in both the distant and recent past. Thus, while they remained open about their feminist critiques during our conversations, they became more cautious about their right and my responsibility to protect their personal and congregational identities. Furthermore, many sisters became even more clandestine about their feminist projects after the investigations in the United States were launched.

That these investigations as well as the prohibition and criminalization of women's ordination have been a major affront to Roman Catholic women cannot be overstated and that they occurred simultaneously in the first decade-and-a-half of the twenty-first century cannot be overlooked. This timing is cause for serious concern on a number of levels, and Joan Chittister (2013b) pointed out the fundamental irony of it all: "it is [over] 2,000 years after Jesus himself modeled [the inclusivity and emancipation of women]," yet the institutional Church continues to restrict and exclude women. Thus, it is in this twenty-first century climate, still ever so closed to women's full participation in leadership within the institutional Roman Catholic Church, that I situate the importance of sisters' experiences, voices and visions. While my effort is inspired by all women religious affected by this struggle, Sister Joan Chittister (2013b) articulated the rationale astutely: "It is about bringing to public visibility and public agency the agendas, the insights, and the wisdom of the other half of the human race."

MOVING BEYOND STEREOTYPES OF NUNS AS SUBSERVIENT

The rising comes when we are able to commit our lives to something worth being condemned for ... (Chittister in Eagan 2014)

Sister Joan Chittister's pronouncement points to women religious' courage and commitment to both resist and innovate despite the gendered constraint and condemnation by the Vatican and the institutional Church's clerical hierarchy. However, actions like rising and resisting, as well as being open to reactions such as condemnation and excommunication are not typically associated with women religious. Yet, it is the women's firsthand accounts of their views and experiences, illustrated by way of numerous quotations throughout this book, that disrupt the widely held stereotypical image of nuns as passive, obedient, silent, and subservient women who are loyally compliant to, and therefore unquestioning of, both Church doctrine and the patriarchal authority that established it (Jackowski 2004, 1; Kristof 2010; Mangion 2008). While there are some sisters "who accept the patriarchal ecclesiology that undergirds their own subordination, the vast majority of women religious ... have definitely repudiated their second-class status in the Church" (Schneiders 2013, 530). In this light, as their own words reveal, the women I interviewed are in solidarity with, and in the company of, a long line of "strong-minded women who challenged bishops and bested them; confronted popes and chastised them;

contested the norms of society and corrected them" (Chittister 1995, 12). By both thought and action, the women in this book pose incisive questions, offer strident critiques, as well as contest societal norms and Church practices that are exclusionary and problematic (Schneiders 2013).

CONTRIBUTING TO SCHOLARLY LITERATURE

Despite mounting international scholarship and activism that have been drawing attention to the matter,[14] the gender discrimination that Canadian Catholic women religious have suffered remains relatively unknown. This is in part due to the widespread silencing effect resulting from the institutional Church hierarchy's pervasive patriarchal power (Schneiders 2013), as well as to the fact that academic research, writing, and teaching, even those focused on women, tend to make little, if any, reference to sisters because of the religious affiliation which is perceived as problematic in a predominantly secular context (Dillon 2003; Ebaugh 2005; Smyth 2007, 10; MacDonald 2003; Mangion 2008, 1). However, as Ebaugh (2005, vi) has argued, academic analyses, and particularly sociological explanations, that ignore religious dimensions altogether remain incomplete and therefore inadequate.

While academic literature, even feminist literature, may not address sisters' gendered plight and potential, the Canadian sisters' voices herein resonate with the views of many other women who have drawn attention to gender [in]equality within Christianity generally and within Roman Catholicism specifically, and that are featured in a wide range of literature genres, including popular, media, and scholarly – all of which are broadly affiliated with "[t]he Magdalene moment."[15] Considered to have peaked more notably at the turn of the second millennium, the "Magdalene moment" is characterized by a renewed recognition of women's leadership roles within Christian traditions that has historically been denied (Manning 2006, Schenk 2017). Through various forms of writing, authors such as Sue Monk Kidd[16] and Dan Brown[17] as well as Sisters Joan Chittister, Elizabeth Johnson, Christine Schenk, and Sandra Schneiders, along with former Sisters Joanna Manning (2006) and Karen Armstrong (2004), among countless others, have been reclaiming and reinterpreting women's potential within and outside Christian traditions. While having begun long before the turn of the second millennium, recent scholarly attention to both the plight and productivity of women religious is undoubtedly related to the popular appeal and profound significance of the "Magdalene moment."

Despite the more recent emphasis, it is important to recognize that feminist scholars and activists have been systematically scrutinizing the androcentric, patriarchal, and misogynistic constraints of the institutional Roman Catholic Church for more than six decades (see, e.g., Chittister 1998, 1983;

Daly 1968; Ruether 1983; Schneiders 1991; Schüssler Fiorenza 1976). The analyses put forth by these authors have been perceptive and penetrating and many of them have drawn attention to how women religious have long been aware of the male monopoly of the Roman Catholic Church and have themselves been deprived, subjugated, and frustrated by it (Chittister 1995; Kaylin 2000, 11; Reed 2004, 76–77). Quoting Rosemary Radford Ruether, Canadian Sister-scholar Ellen Leonard (2007, 241) reminds us that in fact, it has often been women religious, as leading scholars and activists (see, e.g., Chittister (2004, 1998), Johnson (2002), Schneiders (2004) and Leonard (2007)), who have been at the forefront of drawing attention to the Roman Catholic Church's intransigence toward women's equality. Given how scholarship, grounded in experience, offers particularly unique insights, these scholarly advancements by women religious themselves are especially relevant to my analysis.

Shedding Light on the Canadian Context

Illustrations and analyses of dissent among women religious in the United States, Europe, and Latin America have been published relatively widely and certainly more openly (see, e.g., Bonavoglia 2005; Gebara 2002, 1999; Kaylin 2000; Lux-Sterritt and Mangion 2011; Magray 1998; Mangion 2008; Reed 2004). Furthermore, some current and former women religious, as scholars and authors (see, e.g., Armstrong 2004; Chittister 2014, 2013, 2004; Ebaugh 1993, 1977; Gebara 2002, 1999; Johnson 2002a; Leonard 2007; Manning 2006; Schneiders 2014, 2013, 2004), have served as renowned and capable spokeswomen as they have overtly challenged Church authorities and contested exclusionary Church policies. Thus, the notion of subversive nuns may not be novel for some readers.

Yet, like many other faith-filled women, the unique experiences of Canadian women religious have only been "dimly heard from the margins" (Nason-Clark and Fisher-Townsend 2005, 211), if at all, and thus remain comparatively unknown given the relative quietness through which Canadian nuns carry out their work. In addition to being humble about their contributions, as all sisters have been expected to be, Canadian nuns are also relatively less vocal and, as Sister Mabel contends, are "much more placid and much more Canadian" about their public critiques against the Roman Catholic Church. Understandably, not all sisters feel comfortable to criticize openly because they fear repercussions (Chittister 1995, 12; Reed 2004, 85–8). In this light, the study upon which this book is based offered a medium for less outspoken Canadian sisters and former sisters to convey their concerns and critiques anonymously and therefore, safely.

This book thus fills a void in Canadian literature generally by examining women religious' experiential accounts of gender-based discrimination and feminist-oriented activism in the late twentieth and early twenty-first centuries in Canada. More specifically, it fills a gap in Canadian anglophone[18] research regarding the historical and contemporary circumstances of Ontario-based English-speaking Roman Catholic women religious (Smyth 2007). By extension, I contribute to a growing and stirring Canadian scholarship that is seizing a time-limited opportunity to explore women religious' "lives and enterprises ... at a critical juncture in their history" (Smyth 2007, 17). While my research has taken up a broader challenge to sustain scholarly attention to gender and religion (Charlton 2015; Nason-Clark and Fisher-Townsend 2005), it is also responding to a specific call for further exploration of how the tensions between patriarchy and feminism have impacted the lives of women religious in Canada (Smyth 2007, 16). Other Canadian scholars, particularly historians (Rosa Bruno-Jofré 2007; Colleen Gray 2007; Jacqueline Gresko 2007; Heidi MacDonald 2007; Elizabeth McGahan 2007; Elizabeth Smyth 2007) have documented various gendered dynamics among English-speaking women religious in various Canadian provinces, but gender inequality has not consistently constituted the primary emphasis of their studies nor have they addressed the issue incisively. As well, they have not drawn as much attention to contemporary contexts.[19]

In a 1995 publication, Sister Joan Chittister characterized the fundamental transition being experienced by women religious at the end of the twentieth century as a "delicate sociological moment" (Chittister 1995, 14). Back then, she contended that,

> On the one side lies the rupturing of an ancient and valuable institution in the church, on the other side the authentic evolution of the human community along the lines of its highest spiritual aspirations, its deepest gospel values, its truest theological insights. (Chittister 1995, 14)

While Chittister's claim is now more than twenty years old, in some ways that "moment" has not yet passed and remains ever so delicate as the sisters continue to manage the decline in their membership and the innovation of their involvement, all the while negotiating the institutional Church's pervasive patriarchal power (Chittister 2014, Schneiders 2014, 2013). Thus, this book seeks to contribute to further understandings of that still delicate, yet extended transitional period, particularly from the perspective of Canadian women religious whose accounts of their gendered experiences are significant and worthy of becoming better known and understood.

WHO ARE THE WOMEN IN THIS BOOK?

The women shared their perspectives with me during qualitatively based, in-depth, semi-structured interviews and written questionnaires[20] between December 2008 and June 2011. I also became more familiar with their opinions and endeavours as I engaged in participant observation at various events they hosted in their spirituality centres or that they were affiliated with in secular community settings between December 2008 and September 2013. At the time of their interviews, the women ranged from forty-nine to ninety-one-years of age[21] and consisted of twenty-six current and six former[22] sisters affiliated with eight women's religious communities representing the eastern, central, northern, and southwestern regions of the province of Ontario in Canada. In order to protect the participants' identity, their religious community affiliation is not revealed. The views expressed in this book reflect those of the participants and not necessarily those of their religious communities nor all women religious.

When I interviewed them, their years as women religious ranged from twenty-four to seventy-three. Regarding their ethnocultural identification, nineteen were of Irish descent, five were of French descent, two were English-Irish, one was Irish-German, one was Irish-Scottish, two were Irish-French, one was French-German, and one was Indigenous-French-German. Two women were born outside of Canada – one in England and the other in the United States. Two women self-identified as francophone.

The overwhelming majority of the women religious were highly educated; some had multiple undergraduate and graduate degrees. For 6 percent, their highest level of educational attainment was a high school diploma; for 34 percent, it was a bachelor's degree; 44 percent had obtained a master's degree, and 16 percent had earned a doctorate; 81 percent had also completed programs of teacher education. In their professional lives, the sisters worked primarily as teachers and principals; among the participants, there was also a chef, a librarian, a nurse, a social worker, and a psychologist.

They all contributed to varying degrees in their religious communities and in their parishes on committees, leadership teams, vocations, and as pastoral associates, choir members, and spiritual directors. Seventy-five percent of the participants served as councillors on leadership teams and 16 percent served as general superiors of their communities; several sisters did so multiple times, illustrating how women's religious orders are sustained by the numerous roles in which sisters serve in their communities over the course of their lives. For most, their diverse commitments are still carried out during their "retirement" years as some are serving in these roles in their seventies, eighties, and even nineties. For many participants, spiritual direction represents a second career and one through which they conduct specialized counselling and healing based on particular traditions within psychology, theology, social work, and the "New Age" movement[23] which they espouse seriously and enthusiastically.

METHODOLOGICAL CONSIDERATIONS

I recruited participants by contacting ten distinct Ontario-based religious communities that were members of the Canadian Religious Conference.[24] I distributed invitation letters by mail, email, and in person. While approximately half of the participants were recruited through the invitations sent to the religious communities, other respondents were recruited through snowball sampling techniques. Since participants responded readily, and in some cases gratefully to the invitations, the recruitment process was relatively free of challenges. In order to maintain confidentiality and anonymity, all interviews and meetings were conducted on an individual basis.[25] The majority of interviews were conducted in the women's private residential homes or apartments; approximately one-third took place within congregations' retirement homes or spirituality centres; others were completed in my office or theirs.[26] Throughout the official data collection phase, all the women were available for interviews and follow-up consultations.[27]

Participation in this research was open to all women from the religious communities informed of the study.[28] A feminist orientation was not a prerequisite for inclusion. However, the majority of the women who chose to participate in this study have feminist leanings and all are strongly in favour of gender equality. I acknowledge the limitations of the sample and the impact on the generalizability of the results given the participants' predominant gender-based interests.

Interviews were recorded digitally and transcribed by research assistants. Given that quantitative methods do not adequately encapsulate "the subjective, fluid and complex realities of people's lives ... [particularly] phenomena like exclusion and discrimination" (Mander 2010, 255–6) which form the main subject of my study, the participants' accounts were analyzed qualitatively and the data deriving from them were organized thematically. While the themes prioritized and the examples illustrated herein may seem to either favour or critique certain attitudes or approaches, it is important to note that this book is intended as neither an advocacy for nor a disregard against any faith, religious belief, or social choice.

Women-centred approach

> By telling their own stories women appropriate as significant their own experience which they have been taught to view as trivial. (Schneiders 2004, 87)

The absence of women's standpoint in the Roman Catholic religious tradition[29] has been variously underscored by many critics, including sister-scholars:

> Women's experience ... has been largely excluded from the history of mainline religion. (Schneiders 2004, 87)

> [T]he lived experience of women, [has been] long derided or neglected in androcentric tradition. (Johnson 2002a, 61)

Such dearth and derision serve as the impetus for a women-centred approach. As feminist theologian Elizabeth Johnson has emphasized, "[c]onsulting human experience" and listening to people's questions, struggles, values, and hopes are indispensable to shaping inquiry and arriving at new insights and advancing progress appropriately (Johnson 2002a, 61). In this light, and given that women religious' experiences have been noticeably absent from the androcentric Catholic tradition, the inclusion of their voices constitutes an important contribution to scholarly inquiries that seek to shed more comprehensive light on the complexities of people's spiritually oriented and religiously based realities, and particularly on their gendered dimensions (Bruno-Jofré 2007, 256; Chittister 2004; Johnson 2002a; Molesky-Poz 2003; Nason-Clark and Fisher Townsend 2005; Neitz 2003; Schneiders 2004; Smyth 2007).

By enabling women religious to tell their own stories,[30] as well as by genuinely consulting and respecting their standpoint, this study is grounded "in the location of women" (Neitz 2003, 289), particularly in their "everyday world" (Ammerman 2003, 209), and thus provides women religious with a meaningful opportunity to identify the issues, experiences, and aspirations that are relevant and significant to them (Fox 2009; Johnson 2002a; Nason-Clark 1997; Neitz 2003; Schneiders 2004; Smith 1990, 1987). Prioritizing sisters' multiple voices and complex experiences herein is intentional because it has the potential to disrupt preconceptions of women religious and to uncover the range of understandings and occurrences among women religious whose varied positions on the margins shed significant light on the centralized institutional powers of the Roman Catholic Church (Ammerman 2003, 224; Nason-Clark and Fisher-Townsend 2005; Neitz, 2003, 292; Smith 1987). By extension, through this intentionally feminist-informed dialogic text (Smith (1999, 130) in Neitz 2003, 288), readers may recognize the commonalities between women religious' experiences and their own, and may thus feel affirmed as they consider the validity of their own concerns, critiques and questions. Readers may also become aware of broader issues that they can themselves now reflect upon through a wider lens.

Toward an ethic of caring, accountability, inclusivity, and engagement

Words from the Heart (Mander 2010)

Beyond my commitment to university-regulated ethical guidelines, I am dedicated to upholding an additional level of ethical standards – one that brings researchers onto meaningful and arguably essential terrains of responsibility with research participants. Such an inclusive approach is situated within methodological frameworks that promote partnership and reciprocity between researchers and participants (Mander 2010, 2001; Pittaway et al. 2010). As Mander (2010, 252, 269) has cautioned, it is essential to move beyond "detached, impersonal and 'objective' social science research" whereby researchers merely extract information from people, publish it "and then just walk away." Rather, he contends that listening to people's stories and their "words from the heart" and providing them with opportunities to reconstruct and analyze their own experiences enables a study's participants to become partners in research (Mander 2010, 252). By extension, such an engaged and thus undetached approach "democratizes knowledge" and allows for more nuanced and authentic understandings of people's experiences because both the researcher and the researched are provided with opportunities to learn from participants' reconstructions and analyses of their "truth" about their own lived realities (Mander 2010, 253).

Along similar lines and based on study participants' appeal to researchers to "Stop Stealing Our Stories," Pittaway, Bartolomei, and Hugman (2010, 229, 234, 236) caution against the exploitation and disempowerment of vulnerable research participants and favour instead a relationship of reciprocity whereby participants are given opportunities to exercise their agency and demonstrate their capacity to contribute to and benefit from the research process. Pittaway et al. (2010) further acknowledge how non-reciprocal research poses problems for participants who, on some levels, lose "ownership" of their story once it becomes "research data" that is viewed as then belonging "to the researcher and their institution" (Pittaway et al. 2010, 236–7).

My effort to privilege women religious' voices reflects both Mander's (2010) and Pittaway et al.'s (2010) aforementioned approaches to regard participants as more than research subjects, objects, or statistics but rather as real and capable people worthy of being consulted, heard, and included in the research process. My intentions also echo Mander's recommended priority to "hear and value people who are most invisible, voiceless, and powerless ... and to listen to them with empathy, trust, and respect" (Mander 2010, 263). Such an approach has been particularly relevant to my study given women religious' long-standing vulnerability[31] and silencing in the male-dominated and hierarchically structured Roman Catholic Church (Bonavoglia 2005; Chittister 2014, 2013, 2004; Schneiders 2013). I thus endeavoured to ensure that the ethics of inclusivity, care, safety, accountability, and engagement were upheld on a number of levels and in a variety of ways within my study. At the outset, the participants were included in the preparation and realization of this study insofar as they provided input on the content and format of the research instruments, including the questions posed and the language used in the interview guide and the written questionnaire.[32] Prior to and during their own individual interview, each participant had an opportunity to add, edit, or delete questions specific to their own experience in order to respect their voice and to maximize their comfort and safety throughout our recorded conversations.

Several other steps were taken to ensure that the study did not render the women more vulnerable (Mander 2010, 268).[33] For example, pseudonyms were employed to ensure that anonymity and confidentiality were respected. Yet, it is essential to note that anonymity and confidentiality were duly promised not only out of obligation to the pre-established ethical standards relevant to my study but also and especially because the participants and I decided together that particular caution needed to be exercised given how entrenched the patriarchal power of the Roman Catholic Church was at the time that my study began and throughout its duration (Schneiders 2013). In this light and given that I did not want to compromise the work of Canadian women religious, complete anonymity and confidentiality were deemed essential in order to protect not only the individual names of each participant but also the collective identity of the religious communities represented in this study. Such protection allowed the current and former sisters the possibility of moving safely beyond the subtleties and of exposing honestly the subterfuge without fear of potential repercussion (Chittister 2004, 6).

While on the one hand the safeguarding of their identities yielded more detailed explanations of the patriarchal power of the Church, on the other it posed challenges for me as a researcher because I was compelled to remove identifying information (e.g., names of people, projects, buildings, cities, towns, events, organizations, and achievements, etc.) that from historical and contextual perspectives would have attributed significant meaning to the sisters' stories, especially in regard to their spiritual and societal involvement. Admittedly, I found these necessary omissions regrettable insofar as they further conceal the sisters' authorship, ownership, and leadership of certain noteworthy contributions within Canadian society and throughout the world for which they deserve recognition. Such methodological limitations are indicative of how permeating the power of the patriarchal Church remains (Schneiders 2013) and protecting the women from it was absolutely essential. Yet, while there may be losses in terms of factual details, there are certainly gains in terms of the incisive critiques that the women were more openly willing to share with me. As a result, the reader becomes more aware of the nuances and complexities of exclusion and discrimination, and, in my estimation, such details are far more illuminating than the identifying information that was removed.

I took additional steps to uphold my commitment to an ethic of caring, engagement, and accountability, which according to Mander (2010, 268) also implies that researchers have "an ethical obligation not to abandon the person who is the subject of research." Such steps were taken in the post-interview phase of the research process. For example, in addition to offering feedback on the interview experience, all participants were given the chance to review their interview transcripts and thus provide further approval on the use of their quotations. Among those who took the opportunity, some raised concerns about identifying contexts and requested that certain comments not be quoted while others sought to strengthen the tone of their remarks.

I have provided in-person, telephone, and email updates to the participants on the progress of data collection, publications, and conference papers. Participants have been invited to read and approve journal articles, conference papers, and the manuscript of this book prior to publication or dissemination. Such reviews gave participants the opportunity to share analytical commentaries, provide feedback on terminology used and issues addressed, grant the final approval on the use of their quotations, and, if applicable, to edit them if they were still concerned about identifying information or, in some cases, if they wanted to reinforce the point they had originally sought to make. The ensuing editing has generated meaningful and learning-filled post-interview dialogues between the participants and myself as a researcher. The interviewees have also been provided with electronic and/or printed copies of all publications. Wherever possible and however applicable, this ongoing communication with and inclusion of the women has fostered a valuable continuity that has enhanced the manners in which their own voices have been authored, their own experiences have been conveyed, and their own meanings imparted (Molesky-Poz 2003, 23). Based on their feedback, I am aware that through these precautionary and processual efforts, the women who participated in my study have not felt that I (to borrow Mander's term) "just walked away" from them after their interviews. Instead, having had their voices more completely integrated within this book has led to a fuller feminist expression of their agency whereby they, as women, have proven themselves capable of contributing to a context – in this case a publication – that affects them (McGuire 2008; Nason-Clark and Fisher-Townsend 2005). As I note next, beyond the respect that such a methodological sensibility offers the women as research participants, their ongoing involvement was significant not only because it was meaningful but also because it was productive.

Benefits of the sisters' and former sisters' ongoing input

The women's input has undeniably enriched my experience as a researcher, and, more importantly, has given them an opportunity to have their voices included at all stages of the research process. According to the women who provided feedback, they have not only appreciated their inclusion but also view it as essential, especially given that their voices have been silenced within the Roman Catholic Church for so long. Thus, many women enthusiastically seized the safe opportunity to provide commentary.

Their inclusion has enhanced this study in numerous ways. First, it has allowed them to contribute to the data collection process whenever they have felt comfortable to do so. Over the years, many participants have supplemented their original interview or questionnaire data with additional anecdotal evidence, which have served to provide either more complete, up-to-date, or evolving understandings of their experiences and opinions. Others[34] also recommended relevant publications by and/or on women religious. Second, open and ongoing inclusion has encouraged editorial contributions on the part of participants – all of which has enhanced the analyses herein. For example, when Sister Sarah reviewed an earlier version of the manuscript, she noticed that the wording of one of her own quotations did not convey the extent of her frustration over the incident being recounted as clearly as she had originally felt it: "the quote could be made stronger ... It just didn't feel as strong as I meant it." As we communicated, Sister Sarah clarified how she thought it should be edited and she recommended that the analytical commentary also underscore the extent of her sentiment. After we worked together on the edits, she was more satisfied with the revised version because, in her view, it captured the essence of her emotions and the strength of her conviction more accurately.

In addition, when other participants provided feedback, they occasionally identified words that were problematic for them. For instance, as mentioned above, former Sister Naomi expressed her concern over my use of the term "progressive":

> In terms of feedback, I will offer a caution on the use of the word "progressive" to describe one group over another ... there is a reference made to not everyone in the community being progressive. While I am tempted myself to use this word, I think it is a label that is not helpful to the

discussion. In these times, I feel that the old categories tend to promote simplistic and rigid thinking. (Correspondence in 2015)

Naomi's concern about a term implying a dismissive tone is a testament to her social justice orientation; her courage to express that concern is partly indicative of the productive dialogue generated through research inspired by an ethic of caring, engagement, and accountability.

Similarly, in an earlier version of the manuscript, I had used the word "fellow" as a synonym for "peer" because I had been using the latter too frequently in my writing. Yet, upon her review, Sister Theresa informed me politely yet critically, and certainly without hesitation, that my use of the word "fellow" was problematic because it had a masculine connotation which was, at least for her, synonymous with "chap," "guy," or "man." While I had explained that I was using the term as a substitute for "colleague" and although she understood, she maintained that the term was still too associated with males and therefore not appropriate for a book that emphasizes sisters' feminist orientations because it undermined the point of the publication. Upon hearing this feedback, I edited the text accordingly and ever since then, when I am tempted to write the word "fellow," I pause, think back smilingly on Sister Theresa's lesson, especially now that she has since passed away, and do my best to find yet another synonym.

Another helpful critique came from a sister who was concerned about illustrations of the past. Upon review of a section that had described earlier convent experiences, Sister Ella questioned the purpose of such details given its emphasis on the past hierarchical constraints that sisters have tried hard to forget and to move beyond. She wondered: "Why would you bother writing about this? We've moved so far past these old ways. Who would want to read about this?" Other women, like Sisters Shannon and Theresa, who read the same section were not concerned about such details because in their opinion "that's just the way things were." Yet, while Sister Ella's questions did not deter me from writing about previous convent practices, they have certainly encouraged me to reflect on how I portray and analyze the women religious' experiences and particularly on how I now always contrast their past contexts in light of their current priorities and practices of governance, the latter of which has been one of the central objectives of this book.[35]

These examples illustrate that keeping the lines of communication open between the participants and the researcher long after the original interviews allows important feedback to be shared. By extension, such ongoing constructive feedback encourages a researcher to be attentive to participants' concerns, to be open to ongoing discoveries, and to integrate more insightful analytical lenses through which the women's experiences can be most appropriately conveyed, and therefore, understood.

ORGANIZATION OF THE BOOK

In the first chapter, I present the lens through which the women view their own context by illustrating how current and former sisters embrace feminist orientations and advocate gender equality. In the second chapter, I shed light on how the women apply feminist-based critiques to their own experiences of patriarchal control. In chapters 3 and 4, I demonstrate the women's capacities to manoeuver both within and beyond the male-dominated structure of the institutional Church. In chapters 5, 6, and 7, I highlight how women religious practise, engender, and defend their alternative spiritual innovations. In chapter 8, I bring to the fore the women's inclusive governance models and in chapter 9, I draw attention to the women's engagement in feminist activism, including that which controversially counters Catholic dogma. In the concluding chapter, I emphasize the book's contribution to understandings of Catholic sisters across the broader scholarly canvas of gender and religion, and I point to both the concern and potential for the future of women's religious life, which as I discuss next in chapter 1 are variously rooted in past and evolving gendered identities and orientations.

CHAPTER 1

Relating to feminisms

Indeed feminism changes the way we see everything ... It changes what we value and what we seek. It changes the way we see ourselves as women.
(Chittister 2004, 151)

F eminist nuns? Yes! Whenever I have informed relatives, friends, colleagues, and even strangers about my research with feminist women religious, I have often heard one of two responses – one that implies surprise and even critique and the other that conveys certainty and acceptability. The disbelievers or critics often expressed their puzzled reactions through various versions of the question: "Nuns? Feminists? Really? Isn't that a contradiction?"[1] The existence of feminist sisters may seem perplexing to many readers due to the stereotypical imaging of women religious as faithful and obedient servants in their institutional Church (Kristof 2010) and to their indisputable role in the conditioning of gendered subservience among generations of women (Chittister in Bonavoglia 2005).

For others, however, the very presence and purpose of feminist sisters was not only undeniable, but it was also desirable and for some, even memorable. For example, some acquaintances affirmed that "Nuns were the first feminists I ever met" and "Of course! Nuns are among the most feminist women I know." The latter response often included references to how the sisters, as skilled administrators, educators, as well as health care and social workers, had proven capacities for successful leadership and management of complex social, economic, religious, cultural, political, and institutional projects. Such examples are consistent with the observations documented by sociologist Helen Ebaugh (1993, 133), who referred to women religious, particularly those in the pre-1960s era as "unwitting feminists" due to their role modelling as single women with professional careers and, as some acquaintances also noted, educators who prioritized girls' and women's rights to education, employment, shelter, and safety. Such pursuits are indicative of their earnest intentions to promote gender equality among younger generations of women (Anthony 1997b; Coburn and Smith 1999; Dumont 1995) – pursuits that have clearly been informed by feminist orientations promoted by prominent women religious.

For those who are astonished to be reading about feminist nuns for the first time, they may have been even more surprised to discover in this book's introduction that there are renowned and well-published women religious who have not only been asserting their feminist[2] stance for several decades but who have also been incisive and influential in doing so. They have blazed trails both through and around the tough and sometimes treacherous terrain of the patriarchal Church, and they have courageously stood against the hierarchy that reprimanded them for their outspokenness (Chittister 2004; Schneiders 2013). The current and former sisters I interviewed identified these leading women religious as having inspired and informed their own feminist orientations. Among them are prominent theologians and writers including Sisters Joan Chittister (2004, 1998), Elizabeth Johnson (2002), Sandra Schneiders (2013, 2004), Ellen Leonard (2007), and Miriam Winter (2002), as well as former Sisters Helen R. Ebaugh (1993), Mary Jo Leddy (1990), and Joanna Manning[3] (2006, 1999). These nuns, along with many of their predecessors and counterparts (both religious and non-religious), represent "key public voices in the dawning of second-wave feminism"[4] and thus many played pivotal roles in the advancement and application of feminisms in the postwar era and beyond (Sullivan 2005, 3).

While the prominence and influence of feminist sister-authors, as well as the public's newfound awareness that some sisters are indeed feminist, are intriguing unto themselves and would be worthwhile exploring in greater depth, my interest is to shed light on how less well known women religious themselves relate to feminisms – the latter of which is pluralized intentionally to reflect the multiplicity and complexity of feminist perspectives (Nason-Clark and Fisher-Townsend 2005, 211; Neitz 2003, 276; Shih 2010, 222) – many of which the women religious themselves were familiar with. In an effort to be genuinely inclusive of the sisters' voices and to be respectful of their capacity to interpret meanings (Johnson 2002a; Mander 2010; Pittaway 2010), I invited the sisters to convey their own understandings of, affiliations with, and, in some cases, detachments[5] from feminisms. Privileging the sisters' own articulations of feminisms was essential in acknowledging their "multiple subject positions" and in thus both revealing and respecting the diversity of their thoughts, assertions, and practices of feminisms across various locations including both religious and non-religious contexts (Griffith 1997, 205; Shih 2010, 222).

Understandably, the nuns' use of the term "feminism"[6] varied widely as indicated by their consideration of feminism in their lives, and sisters recounted varying degrees of affiliation with the term. While the women did not define "feminism" explicitly,[7] the ambiguous use of the term, as revealed in their accounts, reflects contemporary and historical debates over the various meanings of feminisms and their core tenets. Recognizing its varied use is significant because some sisters who denounced particular versions of feminism, especially the radical variants, still displayed feminist orientations toward gender equity and thus often reproduced liberal[8] feminist precepts (Shih 2010).

It became clear in comments by current and former sisters who were reluctant to identify with feminism at all, that their working definitions were mired in a sort of aggressive brand of feminist activism that did not fit with their preferred style of communicating opinions and pursuing projects. Given the majority of participants' advanced age, their interpretations may stem from the brand of feminist activism of the 1960s and 1970s that is associated with a particularly upfront style of activism (Echols 1989). As is evident in their testimonies, their reluctance to associate with what Sister Edna called "violent" feminism could be read as an affirmation of a more conventional feminism that is not disruptive or overly willful (Ahmed 2014) but more modest (Milestone and Meyer 2011). Still, at a minimum, all sisters expressed what appears as a liberal feminist desire for women's gifts to be respected (Shih 2010).

NON-FEMINIST WOMEN RELIGIOUS

Most sisters and former sisters identified with feminism and almost always in its singular form, however variously defined or understood it was for them. The few (11 percent) who did not[9] identify as feminist still articulated unequivocal support for gender equality and expressed considerable concern over gender discrimination within the Church and in society and thus seemed to hold, albeit to varying degrees, religious liberal feminist beliefs (Shih 2010). For example, Sister Clara, a renowned, strongly opinionated, and published social justice activist did not identify herself as a feminist because she found it exclusionary:

> Well, you see, I don't ever use the word because ... I'm not sure. Like when I went to the women's march, well they call themselves feminists; well I didn't agree. I found it ... wasn't my style at all ... if you're going to achieve anything you have to respect even your opponent ... and you can't knock out half of the population trying to find gender equality ... it'll come in another way.

Yet she was fully supportive of pro-equality activism: "Oh and Stephen Lewis, if I was a millionaire I'd give him my money because he said the other day [in

2008] that gender inequality is the greatest evil of our time. And I thought, boom!" The ever-pragmatic Sister Josephine conveyed a similar hesitation toward the identity due to the presumption of gender-based exclusion, but she was also clearly in favour of egalitarianism:

> It's like the four letter word ... I don't think I'm a feminist as such because a feminist sometimes it's ... [sigh] it's kind of against all humans. I'm not like that. I do believe in equality though ... But the thing is, I've seen many women who are just as hard and so on as men ... and I've seen men who are very gentle and very supportive.

Though she seems to associate feminism with a kind of general antagonism, Sister Josephine's perception of equality echoes a feminist ethic of leadership and a more gender-neutral humanist stance. Comparably, while the ever-so-gentle Sister Shannon did not identify as feminist, her reflection on feminism was indicative of gender equity:

> Feminism is in knowing our value. It is in knowing the gifts that have been entrusted to us and putting those gifts at the service of all ... One gender is only half of the circle. Is it because we can't accept who we are that we attack the other? As Christians, we should surely be able to respect one another.

Sister Edna, a serious-minded woman, also associated feminism with damaging aggression:

> There was a time I didn't like what these feminists ... they wanted to assert themselves as women but I found they were being very violent to themselves ... there are aspects I didn't like about it. It has some good points but there are some points I don't [like].

By contrast, Sister Edna's ideal version of feminism included a liberal emphasis on women's peace-filled originality and dignity: "What I'd like to see is that women would be able ... to exert their creativity and their personhood ... as women without ... tearing down others in the process."

When asked to share her perception of feminism and whether or not she identified herself as a feminist, Sister Benita paused for a long time and then explained the perceived distinction between aggression and collaboration that she deemed relevant: "I don't want it to be like ... Germaine Greer just ... for the sake of being feminine, just using a woman's power ... [but], you know, a way to get people together and ... facilitate."[10] When asked specifically if she identified herself as a feminist, Sister Benita's response was hesitant and indicative of a compromise: "if crunch comes to ... yes I would fight for women's rights." When she reflected on gender equality, Sister Benita, who was a tireless advocate of marginalized girls in her younger years, expressed concern for "women at the bottom of the totem pole."

Although she expressed concern about gender inequality and male domination, the thoughtfully oriented Sister Penelope was also hesitant to identify herself as a feminist because she perceived feminism to be associated with a demanding approach:

> I don't think I'm a feminist in the sense that I don't believe I'm one person to step out and fight for women to have a place in everything, you know, but yet ... I would fight for anything that I believe was our right ... equal opportunity, if I felt [it] was a woman's place, you know. There are certain places, I wouldn't well, in [name of country] for example, on a fishing boat with men, I just wouldn't find a woman ... it wouldn't be safe to begin with, you know; I don't think it's a place for her. But I believe we have all the capacities that men have and I believe that we should have every right too.

Sister Penelope's comments reflect the complexity of some sisters' tenuous identification to feminism, as her description of equal opportunity holds contradictory views. While she reports believing in the equal capacities of men and women, she reproduces the idea of a gendered division of labour in certain spheres – a stance that reveals the complex and sometimes contradictory opinions that are informed simultaneously by multiple feminist orientations (Shih 2010).

Among the current and former women religious with whom I spoke, there were none more aloof to feminism than Sister Nellie. When I asked her to explain her version of feminism and how she related to it, she responded disinterestedly: "I just never think about it." Yet, when I asked if she believed in gender equality, she clarified, albeit unenthusiastically, that she did. While she added that she had helped women to participate more fully in Church activities during her forty-year mission in an economically developing country, she felt the need to point out that she did so but "not with a warrior attitude." Her indifference to feminism was also evident when she expressed frustration with sisters from her religious community who stayed with her for an extended period of time while she was on mission. She seemed to have little regard for their feminist orientation and their attempts at gender inclusive language: "They were so very dominant, and 'she and he,' and that kind of thing, and to me it was just wasting energy." In this way, Sister Nellie's conception of feminist values runs parallel to common perceptions of feminism as something disruptive and unnecessary (Echols 1989).

It is evident that some sisters feel uncomfortable identifying with feminism because they misunderstand it to mean that women's rights are considered superior to the rights of others and that they are championed by way of aggressive tactics (Howard Ecklund 2003). Yet, despite their rejection of, or uneasiness with, the feminist label, all of the women religious (both current and former) denounced patriarchal abuses of power (Griffith 1997), and they expressed what appeared to be an unwavering liberal feminist commitment to gender equality (Shih 2010), which some seemed to regard as common sense. As Griffith (1997, 205) contends, regardless of how contradictory their identities and opinions may appear, it is essential to listen to "non-feminist" women like Sisters Edna and Nellie "who repudiate what they take to be established feminism" because their conflicting messages shed important light on the undeniably muddled realities of gendered experiences.

FEMINIST WOMEN RELIGIOUS

By comparison, 55 percent of participants readily and enthusiastically identified themselves as feminist. Foremost among them was Sister Edith, an accomplished educator and author, who fondly acknowledged the centrality of gender-based issues in her work: "Yeah, actually women's issues is sort of my thing [laughs], I must admit." Her definition of feminism was concise yet encompassing: "Women are ... human beings. Women are equal. Women are made in God's image ... so it's a recognition of the full humanity of women." When Sister Edith provided an update on her experience a year after her original interview, she was proud to share that she had taught a post-secondary course on ecofeminism that year because she felt that "it is an area that needs attention." In addition to illustrating how she seeks to exemplify a broader, earth-centred conception of feminism, her involvement at a relatively late stage of life serves as a testament to her enduring commitment to feminist aims.

While Sister Joelle – a former teacher and superior general who conveyed her views confidently – shared Sister Benita's critique against aggressive styles of feminism, she identified unequivocally with feminism as she articulated a liberal emphasis on gender equity: "I find that some ... feminists, you know, Germaine Greer ... there were some who were a bit exaggerated or extreme to make their point ... but the genuine feminism which recognizes the gifts that women bring on an equal basis ... are something that I value for sure." Sister Joelle further acknowledged the significance of feminism and the ways in which women religious not only implemented it, but also modelled it early on:

> I think feminism has made a very important contribution to women's equality ... to society in general and to ourselves as well. In some ways, even within the traditional structures, we were feminists ... I mean we

were administrators in the health care institutions, and principals, and all that kind of thing.

Similarly, Naomi, who was a sister for twenty-eight years, identified herself as a feminist without hesitation and with much conviction; she offered the following rationale that situates her embracing of feminism within a pivotal temporal context: "Well I grew up in that era of ... I came of age in the 60s, and I think very developmentally came to appreciate that women have incredible potential to be, and to do, in the world ... and that any stifling of that on the basis of gender is just totally wrong." Naomi's version of feminism conveyed women's aptitudes and entitlement: "Well for me I think feminism is embracing women as full human beings with all who have a right to everything, to accomplish, and to be about and to realize their potential in every way."

Three sisters and one former sister, who readily identified as feminists, also reflected on others' reticence. For example, as she questioned the resistance against feminism, Sister Jeanette, a caring and conscientious woman, expressed enthusiastically what feminism meant to her and what she gained by it:

Some sisters too have this thing that feminism is against the Church. It's not against the Church. It's not. It's like they say you're protesting. That's not protesting ... It's an energy! It's an energy! It's a gift! ... Feminism to me is the gift of creativity ... And I feel like I have opportunities to use my gifts as a woman and opportunities to ... support others in using their gifts.

Comparably, Sister Adele embraced the identity wholeheartedly: "Well, I would call myself a feminist." As a discerning woman, she then clarified how she had proudly acknowledged her feminist identity against a fellow sister's questioning:

One of our older sisters one time ... she trusted me and ... I was on the leadership team and she was telling me about somebody else and she said, "You know, she's one of those feminists," and she said, "Are you one of those too?" [laughs], and I said, "Yeah I am!" And she said, "Ah!" She didn't know what to do with it, you know ... Well ... what I sensed [from her] was kinda the shock that "oh my gosh, even this person I thought was good would speak in this way." I think it got her thinking ... we had a very good relationship of mutual respect ... I think ... it was just to see that she thought that oh well now I have to think about this because ... she knew ... I wasn't flighty! [laughs]

Sister Adele's openness with her identity clearly stimulated another sister to pause and reflect – an indication of the tensions and uncertainties regarding women's roles and ambitions and the nuanced ways in which sisters negotiated their more-or-less feminist projects.

When asked if she identified herself as a feminist, former Sister Judith confidently and enthusiastically replied, "Yes I do! Yes!" She was also swift and clear about her liberal version of feminism: "I think that feminism is believing in the equality of women and men and in the possibility of women ... being able to do what men can do." In a discussion on the hesitancy of other sisters to identify as feminists due to negative connotations, Judith, who is empathetic and sharp-witted, expressed sadness and caution: "Yeah isn't that too bad and ... all the gains are never gotten for good! That's one thing I have learned for everything, for feminism ... for every human right, if you're not watching every single minute, you lose them."

Similarly, as one who readily identified herself as a feminist ("Yes I do!"), contemporarily oriented, eighty-year-old Sister Maureen offered an affirming explanation of feminism while recognizing the critiques against it: "I think Jesus was a feminist ... I think ... to realize the gift of feminism and to speak about it. You know, people sometimes when you speak about it, 'Oh, you're a feminist' right away, you know ... it's not a positive thing but it's a negative kind of thing." Yet for Sister Maureen, the feminist identity was positive, so much so that in her view it was a compliment to be proud of because of the inclusivity and openness associated with it: "I think a female, a woman is able to be more open to nurturing people who like say ... same-sex marriage or ... lesbianism ... I mean women are a lot more open to help trying to ... bring it to a new place ... I think Jesus is our model for being feminine."

Sister Maureen did not elaborate on her sense of Jesus modelling feminism and femininity, but her positioning of Jesus as a feminist figure is a view held by many scholars and activists. For example, in *Jesus Was a Feminist,* Leonard Swidler (2007) reminds us how Jesus challenged societal convention to treat men and women equally. Similarly, in *Jesus Feminist,* Sarah Bessey (2013) presents Jesus as a proponent of gender equality. Chittister (1995, 153) also linked feminism and Jesus by pointing to the way in which he valued women's worth and empowered women by assigning them important tasks, including announcing his resurrection.

The confidence and pride with which Judith and Sisters Adele and Maureen not only associate with feminism but also repel critiques against it are testaments to their belief in and commitment to the advancement of gender equality. Yet, the existing critiques among some women religious, as well as the qualifications presented below, are indicative of some sisters' reluctance to embrace certain styles of feminism and feminist activism that they believe to be antagonistic. Other sisters identified themselves as feminists but qualified either the extent of their association with the identity or the nature of their feminist engagement. For example, Sister Theresa, a former teacher and principal who was very forthcoming with her incisive critiques against the Church's patriarchal structure, shared that: "I'm not out there on the street corner but I think I'm living from a feminist stance ... and standing up for it." Similarly, while Sister Rita, a pensive and practical woman, distanced herself somewhat from a feminist identity, her concern for gender equality was unmistakable and she drew on more renowned voices to demonstrate her conviction, as did many of the other sisters I interviewed:

> To say would I call myself a feminist? I'm not right out there in front pushing for, but I know it ... I know it can be loaded but ... it's needed and I would want to see it more and more all the time. I don't see it as equal ... I think there's a long way to go with that ... in the Catholic Church ... And I think a lot of sisters too are really showing the need for women; like, you know, we've got Mary Jo Leddy, and we've got Joan Chittister and Barbara Fiand and so many of these fine, fine women.

Others similarly identified themselves as feminists but distanced themselves from what they considered confrontational qualities:

> Well, not a roaring one. (Sister Marian)

> Not an extreme feminist ... I guess I consider myself as a feminist when I hear about things that are putting down women but I'm not ... a fighter ... yet I admire those who do. (Sister Sophie)

Sister Corinne, a considerate woman who is cautious about when and where she discusses gender justice, also moderated her position. On the one hand, when asked how she felt about feminism, she promptly responded, "For me it's positive ... it's a gift to be a woman. It's a gift ... it's beautiful. It's positive." Yet, when asked if she considered herself to be a feminist, she instantly felt the need to clarify her position: "Yes but ... I would say mild [laughs] ... a peaceful one."

Even Sister Kelly, who is known as an uncompromising promoter of women's equality and feminist spirituality, who authored a feminist-oriented book that advocated for greater inclusiveness in the Catholic Church, and who also embraces some radical religious feminist precepts including female Goddess wisdoms (Shih 2010), qualified her feminist stance: "I am not one of those, what's defined today as a radical feminist, although I believe I am a radical feminist because of getting at the root of what it is ... no, not the kind of ... harsh ... That's not for me, and I kind of lead from behind rather than in front [laughs]." As I exemplify further in the chapters on spirituality and activism, the way in which Sister Kelly, along with other sisters distinguish their feminist identity from their feminist practices is curiously perplexing. In the meantime, some of her additional interpretations remain illustrative here. For example, when asked to clarify her negative interpretation of feminism, Sister Kelly offered this explanation that viewed feminism and femininity as conflictual: "I think that a lot of ... people in the 70s ... when women woke up, you know, that they ... actually were being moved by what Jungians would call their negative animus. [sigh] Not, not really feminine."[11]

Like the above-mentioned women, Sister Kelly too disavows a sort of wilful assertiveness that is associated with feminist activism (see Ahmed 2014). Many of the sisters appear to separate this wilfulness from supporting women's rights or gender equality, a position that is not expressly feminist but contains strands of a broader feminist project or, at minimum, a religious liberal feminist form of it (Shih 2010). Fittingly, when asked if she believed in gender equality, Sister Kelly's commitment was unequivocal: "Oh! Yeah! Of course, of course yes." When asked if she thought gender equality was possible in the Roman Catholic Church, Sister Kelly seemed optimistic in light of how she positively perceives the current scandals and controversies as leading to an eventual collapse and regeneration of the patriarchal Church: "I hope it is. I pray for that. I hope for that. I work for that and I think it will come. It has to because I believe the Spirit is at work in history within our Church or this fermentation that's going on now wouldn't be taking place."

Similarly, Sister Loretta, a former general superior who was very open with her critiques against the Church's male hierarchy, was also averse to being identified as radical:[12] "I think so. I hope so [laughs] ... I don't think I'm a radical feminist ... I just feel that we ... try to be present to people, to try to be relational and ... not to be judgmental." The latter part of her explanation is indicative of her recognition of what feminism is generally more associated with – inclusivity rather than merely a shifting of gender norms. When she described what feminism meant to her, Sister Loretta further emphasized the importance of human connectivity, also affirming an essential femininity related to community building:

> Well, first of all, it means a relational person. I think that women have that capacity sometimes that even a lot of men don't but that priests certainly don't. Well I shouldn't say that. Some are very relational too. I mean I'm not making ... a generalization. But I think that as ... a woman, we're much more relational ... and try to build relationships ... try to build community, try to listen, try to be present ... I think those are all feminine qualities for me anyway. Stand up for what we believe in.

Sister Loretta's critique against priests, while seemingly exclusive, must be understood within the wider context of the Church's patriarchal structure, which has undoubtedly been more hierarchical than relational. Nevertheless, Sister Loretta does acknowledge and appreciate the male priests she knows who are progressive and inclusive.[13]

Sister Mabel, an incumbent general superior who conveys her strong opinions and compassionate considerations unequivocally and who aligns herself with feminist orientations, also emphasized co-operation and ingenuity in her interpretation of feminism, further cementing an essential femaleness in her sense of women's gifts:

> I believe that ... whatever gifts I have as a woman, these gifts need to be used for others and ... women are much more collaborative. Women are much more inclusive ... I'm thinking generally now, but a true feminist I think would be that kind of person, to be creative, engage others in the sharing in the works. It's like a collaborative effort, mutuality, all trust, all those kinds of qualities.

Sister Marian, who was both candid and sensitive, also uses the word "gift" to celebrate her strengths, but unlike Sister Mabel and others who distance themselves from assertiveness, Sister Marian's expression is wilful and proud. She interprets feminism as a reflection of her groundedness and self-confidence, particularly in terms of what she has to offer as a woman:

> Well it means I know who I am and I am a woman gifted to love and to create and ... to spread joy and to be encompassing and receiving ... no matter where I am and not to be shy about that or denigrated in any way and ... that's who I am and I'm loved by God and sustained by God in life and that's all I need to know.

Taking wilfulness further, former Sister Darlene, an insightful and reassuring woman, as well as a self-identified active feminist, describes her entry into feminism as a "loyal dissent" against the Church. As she explains, her unequivocally feminist identity originated in a direct encounter with the blatant mistreatment of women by Church officials which had a profound influence on her spiritual and theological world view:

> I began to see myself in loyal dissent [laughs] pretty early on ... Feminism was an important part of it for me. Like, I realized very dramatically that our Church wasn't very good to women ... I can tell you exactly. It was very dramatic. I was doing spiritual direction in a small renewal centre that we had ... and I was out one day just roaming around in the garden ... and this woman came by and she said, "Are you a nun?" And I said, "Yes I am," and she said, "Could I talk to you?" And I said, "Of course." So we went in and we sat in my office. Well the woman ... was going to

jump off the bank ... to commit suicide and I was sitting on a rock and so she talked to me instead because of who I was. It was pretty dramatic.

Now her story was quite awful ... [it] was a lifetime of abuse ... sexual abuse by a drunken husband, and he used to work as a logger in the woods ... and she dreaded his coming back because he would always drink and ... rape her ... there was no tenderness ... in that marriage. It was absolutely dead and full of violence and she had gone to the parish priest ... [who] had said, "Well, you've made your bed, you married him, so you've got to lie in it so what you need to do is pray more." So ... she joined a charismatic prayer group ... it was a great escape for a little while and she went back to the parish priest after a couple of years ... and she said, "He is still beating me up; he's still raping me. I try to pray and I try to trust God but you know ..."

The other part of it was she was beginning to be fearful for her daughter ... and the priest said, "You have to do your duty to your husband, you have to be available to your husband, and if you are available to your husband he won't go after your daughter." And she realized that she couldn't accept that. So she sent her daughter to the grandmother's for the summer and ... she was going to end her life. Well, I knew I had to act pretty fast on that so I had to get her out of that situation; that is what I helped her do. So she went out of the province to her sister where she was safe and she filed for divorce and she did get divorced and she got money from the husband ... then she got her children.

So that turned out very well, but it left me with, here ... was the parish priest; I knew him very well; he's a nice man and it was ... my first encounter with ... the realization that the Church doesn't care about its women and the clerical culture is ... that women were needed in the priesthood ... I joined CNWE after that. But that's the beginning of what for me was a journey of working at Church renewal and I joined a lot of things at that time ... We are the Church International Movement and Catholics of Vision ... the CCCC, the Coalition of Concerned Canadian Catholics.

It was a jolt ... for me; that was a formative event ... because I was slightly feminist before that but that pushed me to be an activist feminist in the Church. So I studied feminist spirituality and feminist theology after that, which was only just beginning. Like the first feminist theologian was Mary Daly, she was my age ... So that was all pretty exciting ... and it wasn't just the critique on the male patriarchal. It was a whole new way ... of seeing the world differently, and after that, it was the womanist thing, you know, there was all kinds of things going on, but ... my world view shifted; my philosophy, my theology, my spirituality shifted in major ways at that time.[14]

When I asked Darlene whether the woman was aware of the impact that their experience together had on her feminist orientation, she replied affirmatively: "Yeah! Yeah, like we mediated God for each other, you know. It was wonderful, yeah, yes!" Evoking the mutuality of the women's exchange, Darlene added that the two have remained in touch over the years, and thus Darlene receives updates on the family's progress, including the well-being of the mother, daughters, and grandchildren.

Darlene's view of feminism has become all-encompassing and, in many regards, intersectional (Collins 2015; hooks 2000), and she credits feminism for having brought her toward other approaches including racial inclusivity and earth-centredness:

> Well, as I say, it's a whole world view of the equality of all … like the divine milieu is really important to me but in the divine milieu, you know, I am no more equal than anybody or anything else is equal as God's creation … All of us one in that great [pause] wow! So yeah, I just feel totally, I mean gender equality, races, nationalities, species … I just see everything is one in God … But it was feminism and its critique of the one way that led me there.

In addition to illustrating how one's "incremental growth in awareness" regarding feminisms leads to intersectional perspectives (Collins 2015; hooks 2000; Shih 2010, 240), Darlene's testimony also echoes Sister Joan Chittister's contention that feminism "revisions the world from the perspectives of equality, humanity and dignity of every living thing" and is particularly ecological and global in its outlook (Chittister 1995, 151). Yet, Darlene's experience also serves as an example of how there was a limit to which feminist projects could be actively pursued within her Church and religious community at that time. Once Darlene's feminist identity had moved beyond a liberal orientation and had thus reached a point of outsider status, she could no longer feel at home either in her community or, eventually, in her religion. Darlene's emerging predicament serves as an important reminder of how one's shifting religious identity and secular affiliation must be understood within the context of institutional power and domination (Ammerman 2003, 223).

It is clear that sisters, both non-feminists and feminists, have conflicting notions of feminism. Many sisters distanced themselves from radical feminism because they associated it with confrontation and unfeminine wilfulness. However, given the majority of the women's advanced age, their interpretations may be related to a particular brand of 1960s and 1970s radical activism (Echols 1989). Yet, others embraced the term feminism and many of its facets wholeheartedly and, in particular, the liberal forms of feminism that for them celebrate the giftedness of women as essentially peaceful and inclusive (Shih 2010). As I explore later, these variously feminist projects were deployed strategically.

POST-FEMINIST AND HUMANIST WOMEN RELIGIOUS

The remaining third (34 percent) of the women interviewed acknowledged their feminist stance but advocated what they referred to as post-feminism, mutualism, or humanism whereby they sought feminine and masculine reconciliation as a basis for authentically inclusive processes (Chittister 1998; Manning 2006). For example, while retaining her self-identification as a feminist, the always-animated Sister Agnes illustrated the complexity of terms as she pondered moving beyond using the word "feminist" to using more humanist language:

> Well, isn't it funny all the studies I've done and reading, I don't really ... it's hard to know ... Some people feel that the feminist movement has gone as far as it can go ... I guess I consider myself kind of a humanist, a human, a female human who is stifled in the Catholic Church, and I know that ... female humans ... struggle in society too in many, many professions ... Ah, being a feminist has such a negative tone for a lot of people. So I would like to think of myself ... as a humanist, as everybody having a right, male and female ... but I know I'm a feminist.

While Sister Agnes recognized her feminist standpoint and while her propensity toward humanism seemed motivated by an intentional distancing from negative connotations related to feminism (Manning 1999), it is evident that her embracing of humanism was rooted in a wider sense of equality, and yet was also informed by her own gender-based stifling.

Comparably and perhaps somewhat ironically, Sister Carmen, whom I was strongly encouraged to contact to participate in this study because of her allegedly renowned and feisty feminist stance, did not actually identify herself as a feminist: "I am called a feminist but ... I don't call myself one. I don't care what they call me! [I am] in favour of humanity." Clearly Sister Carmen's wilfulness was intact, yet for her, not related to the presumed feminist label and as Ammerman (2003, 209–10) reminds us, such a seemingly inconsistent stance is often filled with tensions between assumed roles and declared identities as one emphasizes their own uniqueness. Similarly, Sister Noreen, whose belief in gender equality was as fervent and absolute as her ever-enthusiastic disposition, actually distanced herself from a feminist identity. Rather than leaning toward an essential femaleness as reported by some of the other sisters, her reasons reflected a discontent regarding what she perceived to be unproductive divisions:

No, well I don't believe in categories, I don't believe in isms. I'm a woman, and that's it. I'm not interested in feminism; [it's] about the universe, our place and our connection about the divine and the universe. I studied at ... university, the structural approach, you know, in feminism ... to me, feminism is another discrimination thing, okay. If you're going to speak of feminism then you're going to speak of masculinism and you're going to go into the isms. No! Let's stay with human beings. Whatever, words ... these are artificial boundaries; they scare me, as a matter of fact; this one-sided thing like this scares me because it divides people; sure women had to fight, they had to get together ... and I think strides have been made but don't label me a feminist because I'm standing up for a woman; I'm just a human being who is seeing something that's right here. If you say pants or skirt ... I'm going to say no difference!

Echoing a similar view of gender distinctions as overdrawn, Carol, whose critiques against the institutional Church are trenchant (as expressed in her interview by emphatic fist-pounding), distanced herself from a feminist label; yet her reflection was grounded in both equality and mutualism: "I don't know if I'm a feminist. I believe in the equality of the sexes but I think that both the feminine and the masculine needs to be honoured within the person."

Sister Ella, a faith-filled and affirming person, as well as a strong critic against the Church's male hierarchy, had clearly discerned her broader position on feminism, which also includes the mutual embracing of masculinity and femininity across genders:

I find that's a hard question ... It's just ... a fact of life that half the population are women and that I feel gifted as a woman to live out my life using my gifts ... as men need to live out their lives using their gifts. I kind of hate to be talking even about feminism and masculinity. Like ... it's a fact of life and of course it's because of the lopsidedness of the culture that we would concentrate on it now trying to right the balance but I don't think a lot about it really.

As Sister Ella raised the idea of mutualism in our conversation, she expressed ease and enthusiasm: "Well, that's where I feel more comfortable and where we help men own their femininity and help women own their masculinity and become whole in that. That's where I would use my energies." Comparably, Sister Kelly, who distances herself from "radical" feminist tactics, yet tenaciously advocates for women's rights within the Roman Catholic Church, also nuanced her view on gender parity by emphasizing balanced reciprocity: "I like to use the word mutuality rather than equality." While they did not self-identify with particular brands of feminism, by their reference to mutuality, Carol and

Sisters Ella and Kelly are nevertheless, and perhaps even unbeknownst to them, articulating contemporary tenets of intersectional and to some extent critical feminisms (Chittister 1998; hooks 2000).

Former Sister Mildred, whose perceptiveness is palpable, assertively articulated what appeared to be a well thought out post-feminist position that advocated equilibrium as well: "I'm not a feminist in that I need to go out and fight with the Church and that. But I do believe in the whole balance between ... the intellectual side, the rational side, and the emotional side and the understanding of it ... the empathy." While Mildred claims that she does "not outrightly" engage in feminist work, she believes firmly in gender equality, and her counselling office's shelves that are filled with books on women centredness are a testament to that commitment.

Sister Sarah has been exposed more recently to evolving versions of feminism in her advanced university studies. Her deeper understanding is indicative of wider and more inclusive feminist debates. Thus, as a mindful and considerate person, she held a similar view on mutualism between both women and men through what she referred to as a post-feminist approach:

> There are so many branches of feminism today that I don't really know where to put myself. But I think I feel most comfortable at this moment calling myself kind of a post-feminist in a sense that I always find that the word "feminism," although I don't personally have a problem with it, I find it creates a barrier with a lot of people. So I tend to see myself more as a post-feminist and I also say that because I really believe that men as well as women have been equally damaged by patriarchy, and ... it's about the flourishing of all of us not just about the flourishing of women, although I think women proportionately have suffered more, they're not the only ones who have suffered.

In contrast to other sisters who view feminism as antagonistic, it is evident that numerous (72 percent) sisters and former sisters are well educated about feminisms and embrace components of its strands and evolutions to various degrees, including third-wave and, to some extent, fourth-wave dimensions.[15] Taken together, the women's diverse views on feminism reflect the dynamic complexities through which they consider the multiple relational and institutional conditions that impact their own and others' lives (Ammerman 2003, 224; Shih 2010).

CONCLUSION

Given that some sisters do not identify themselves as feminists, this chapter's analysis of their simultaneous commitment to feminism and Catholicism may seem problematic. Nevertheless, despite their varied affiliations with feminisms (Neitz 2003; Shih 2010), all of the current and former sisters interviewed aligned themselves with feminist principles, and they advocated for and/or partook in feminist forms of circular models of governance, gender inclusive liturgies, and women-centred activism that their religious communities organized. Therefore, their support of feminist-oriented activities and their "across the board" frustration with the patriarchal constraints of the institutional Church serve as sufficient examples of their embracing of feminism(s). This actuality, at least in part, affirms Dumont's (1995, 183) argument that if historically women religious were not feminists, they have become feminists, albeit to various extents. As the remainder of this book illustrates, it is through feminist understandings that patriarchal institutions, like the Roman Catholic Church, are "intrinsically oppressive" (Schneiders 2013, 428), and it is through feminist values of "equality, relationships, life, creation, nonviolence" that current and former women religious offer their critiques, carry out their decision-making processes, and advance their human enterprises (Chittister 1995, 166).[16] In the next three chapters, I shed light on how the women's feminist lenses have not only informed their own recognition of and critique against patriarchal domination but have also enabled them to conceive of and engage in ways to move beyond it (Gervais and Turenne Sjolander 2015; Johnson 2002a; Schneiders 2013), often in critical, diverse, and intersectional ways (Collins 2015; hooks 2000; Shih 2010). As will become evident, the women's application of feminist analyses to their own circumstances brings to light with cogent clarity their own experiences of patriarchal power – many of which have never been revealed until now (Dumont 1995, 183; Peddigrew 2008).

CHAPTER 2

Experiencing patriarchal domination

*Restrictions and intrusions, coercion that sometimes reached the level of bul-
lying ... unilateral demands for submission without dialogue, and outright
psychological and spiritual violence ... began to appear clearly for what they
were: totally unacceptable domination of women by men in the name of God
and sacred power.* (Schneiders 2013, 530)

W ithin the Roman Catholic Church's entrenched patriarchal structure
and its corresponding "sexual apartheid" (Schneiders 2004, 3), women
religious have long been marginalized, degraded, and oppressed by male clerical
authorities, as well as systemically excluded from leadership and decision-making
(Bonavoglia 2005; Chittister 2004; Ebaugh 1993; Leonard 2007; Mangion
2008; Schneiders 2013, 2004). Among the countless instances of patriarchal
domination throughout the history of the Church, a major change in Canon
Law in 1917 led to particularly excessive and repressive restrictions over the
governance of women's religious orders by the Church's male hierarchy (Coburn
and Smith 1999).

While others (see, e.g., Gray 2007, Lux-Sterritt and Mangion 2011,
Magray 1998, Wittberg 1994) have duly documented sisters' ceaseless struggles
with clerical control and episcopal interference elsewhere in earlier centuries,
uncovered mainly within archival records, in this chapter, I present Ontario-
based sisters' own experiential accounts of denials and exclusions which constitute disconcerting evidence of "systematic institutionalized sexism" (hooks
2000, 1). As such, late-twentieth and early-twenty-first-century examples of
Canadian sisters' pain and frustration associated with the Roman Catholic
Church's intransigence toward women's equality are made known.

SISTERS' PERCEPTIONS OF PATRIARCHY AND MISOGYNY

The Church is a patriarchal institution. Women were not permitted to take leadership roles in the Church. (Sister Shannon)

Every current and former sister I interviewed contended resolutely that the Roman Catholic Church is a patriarchal institution. Their perceptions were by no means surprising as I was already aware of their feminist inclinations. However, the laughing tones, the subversive smiles, the disapproving eye-rolling, the facial expressions, the hand-raising motions, and sometimes the fist-pounding gestures through which these elderly and pious women conveyed their opinions in response to the question "Do you think that the Roman Catholic Church is a patriarchal institution?" were both affirming and amusing:

I do! I do! (Sister Adele)

Oh yeah! (Sister Josephine)

Oh yes I do! (Sister Jeanette)

Oh I sure do! (Sister Sophie)

Oh definitely, definitely. (Sister Penelope)

You couldn't write yes big enough! (Sister Loretta [laughing])

How loud do you want me to shout it? (Sister Kelly [laughing])

Is that a rhetorical question? Of course, of course. (Sister Joelle [laughing])

Absolutely! Absolutely! It's pathetic. (Carol)

Well, naturally it is; I mean it's obvious. (Sister Carmen)

Oh yes it is. I think it would admit that itself. (Sister Sarah)

Absolutely ... Certainly it's a "power over" understanding of authority, and I don't see much servant aspect to it. (Darlene)

It still is, yes. Oh yes it is, and it is still especially Rome that is still hanging on to that. (Sister Corinne)

Oh yeah! It's a pyramid structure, and it's wrong! It's outdated! (Sister Ella)

Some sisters offered even more sarcastic rejoinders:

Isn't it!? (Judith [laughing])

Oh no, Christine! How can you say that!? (Sister Agnes [laughing])

Do I think? I know! (Sister Maureen)

Is it? [rhetorically and laughingly] Oh absolutely! (Sister Mabel)

Still others conveyed their perceptions of the Church's patriarchal dimensions through poignant visual images that had clearly troubled them. As Sister Theresa remembered a televised depiction of the Vatican that she had seen shortly before I interviewed her in 2009, she verbalized her emotionally charged critique against the androcentric dimensions of it rather emphatically: "I'm disheartened by the maze of males ... the rows and rows and rows and rows of men! There wasn't the sign of a woman. The pope was up there surrounded by all these cardinals. It just made me sick."

Similar images were evoked by those who perceived the Roman Catholic Church as a misogynistic institution (Schneiders 2011). For Judith, the Church's misogynous structure was indisputable: "Oh God! Definitely! Absolutely! ... And it's right from the top! Yeah ... they take their lead from there." Judith remembered how this perception was shaped by a compelling image that she had seen more than thirty years prior to that of Sister Theresa's but whose content portrayed the very same male-dominated scenario, and it was this particular patriarchal portrayal that prompted her to eventually leave the Roman Catholic Church:[1]

> I had my *big* awakening when I saw ... *Time* magazine had a picture of the funeral [of Pope Paul VI in 1978] ... it was an aerial view. Oh my God! ... It was the first time I noticed nothing but ... men! Nothing but men! Nothing but bishops! And that struck me like it had never struck me before, and I just said to myself "Why do I want to belong to this organization?" There's nothing in it for me! Nothing!

While the majority of sisters shared Judith's opinion completely, some felt that labelling the Roman Catholic Church as a misogynous institution was "going too far."[2] However, Sister Sarah qualified her hesitation by recognizing how the Church plays a promotional role: "I think in some ways some of the attitudes can contribute toward misogyny." While fully regarding the Roman Catholic Church as misogynous, Sisters Edith, Noreen, and Joelle were cautious about generalizing and thus specified that it is "the structures" and "the institutional" aspects of the Church that are problematic because they are, as

Naomi declared rhetorically, "still sufficiently masculine-oriented." Sister Edith also added that the resulting sense among the sisters is one of "powerlessness." In reflecting on the misogynous nature of the Church, Sister Rita also made particular reference to the hierarchical dimension when she specified that it was "coming from Rome."

The current and former women religious (65 percent) who firmly believed that the Church is a misogynous organization were emphatic in their explanations. For example, according to Mildred, the problem is blatant: "Hater of women!? ... Well, I think it is that, obviously." After insisting that the Church is "definitely" misogynous, Sister Kelly explained that it is evident in "the way they treat women; they don't even listen to women, you know! ... They don't even bother including how women feel ... or what they think ... *that's* misogynistic."

Sister Noreen related the institutional dynamics to power:

> It's a power issue ... There are some women in the Church who are very competent, theologians who are very outspoken, very well prepared, and they are a threat. So ... if you're guarding your power, you're just like ... Gaddafi or all those dictators ... that we see falling one after the other, right? You're going to do whatever.

While she is not at all interested in gaining clerical control for herself because she prefers to avoid a hierarchical system that would place her on a pedestal, Sister Noreen is very aware of the limiting and even sidelining implications of the Church's patriarchal power over women religious: "A sister has no power whatsoever. I have no power whatsoever, from that angle, you see? So if I was hung up for power, I certainly couldn't pull out my sisterhood as a power thing. Forget it! What are you gonna be, shut out?" Sister Noreen's contextualization is further illustrative of the extent to which institutional power impacts how religious identities are both perceived and practised (Ammerman 2003, 223).

After exclaiming "Oh yes! Oh God yes!" when I asked her if she viewed the Church as misogynous, Sister Agnes explained how she saw it manifested, again linking it to power: "Well, in not using women's gifts [and] in being afraid of their power, their fire, their drive, their passion ... they're afraid of women ... they don't understand women." Sister Agnes elaborated on how the misogynistic attitude is counter-intuitive to the teachings of Jesus, yet seemingly ingrained in the institutional Church: "It really bothers me that ... the Church seems to go out of its way to not do some of the things that Jesus did like his hanging around women so much, you know! His high regard for women!"

Sister Mabel takes this outlook even further, framing issues of patriarchal power as a form of abuse (Schneiders 2013). In conveying her view on the

Church as a misogynous entity, Sister Mabel explains how it is so foundational to the Church as an institution that misogyny will only be eradicated when the institution crumbles, evoking Audre Lorde's (1984, 110) famous words, "the master's tools will never dismantle the master's house":

> Well, I think it is a form of abuse because there's gifts that are being squelched and not used. I call that abuse ... there's no consciousness that there's a whole other half of the population or more, and I don't think that's going to change in our [lifetime]. It's going to change but it'll be in the fall of [the Church]; I mean they're holding on like this now [grips armrests of chair] ... but I don't I don't feel [it] personally.

In one extended sentence during our conversation, Carol listed more specifically how she and other women were personally deprived as a result of this "absolutely" misogynous structure, as it:

> Did not recognize my creativity in liturgy ... Did not allow me to perform liturgies in a public setting ... Would not ordain me, not that I wanted to be ordained but I was doing the work of a priest, you know, all the way along ... [and there was] no recognition of women's roles; I mean bright, bright women.

Sister Loretta also made reference to the ordination issue as she shared her frustration over the Church's misogynistic character: "Well, when you can't even talk about women's ordination; I mean that's pretty extreme!" Similarly, Sister Theresa did not think that the views held about the Church as a misogynous entity were "too strong." When she clarified, with an air of provocation, she echoed concern over the deprivation of ordination, and she drew attention to the scarcity of women in biblical teachings which Stone (1976, xxvii) refers to as actualities that were "intentionally hidden": "Well, the whole bit ... that women can't be priests ... and what they've taken out of the gospels, the scripture, the old, and the new testaments. Women aren't there anymore. They've just somehow disappeared."

Sister Sophie, a perceptive and supportive woman, also felt that the Church is misogynous not only "in some cases" but "in many ways." One of her examples echoed what scholars and journalists (e.g., Bonavoglia 2005; Bouclin 2006; Peddigrew 2008; Schneiders 2013) have also documented: how priests have manipulated their positions of power when they have abused women sexually. Likewise, Sister Ella saw the Church as misogynous "in many, many parts" adding that "it's lopsided and it's bound to be very dysfunctional because it is so lopsided." Taking the dysfunctionality of the Church's patriarchal structure further, Sister Mabel emphasized its contemporary irrelevance:

> Well, I don't believe in patriarchy, period ... That whole thing is gone;
> that's an age past and they just haven't caught up with it yet ... and it's
> not working. It doesn't work in anything anymore ... [but] that's all they
> know. They wouldn't know how to ... share or talk about ... the heart,
> how grace is working in you.

Distinguishing between what she knows to be the decentralized governance
currently practised within many women religious' communities and the rigid
hierarchical Church, Sister Mabel reminds us of the lost opportunity for self-
expression and sharing of thoughts and feelings within the patriarchal Church's
structure and culture.

As Sister Sarah elaborated on her view that the Church is both a patriarchal
and a misogynous institution, she situated her explanation historically and
theologically with a partially genealogical dimension. More specifically, she
pointed to the lack of attention to the matriarchal history of the Church, as well
as to the differential status of men religious and women religious as exemplified
in how male priests are designated a paternal parental role as they are referred
to as "Father" whereas women religious are assigned the role of sibling as they
are referred to as "Sister":[3]

> Another thing I thought of too around ... women in the Church ... we
> talk about patristics and the fathers of the Church and we don't so often
> hear ... about the ... mothers of the Church and even in the language
> we use in religious congregations ... a priest is "Father" whereas we are
> "Sisters" ... and the priests, I don't know how they get into the role of
> father ... because they're supposed to be in the role of Jesus who was ...
> brother, the son. So ... the language that we have really does ... reinforce ...
> those relationships.
>
> And ... it's okay for women to be mothers if they're married women,
> but they can't be a mother if they're part of the institutional Church in a
> religious congregation ... so their voice is ... lowered to sibling in a sense ...
> so it's ... interesting that ... we've had a lot of mothers of the Church ...
> but they're not [spoken about] ... but ... there's a whole discipline called
> patristics which is this study of the works of the fathers of the Church ...
> I don't deny the importance of those ... but ... it's very ... ecclesial.[4]

Sister Sarah's illuminating example of gender inequity is indicative of women
religious' acute awareness of the structure and nomenclature of the institutional
Roman Catholic Church that both produces and maintains the hierarchical
divide between men and women, and thus determines whose voices and which
narratives are either valorized or dismissed (Ammerman 2003; Chittister 2004;
Johnson 2002a; Nason-Clark 1997; Schneiders 2013).

While the extent to which the sisters viewed the patriarchal and misogynous dimensions of the Church varies, their testimonies confirm, and indisputably so, the existence and entrenchment of the Church's sexist control in the Canadian context. Their critiques of the patriarchal, dualistic, and hierarchical nature of the Roman Catholic Church parallel those expressed by other sisters in Africa, North America, and Europe.[5] As I illustrate in the next section, many of the women religious' experiences are also analogous to those of other sisters who have struggled with subordination, abuse, inferiority, and exploitation – experiences – and often traumatic ones, which have led to feelings of sorrow, confusion, and resentment (Bruno-Jofré 2007, 262; Schneiders 2013, 531).

SISTERS' PAINFUL EXPERIENCES WITH PATRIARCHAL DOMINATION

I also felt the pain of bumping up against those Church structures all the time as a woman. (Sister Adele)

The majority (75 percent)[6] of the sisters and former sisters recounted numerous instances of sexist discrimination, humiliating disrespect in public, patriarchal interference, and patronizing denials by bishops and priests that they themselves experienced in their mid- to late-twentieth- and early-twenty-first-century work as school principals, teachers, pastoral associates, feminist authors, liturgical coordinators, and conference organizers. For example, in an emphatic tone that conveyed both anger and impatience, Sister Clara recalled struggling over the male-dominated supervision and facilitation of her community's chapter:[7]

[T]he thing that drove me nuts was the bishop coming to supervise our chapter. Can you imagine? That only ended after Vatican II. It's like we couldn't be trusted around our own chapter ... the worst one was ... not dealing with the sense of belonging [as a woman] in all those years. That was quite painful ... I couldn't function. All these Jesuit priests coming to give retreats ... I was so angry! ... I mean just the thought that we couldn't do it ourselves.[8]

While Sister Clara's concerns pertained to a chapter meeting several decades ago, Sister Marian, who is from the same religious community, felt that the Church's control over the sisters' affairs is still ever-present: "I just know how tied down we are as a congregation; we can't ... it would appear that we're not trusted to make any sensible decisions whatsoever and we have to go through the ordinary of the diocese and all of this stuff you know!"

These twentieth-century and twenty-first-century examples shared by Sisters Clara and Marian illustrate nuns' limited self-determination in their own communities and are consistent with the clerical domination over women

religious' corporate affairs and decision-making across several centuries including the twelfth and thirteenth centuries (Schneiders 2013, 2004; Wittberg
1994). As others have found elsewhere and across time (Kaylin 2000; Mangion
2008; Schneiders 2013, Wittberg 1994), such stifling took place not only
within convents but also in parishes and schools where sisters contributed
considerably but without much recognition.

Challenges in parishes and at church altars

We're not considered ... [but] we built the diocese, you know! (Sister Kelly)

In the Roman Catholic tradition, sisters have historically been a vital, albeit
under-acknowledged, part of Church parishes (Ebaugh 1993; Mangion 2008;
Smyth 2007; Wittberg 1994). In earlier centuries and up until approximately
the mid-twentieth century, their parish roles were defined by traditional gendered divisions of labour that were similar to those governing patriarchal family
structures during the same historical period (Mangion 2008; Schneiders 2013;
Wittberg 1994). Thus, as women, sisters were typically only "allowed" to assist
with domestic chores involving primarily the housekeeping of churches and rectories,[9] the cooking of meals for priests and bishops, some secretarial duties, as
well as the preparation but never the offering of Mass – the latter being the most
visible role because it was performed publically at the altar where historically
women were not even allowed to be near, and it was thus the most recognized
position (Bouclin 2006; Dugan and Owens 2009; Ebaugh 1993; Mangion
2008; Roll 2015b; Schneiders 2013). By contrast, sisters' work behind the
scenes was not only unrecognized by Church authorities but was also rendered
invisible to parishioners compared to the priests' roles. Sister Kelly, who had
longed to be a priest since childhood, described resentfully the various "behind
the scenes" and thus mostly unseen tasks that sisters carried out:

> You had the choir; you played the organ [sigh]; you counted the collec-
> tions ... you cleaned the church; you were the sacristan ... and some of
> those you did simultaneously. You did them all! You took off ... the bul-
> letins. I did that every Saturday ... [and the acknowledgement?] Nothing!

Carol also grudgingly recalls the extensive groundwork that she often provided for the parish priests who would then take centre stage at the altar with
her liturgical creativity:

> I used to write liturgies ... when I was doing pastoral ministry and they'd
> tease me saying, "When Carol's written the penitential rite, we're going
> to need boxes of Kleenex in the pew!" But what would really piss me off

is yeah I would pour my gut out trying to create liturgies, spend hours on it, and these guys [male priests] would walk in five minutes before the ceremony and say, "Where's the stuff?" ... and just read it off ... No feeling ... and I couldn't perform it. I could not lead it. I was very much subservient ... so my creativity was ... being misused by a Church that was just going ... by rote going through the movements. Yeah. ... absolutely not credited. No!

In other instances, not only were sisters' contributions not acknowledged but they were also often not welcomed or, in some cases, subject to sexist denial and disrespect. For example, in addition to having felt disregarded by priests who nonchalantly and unapologetically showed up hours late or not at all for liturgies and retreats she organized with youth, Sister Maureen also recalled how she felt overlooked as the leader of a program for lay people in a parish:

He just took right over and totally ignored me. He totally disregarded me ... I always wanted to do something for the lay people but when the bishop set this up, I was doing it but the person in charge was "Father" ... there had to be one [a priest] in charge, you know ... and I really stewed over that for a while.

Similarly, Sister Theresa who worked as a pastoral associate, was belittled behind her back by a parish priest with whom she worked: "He was floored that I was actually talking to him about the liturgy and all this stuff and ... he told some of the women [in the parish] who told me that he said 'you know, she's not really a nun, she doesn't wear a habit.'" Comparably, Sister Edna who also worked in a parish, recounted feeling hurt and enraged when she overheard a priest telling parishioners: "it's just a sister" ("c'est juste une soeur"). "Well, for that I was angry at him ... that's the way he worked ... [and then] they [parishioners] never trusted a sister being in charge of the parish." Such blatant undermining demonstrates the rippling effects of priests' patriarchal attitudes, which can also skew lay people's perceptions of women religious (Bouclin 2006).

Whereas Sisters Theresa and Edna felt dismissed by verbal remarks, Sister Marian sensed rejection by the overwhelming presence of male clerics. She recounted a paralyzing feeling when she entered a church to prepare as a reader during a Mass which was a task she had been officially scheduled to fulfill: "I opened the doors to go into the sacristy and it was wall-to-wall priests like it used to be back in the '40s ... priests and altar boys. There wasn't a woman and I froze in the doorway ... It was like a wall ... The Bishop was there right in the group among them all ... I turned around and left." Sister Marian's immediate exit from the sacristy resulted in her being deprived of the occasion to be both present and participatory near the altar up within the sanctuary. While her actions may be perceived as self-directed deprivation, the debilitating impact that the male-centric space had on her temporary immobility in the doorway cannot be overlooked.

Further illustrative of how the spaces at and around the altar are male-dominated (Helman 2012; Roll 2015b), ninety-one-year-old Sister Shannon's reflection on exclusion captures the essence of sisters' gendered experience: "At times I have felt 'put down' for being a woman, especially when women have been refused the opportunity to take active part in the liturgy. Men are given active participation while many women were willing and better qualified to do so." While also underscoring how women's qualifications are not valued at Church altars or within Church sanctuaries, Sister Agnes drew attention to a particularly troubling dimension that she feels undermines women religious' liturgical potential:

> [There is] something I wanted to say about … the priests who have sexu-
> ally abused and it's got to do with the putting down of women again …
> In some of our motherhouses … the person celebrating Mass cannot be
> in a regular parish [because of sexual abuse], so he's with older women. So
> here's this person up there [at the altar] and we're down here [in the pews].
> We're very gifted women who could be celebrating Eucharist, who could
> be doing wonderful reflections, you know [louder], and I guess that's
> when it really, really bothers me especially!

For Sister Agnes, this example of undeniably blatant exclusion of women religious from the altar within the context of their not-so-subtle responsibility[10] to contain abusive priests is further indication of women's relegation to the margins of power within the Roman Catholic Church (Gervais and Watson 2017).

These problematic altar-centred and parish-specific incidents among Canadian women religious are similar to the job dissatisfaction experienced by nuns in the United States, who also encountered blocked mobility and powerlessness, despite, as Sisters Agnes and Shannon point out, often having been more competent and, arguably in some cases, overqualified compared to the male clergy who were in charge of the parishes or "relegated" to say Masses in motherhouse chapels (Ebaugh 1993, 143; Wittberg 1994, 1989).

Undermined and underestimated

Such appalling and dismissive treatment, clearly intended to maintain the patriarchal status quo in the Roman Catholic Church, have left many sisters feeling undermined intellectually, underestimated spiritually, and dislocated institutionally:

We don't seem to have a place in our Church ... I feel that we haven't received full recognition of who we are as women. (Sister Loretta)

We are ignored completely; we are really put down, oh, put down by the Church, by the hierarchy. (Sister Sophie)

Certainly in the Church circle it's the men who matter. Women don't matter that much. (Sister Agnes)

I felt that we were second-class ... our opinion was not considered. (Sister Corinne)

Sister Corinne's comment echoes the perception of countless sisters who feel like "second-class citizens"[11] and who thus reconsider their affiliation with the Church (Ebaugh 1993, 154). Although numerous women religious have rejected their second-class status (Schneiders 2013), many sisters continue to feel dejected by their ongoing subordinate position in the Roman Catholic Church. Although Sister Corinne did not recall any personal experiences of overt patriarchal discrimination, she did feel uncomfortable in the presence of some of the Church's male authority figures. An example revealing her uneasiness came to mind when I asked her if she felt frustrated by expectations to obey a Church that did not represent her views of gender equality. Her response also illustrated how she experienced paternalism as domineering:

Well, yes I did ... I always felt a little bit strange ... I never really felt comfortable in the presence of a bishop. I don't know if it's his attitude or what ... sometimes we had visits or ... we had an interview with the bishop. But I never felt ... that he was fatherly ... I felt like it was more of an inquisitor ... that was my feeling so I was never close to him. No.[12]

The aforementioned testimonies demonstrate how the hierarchical Church's conservative approach to women has provided women religious with very little room to manoeuvre (Bruno-Jofré 2007, 268) and as a result have restricted women from specific spaces within the Church (Dugan and Owens 2009). Such experiences among Canadian women religious resonate with those of their counterparts in the United States (Chittister 1995; Coburn and Smith 1999; Ebaugh 1993; Kaylin 2000). Furthermore, not only are women religious held back from particular Church spheres but sometimes in the locations where they are "allowed" to be, their experiences within them are eclipsed by the male hierarchy and, as a result, the sisters are often left feeling alienated. In some instances, since the hurt is so profound and the memories of those locations are so tainted with sentiments of rejection, many sisters no longer seek out, and in some cases intentionally avoid, those Church spaces, including altars, sanctuaries, sacristies, confessionals, chapels, the pews in the naves, rectories, and meeting rooms.

Denial of sisters' rights as women

One of the ways in which the sisters articulated their experiences with patriarchal denial, discrimination, and disrespect was through rights-based language, as prompted by some of the interview questions. When asked if she felt that her rights as a woman had been violated as a result of patriarchal Church practices, Sister Joelle immediately replied affirmatively and added readily: "I can give you an example." She went on to disclose her experience of overt differential treatment in public, which resulted in her being quite visibly excluded from the altar and the sanctuary when she and a fellow sister were being introduced as ministers to parishioners at the same time as a male deacon:

> So the three of us were presented at a parish Mass in September at the beginning of the year and he [the male deacon] was in the procession, he had the robe and so on, in the procession and up in the sanctuary; we sat at the front of the church but, you know, in the pews. So we were not nearly as evident to people … I was very angry about that, and you know we had to work harder to make connections and so on … so that was a moment that I really got in touch with my anger.

Sister Joelle's infuriating experience of having been relegated to the pews while the men, of varying clerical ranks, were elevated to the altar "up in the sanctuary" is indicative of how gendered undercutting against women religious and other lay women by male religious has been manifested systematically and publically within formal Church practices (Chittister 2004; Dugan and Owens 2009; Schneiders 2013) and particularly *at* or rather, in this case, *away from* significantly symbolic spaces like the altar, which evidently remains a focal point of male domination (Helman 2012; Roll 2015b). Despite her anger toward this incident and her overall resentment related to being deprived of the vocation to ordination, Sister Joelle admitted that she did not raise the incident with the presiding priest because she felt hushed within the patriarchal climate: "I was silenced but … I guess we've just been so used to that kind of treatment."

The same sense of exclusion was echoed by the majority of the sisters I interviewed. When Sister Agnes reflected on the denial of her rights, she explained: "My gifts are not welcomed in the Catholic Church … I'm a woman. I don't have the right body parts so my gifts aren't used! Call it what you'd like! The Catholic Church seems to be afraid of the gifts of women." Sister Edna's response revealed a similar sense of disregard: "Well, I feel like we haven't received full … recognition of who we are as women." For Naomi, a calm, contemplative, and caring woman, the denial of rights manifested itself through concrete deprivation and has led to an embarrassing association with the official Church: "Well ... in as much as if I wanted certain things, I couldn't have them ... and in as much as ... I am ashamed of the institution. So that's pretty horrible."

When asked if she felt that her rights had been denied, Judith referred not only to her own sense of deprivation but also to that of other women: "Oh I do ... every woman I think ... most women in the Church, especially religious women, are far more educated, far more open ... maybe more intelligent, at least I mean they're women after all! ... and can never have a leadership role yeah ... I mean it's inhuman." Whereas Sisters Maureen and Joelle were similarly frustrated with the repercussions for women, they were also concerned about how others have been cheated out of the benefits of women's liturgical capacities as a result of the patriarchal-based barrier:

> Sisters are missing out, but also that the lay people are missing out ...
> Yeah, that is a great [loss]. Like, to see that happening in the Church and
> nothing done about it! (Sister Maureen)

> There are so many needs ... I really resent the fact that so many people
> are being deprived, not only of the Eucharist, but of ministry, because of
> the limitation of ... ordination to ... women. (Sister Joelle)

In her response to the question on women's rights, Sister Sarah reflected profoundly on the unknown effects related to the restraints against her and other women's potential: "Well ... I guess I would answer that ... around that whole notion of human dignity ... and the flourishing of the person that I can't ... I don't know what it would have been like for me or what it would be like for me if there was ... no constraint put on the gifts that I could use within the Church."

As part of the same reflection on the violation of their rights as women within the Church, several other sisters emphasized the obvious ways in which their full participation in the Church is denied. Some made reference to the priesthood, while others spoke of particular sacraments or ministries that they were not allowed to practise:

> Well ... in that I couldn't be a priest, yeah. Oh, and I wrote ... in to ...
> the Diaconate, that program in Scarborough, just for the hell of it I
> should say! [laughs] ... and they wrote back and said, "Oh! You have all
> of the necessary qualifications but we ... can't." Yeah, so I mean I didn't
> want to be a deacon. I don't believe in them. Why not go the whole way?
> (Sister Carmen)

I'd love to hear confessions. I'd love to be able to do that. (Sister Josephine)

In our diocese like there was a ministries program … they would have various speakers from lay people to sisters … and all of a sudden – I think it was when Bishop [name removed] came here, the only people who taught in the ministries program were priests, and I remember how hurt [name of sister colleague] was one of them who used to do a lot of teaching there and … she was cut right out of it. (Sister Loretta)

Of course! [laughs] … [The denial of our] abilities … the priests have made rules that we can't have … ritual communion service … I think it was the bishop that said [it] … 'cause we could … go through a liturgy, everything in a liturgy except the consecration, and have a liturgical celebration and we're not allowed to do that. (Sister Maureen)

While the denial of women's and women religious' full participation in Church sacraments and ministries, including the denial of the ordination to the priesthood, "led a number of women religious … to pursue the academic study of theology" (Leonard 2007, 241), even the alternatives to the restrictions were denied to women early on.[13] Similar to what American women religious encountered (Chittister 1995, 164; Kaylin 2000, 136), many Canadian sisters were denied access to theology classes and degrees up until the 1960s because they were both female and part of the laity. Sister Edith, who has had a life-long passion for theology, recalls "having had to wait a while" to study it in the 1970s because she was a woman.

Furthermore, while other sisters confirmed the undeniable reality of daily discrimination, some shed light on deeper layers of marginalization. For example, as she reflected on the violation of her rights as a woman, Sister Kelly emphatically implied its inevitability: "Of course … Oh! Oh yes!" Carol was comparably unequivocal: "Absolutely. Absolutely." She then shared an example that shed light on an additional level of marginalization that she experienced as a lesbian: "Well, my whole sexuality is denied, you know. I'm intrinsically evil … made in the image and likeness of God but, oooh, just a minute! Not if you're gay! You know. Taught, like duped."[14]

While some (22 percent) current and former sisters felt that they had not faced violations of their rights personally, they had observed gendered mistreatment against other women and women religious by Church officials. For example, Sister Noreen was incisively honest about her own experience, yet sympathized with other women. When I asked her if her rights had been denied under the Church's patriarchal regime, she responded: "I cannot speak to that … well, I see it among some of the people, and I respect other people's experiences okay, but for me I would be making it up." When I asked Sister Nellie if she felt that her rights as a woman had been denied, she replied "more or less but I don't have that much … direct experience." Yet when I asked if she felt that women's rights overall had been denied within the Church, she responded emphatically: "Oh most definitely." Ninety-one-year-old Sister Shannon's experience and opinion were comparable to Sister Nellie's: "I have not encountered issues of human rights being violated [but] … women's rights have been violated for a very long time by attitudes within and outside the Church."

Sister Edith also distinguished between her own circumstances and the wider patriarchal context: "I don't know that I can go that strong … there's certainly … people … there's attitudes." Sister Edith's extended response revealed the complexity of her experience. On the one hand, she spoke of how she had been deprived of the opportunity to become a priest, yet, on the other hand, she explained how she may have been spared from direct violations of her rights as a woman due to the respect she had gained through her academic and pedagogical success. Still others, like Sister Mabel, claimed to have protected their rights as women through their strong personalities. Yet, when asked if she was aware of other women's struggles, she was unequivocal: "Oh yeah! Yes, I have!"

While other sisters did not feel that they had faced gendered challenges directly, they pointed to broader patriarchal contexts that impacted their experiences. For example, Mildred did not recall a personal encounter herself, but she immediately thought of the wider context: "I think it's broader than that; I don't think it is just priests; it's men in general." Similarly, when asked if her rights as a woman had been denied as a result of the patriarchal power of the Roman Catholic Church, Sister Rita responded, "No, I don't think so, no." But she then noted how patriarchy has permeated her experience as a nun since the beginning: "All the stuff we were told in the novitiate, all our books were written by men and all that kind of thing too, you know … like [in] our training … we more often heard of the men than the women." Sister Rita's observation echoes that of other feminist critics of Catholicism like Molesky-Poz (2003, 26) who have pointed out that the majority of religious resources including texts are "the product of male transmission."

With a view to widening the context of rights beyond those specific to women, Naomi emphasized how many other populations were negatively impacted by the exclusion resulting from the Church's patriarchal practices:

> It is patriarchal and hierarchical and … not indicative of gospel living. I am ashamed to be associated with the institutional Church, that is, knowing people who suffer from all of the power, the use and abuse of power. So whether it's people who are feminists or people who are gay or lesbian or are divorced or people who have been abused, like I find it very difficult to know the wrongness of … what is happening and has

happened there and still be associated with that same institution. That's very painful for me.

That Naomi not only widened the scope pertaining to the denial of rights but also was deeply embarrassed and distressed by the Church's rejection of marginalized individuals is a testament to the broader and profound sense of injustice that both former and current women religious attempt to uncover and overcome. Nevertheless, as I show next, given the prevalence and complexity of gender discrimination within the Church, it remains a preoccupation among feminist women religious.

The Church's exclusion and exploitation of the sisters' femininity

The Church is entrenched in a ... spiritualized notion that the male is god. Therefore, anything other is less than. So no matter how good you are, you're always in another category. (Naomi)

Naomi's reference to "male is God" echoes the variously referenced feminist critique of the patriarchal context of the Roman Catholic Church whereby the notion that God is male and male is God has prevailed (Chittister 2004, 150) and has inevitably shaped perceptions and experiences of both femininity and feminism. During my numerous conversations with women religious, it became apparent that their feelings and experiences pertaining to inequality were related to both the denial and exploitation of what they referred to as their "feminine" attributes.

Many feminist scholars have duly problematized the concept of the "feminine" as a socially constructed patriarchal category that reduces understandings of femininity and masculinity to biological levels.[15] There is no doubt that such critiques are warranted. Furthermore, the presumed tenets of femininity, including obedience, docility, and domesticity, that have long been imposed upon women throughout *his*tory (Mangion 2008, 213), and that have generated antiquated yet stereotypical and "idealized versions of pious femininity" among nuns (Kristof 2010; Sullivan 2005, 223), are still problematically subsumed in papal exhortations on the expected roles of women and men within the Roman Catholic Church (Case 2016; Leonard 1995; Pope John Paul II 1988). For example, the Catholic hierarchy has praised the "feminine genius" of women and has continued to promote gender complementarity which maintains differences between men and women despite regarding them as equals (Case 2016; Pope Francis 2015), all of which serves as a condescending justification for the Church's exploitation of women's labour and for its ongoing prohibition and criminalization of women's ordination.

Against such a problematic backdrop, it may seem contradictory to explore how women religious feel about their "feminine" attributes. However, I did so intentionally for two interrelated reasons. The first purpose was to respect the positive significance that "the feminine" held for the sisters, regardless of how it may resemble second-wave feminism's essentialist view of femininity. The terms "feminine" and "femininity" were employed in the interviews with the women religious because they themselves used them and related to them as they conveyed their pride in *their* "feminine" qualities and in how they shaped what they consider to be their unique contributions within an excessively patriarchal Church context. In this sense, the sisters were proudly laying claim to and, in some ways, reclaiming attributes that they felt had been taken for granted, disregarded, and exploited for so long. This stance is affirmed, and in fact implored, by renowned feminist author and storyteller Chimamanda Ngozi Adichie (2014), who contends that femininity and feminism are not mutually exclusive and that women should neither be ashamed of nor apologetic for nor be expected to reject their own femininity if they identify or want to be recognized as feminists; rather, their choice to celebrate it should be upheld and respected.

Secondly, as the sisters shared examples of both gendered exploitation (below) and of recovered feminine spirituality (see chapter 6), they revealed the complex ways in which they have negotiated the paradox of femininity which must be recognized, at least in their lives, as both imposed and [re]claimed. While the sisters' views and actions may have been conditioned by centuries of forced feminization and, however problematic the historical imposition of feminine tenets upon women religious by the Church's male hierarchy remains, the sisters' own illustration and negotiation of the paradox point to the varying degrees of agency and innovation they exert within the highly charged and arguably tightly roped context of male privilege and female subordination (Griffith 1997; Holtmann 2011b; Neitz 2003).

As Sister Ella reflected on how her femininity was stifled in the Church, she explained how the disregard is manifested quite concretely: "Just the … numbers of men that dominate a service. An ordination … well the Easter celebration sometimes, you know, right up in the Cathedral. Those kinds of things … that's where I see it the most."

Echoing wider understandings of the asexualization of women religious in the Roman Catholic Church (Chittister 1995, 148), several sisters found that their gender was denied and their sexuality was erased both physically and symbolically through the habit – the uniform that most of them wore until they decided otherwise in the late 1960s or early 1970s post–Vatican II renewal period. Darlene conveyed what many sisters shared in this regard:

Well, they covered us up in habits ... So you denied your ... sex, in a sense, your gender. You were supposed to be ungendered [laughs] ... I was aware of that various times ... I was the first one in my community to take off the veil ... so that caused quite an upheaval ... by the end of five years, they all had it off [laughs]!

Similarly, Sister Adele felt that the organized communal arrangements within the broader institutional Church parameters also stifled feminine attributes through the use of the habit:

Oh yeah! I would say it was stifled in religious life early on too. I mean the habit was ... a way of ... neutralizing you [laughs] ... So I think it was in the tradition ... That's why it was changed in '65, I guess, to a modified habit which was pretty much a habit still. But in '69, it was really interesting; it was kinda fun to watch each other expressing our femininity in dress [without the habit] and very ready to change.

When Sister Theresa reflected on femininity, she emphasized the Church's limited tolerance: "Oh ... it's allowed. I mean we're there. What can they do about it? That's about it." While Sister Theresa may appear resigned to the intolerance, she seems simultaneously resistant to it. Sister Rita was less sanguine and expressed concern about the lack of progress: "I think there's ... a long way to go with femininity in the Catholic Church." Seventy-three-year-old Sister Loretta's critical view on how femininity is regarded in the Church was emphatic: "It's not! [laughs]." Similarly, Naomi held a rather sceptical view as she commented on how femininity was regarded in the Church: "Oh well, it's suspicion and with very narrow parameters."

It is clear that the sisters I interviewed felt this gender-based "othering" palpably. For example, whereas some sisters thought that their feminine attributes had been denied, others felt that they were exploited within the Church. Several sisters shared how they felt that, for its own convenience, the Church took advantage of their feminine attributes, which are stereotypically linked to socially ascribed and, in this case also religiously ascribed, gender-based roles of servitude. For centuries, similar to women in the domestic contexts of marriage and families, sisters have worked, most often unpaid or underpaid, in male clerics' residences (rectories), in churches, as well as in parish, diocesan, and Vatican offices, as cooks, cleaners, and secretaries (Chittister 1995; Mangion 2008; Létourneau 1978; Schneiders 2013). The exploitation inherent in such conditions of domestic servitude has been painfully obvious to all the sisters with whom I spoke. For example, when Sister Kelly reflected on being a woman within the Church, she protested loudly: "We were slaves of the clergy, that's who we were!" Sister Kelly made that statement after she shared that she "had good relations" with priests growing up, "but it was only later ... when I got into parishes as a grown-up religious woman and realized" the exploitive conditions. Sister Joelle held a similarly dispiriting view when she talked about how women's "feminine" gifts are regarded in the Church:

> Well, they were appreciated ... in terms of doing all the slave labour ... making good pies, and being nice to Father and so on ... A lot of people think that priests support us [laughs]; it's so ironic, honest to God, it's so much the other way around [laughs].

Judith echoed Sister Joelle's and Sister Kelly's frustration over what they perceived to be the Church's expectation of women religious through gendered domestic servitude that priests and bishops took for granted: "It's not regarded in the Catholic Church, you know, I mean ... as subservient, as a minor role, you know, as ... the helpmate ... the silent one who keeps the man." These Canadian sisters' examples reflect what Wittberg (1994) has coined the dual labour market in Catholic parishes in the United States and are consistent with what Nason-Clark (1993) and Nason-Clark and Fisher-Townsend (2005, 210) observed across other Christian organizations whereby the gender division of Church-based labour relegated women to domestic duties (e.g., polishing brass and cleaning linens) and elevated men to the pulpit and policy-making. They are further indicative of how the domestic dimensions of the gendered exploitation inherent within the Church's exhortation on sexual complementarity and the so-called "feminine genius" have been manifested concretely in the lives of women religious (Case 2016).

While some sisters emphasized the denial and manipulation of femininity, others drew attention to the fear that they perceived to be associated with its positive and creative potential. For example, Sister Noreen felt that femininity within the Church "is not valued ... but feared." Similarly, when asked how she thought femininity was looked upon by Church officials, Sister Ella grinned with pride and exclaimed: "Oh I think people are afraid of us!" The same sentiment was repeated by spirited Sister Agnes: "The Catholic Church seems to be afraid of the gifts of women." The remarks by Sisters Noreen, Ella, and Agnes here, and the illustrations of the nuns' celebrations of the Sacred Feminine in chapter 6, shed further light on the paradox of femininity because they demonstrate how, as the sisters have repossessed and repurposed their "feminine" gifts, they have simultaneously engendered a reappraisal of femininity (Sullivan 2005, 223) and, in doing so, have amplified the trepidation among those who have sought to impose and control it. Church officials have been responding to this fear not by opening up a dialogue toward understanding and inclusivity but rather by intensifying their patriarchal tactics.

Intensification of patriarchal domination

The sisters' testimonies have no doubt substantiated the patriarchal dimensions of the Roman Catholic Church. Yet, one could be led to assume or at least hope in the late twentieth and early twenty-first centuries, given the recent, albeit relative, gains in women's rights worldwide that patriarchal power would be losing ground in the Church, as it has, although only partially, in other social, economic, and political institutions. Indeed, since the mid-1960s women have been increasingly included in various Church roles and activities where they had not been in the past. However, some women religious feel very strongly that rather than retreating, the patriarchal conditions became exacerbated particularly under the reigns of Popes John Paul II and Benedict XVI. When asked if the patriarchal power of the Roman Catholic Church had diminished since Vatican II, Carol responded by insisting that the opposite was occurring: "Worse! Worse! There was hope for a period of time. There was hope." Judith's response pointed similarly to the lack of progress: "No! Not a bit! Listen, they just get worse. Too bad! … They've lost every opportunity and then to put in this guy [Pope Benedict XVI], the enforcer."

Although the demeanour through which ninety-one-year-old Sister Shannon expressed her views was much quieter than that of Carol and Judith, she certainly shared the same opinion on the resurgence: "Patriarchal power has diminished somewhat but it seems to be reviving." Sister Mabel who claimed to have never had a confrontation with male clerics until she was general superior in the twenty-first century, also noted the recent intensification:

> I would say for a few years it … diminished but it's like anything when there's a fear, you grab on and it's accelerated now beyond … humanism; I mean it's just craziness. It's like after Vatican II they got so frightened. You know, people were free. People were leaving who maybe never should have been there in the first place. So then they excommunicated everybody who had a different idea … I think there's an awful lot of fear. I think a lot of the things that come out of it are fear. Trying to make people, you don't make anybody [do anything] today. They're so far behind the times; it's like they're not in touch with the culture, the world they're in, you know. Like where the Church should be at the forefront.

Sister Loretta drew attention to the paralyzing impact that the increased patriarchal control had on some sisters:

> Oh I think it's gotten worse. I think after Vatican II … there was some hope and I think that … a lot of things started to happen and then they pulled in the reins. That often happens, you know … even with some of our sisters. We've had some of our sisters who were right on the front

lines after Vatican II and then somehow or other got scared and became more conservative than ever!

Sister Penelope was concerned about the perceived regression: "I think it's getting worse now; it's gone backwards especially in our diocese anyways; our men coming out of the seminary right now are so conservative, it's unreal … it's very scary." Sister Jeanette, who belongs to the same religious community as Sister Penelope, also observed a reversion to patriarchal ways: "We as sisters are not involved in the Church as we used to be … and it disturbs me … it's going back to where it's the priest who is the dominant person in the parish."

Both Naomi and Sister Corinne also claimed that the Church's patriarchal power has "increased" particularly "in recent years." Sister Theresa who had what she referred to as "ins and outs with some of the priests" in her diocese when she was a school principal, echoed a similar concern: "Well I think they're trying to backtrack on it. That's what I'm annoyed about now … I think they realize that … the roots of the Church are rebelling and so they're trying to tighten things up. And it's just going to backlash. It is in a way."

Sister Adele situated her own personal experience with the rise of patriarchal domination within its broader context:

> That's certainly what I bumped up against when I worked in a parish … and I think it needs to change, that's for sure … now it's really out of fear. That … there seems to be a closing in and a pulling back, an emphasis again and more on this patriarchal [attitude of] "I have the answer and we have the answer and you obey!" Like it seems to me … it's going backwards rather than the way Vatican II opened things up.

Sister Joelle reiterated the obstacles in a tone that conveyed both disappointment and discouragement: "I don't think there's a great deal of change … I think that John Paul [II] put us way back, and certainly increased the … patriarchal dimension." Sister Corinne qualified her interpretation of the increase in patriarchal domination by specifying the Church's structural levels that are most responsible for it:

> Ah it depends at the level … I think at diocesan yes [it has diminished] … they're trying a lot to involve women in dioceses … well in some departments … But I think the top is still very, the Curia are there, you know, the top, so they're still … very, very patriarchal.

Sister Marian held a similar view and was worried about the generational effects:

> I think it [patriarchal power] stayed the same … I'm surprised at how conservative the bishops are, you know, really, I really am and … Rome

is appointing them so I don't see too much … hope out of Vatican II. I
think there was hope and great … joy, but I think it's been kind of shelved.

Sister Sophie emphasized how the implications of the intensification were palpable and persistent:

Right now [in 2009] … the men are so powerful that it's pretty hard …
Certainly with … women religious, they are trying to keep their thumb
on us … they're trying to rule our lives … I don't think they're succeeding,
but they're going to continue trying.

While Sisters Corinne, Kelly, and Marian attributed the intensification to the
upper echelons of the institutional Church, other women religious felt that
the patriarchal control had decreased somewhat. However, all were quick to
clarify the partiality of the alleged decline and to point out how ubiquitous the
Church's patriarchal control remains:

I think it has diminished … but it's kind of stalled. (Sister Ella)

To a certain degree. Yeah. It's still there and it always will be. It's not going
to change. (Sister Josephine)

Well, I think that it has diminished. I mean when I was growing up in
the Church, there was no woman on the altar, and my brother was an
altar server, yet I was not able to be, but my [younger] sisters were … I
was born right … during Vatican II … so there has been a diminishment,
but I think then there was a levelling off. (Sister Sarah)

Regardless of whether or not some sisters perceive a partial diminishment or an
undeniable intensification[16] of patriarchal power within the Roman Catholic
Church, all contend that patriarchal conditions are deeply entrenched within
the institutional Church, and as Sister Sarah reminds us, altars have constituted
the Roman Catholic Church's epicentre of male-domination at least at the local
parish or diocesan level (Helman 2012).

"The bent woman": painful consequences

While some women religious feel angry and frustrated by the patriarchal control, others have felt silenced by it. Such was the case for Sister Marian who,
despite her self-identified confrontational demeanour, felt hushed: "I may have
given up opinions." Similarly, a more timid Sister Corinne stated: "I felt like not
giving my opinion anymore." In addition to certain sisters having felt silenced,
others admitted that they felt stifled by the male domination (Peddigrew 2008).

Such a sentiment was expressed particularly by Sister Kelly who referred to the male-led Mass as "the most painful experience" and who declared that "my desire to be a priest from the time I was little – I used to say Mass on the stairs steps, you know – has never died in me." During our conversation, she also spoke of the profound impact that an image of "the bent woman" had on her as she reflected critically on her gendered position in the Church. Referring to the description in the Gospel of Luke (13:11) of the woman who "was bent over and was quite unable to stand up straight" (*New Revised Standard Version* of the Bible 1989),[17] Sister Kelly shared that "it was a very emotional experience to see that woman, you know, and it was just 'Oh God that's how I feel in this Church' ... and the old theology and ... the preservation of the Church, you know, is still strong in people." As Sister Kelly described her own drawings[18] of the woman bent double that she still had in her office in 2009 from the late 1980s, she underscored again the personal pain associated with patriarchal power: "Yeah, this is the bent woman where we allowed patriarchal power ... to do that to us, you know, yeah. That's what I saw in the Church, you know, and it just went right through my heart."

During her interview, I recall feeling puzzled as I heard Sister Kelly share about her "bendedness" and by extension her brokenness because she spoke and wrote so openly and courageously about women's unequal position within the institutional Church. Yet, as I considered her words in greater depth, I was reminded that if a woman like Sister Kelly, who is outwardly confident and vocal in her critique against the Church and who has seemingly moved beyond the institutional Church on so many levels by advancing numerous spiritual alternatives, can still feel so harmed and impaired, then the pain and pervasiveness of the Church's patriarchal power certainly warrant much further scrutiny.

CONCLUSION

Down the road, they're going to be apologizing ... for their sin of sexism.
(Sister Agnes)

This was the passionately spoken opening remark of Sister Agnes' interview that she declared even before I began to ask her questions. Her reference to the "sin of sexism" echoes the tenets of religious feminism that critique the patriarchal and hierarchical dimensions of the institutional Church for being not only problematic and dysfunctional but also sinful (Chittister 2004, 169; Schneiders 2013, 428–9). To use the Church's own morally charged language against it in order to describe and challenge its transgressions is a trenchant tactic indeed. Yet, regardless of how the Church's patriarchal domination is defined or constructed, it is essential to underscore that its consequential harms are penetrating and long-lasting.

The sisters' subjection to bullying and disempowerment tactics at the hands of male leadership serves as one among countless examples of how religion, and particularly its hierarchical form, has shaped social interactions between men and women, particularly to the detriment of the latter (Nason-Clark and Fisher-Townsend 2005, 208; Schneiders 2013). The exclusions, losses, and senses of inferiority resulting from the Roman Catholic Church's patriarchal structures, policies, and practices have constituted sources of pain, anger, and resentment and they have inevitably impacted sisters' sense of belonging in their own Church (Bonavoglia 2005; Bruno-Jofré 2007; Schneiders 2013, 2011). Such troubling conditions comprise the basis of tensions that women religious sense as they reflect on the relation between their raised feminist consciousness and their deep-rooted faith in Catholic spirituality (Gervais 2012).

As the next chapters illustrate, just as feminist analysis helped women religious realize the systematic subjugation they endure within what Schneiders (2013, 564) considers "the most relentlessly patriarchal institution in the Western world" and what Radford Ruether (2003, 5) deems "one of the most oppressive of all religious superstructures," so too have feminist ideals empowered them to overcome such patriarchal control.

CHAPTER 3

Understanding how and why they stay

And why do we – I – continue to align myself with an institution so closed,
so heretical, so sinful? (Chittister 2004, 169)

W omen who are both Catholic and feminist face both spiritual and institutional challenges because their membership in the official Church has been simultaneously shaped by patriarchy and called into question by feminism (Schneiders 2004). Some women, including Judith and Mildred, have removed themselves from the oppressive[1] environment by abandoning the Catholic tradition altogether. Judith clarified her rationale for leaving the Church: "I just said to myself 'What am I doing in a place that doesn't want us to start with?'" Others who have remained acknowledge that staying is a tightrope-like experience fraught with tensions and dilemmas that lead to profound struggles and numerous questions (Coco 2013; Molesky-Poz 2003, 29; Schneiders 2004, 95).

Among those numerous questions, Sister Joan Chittister's abovementioned self-reflexive pondering is one of the most fundamental ones that women ask, and it echoes Mary Daly's (1991) renowned and decades old question "why stay?" It is a recurring[2] and duly posed question in light of the Roman Catholic Church's intransigence toward gender equality and of the consequent troubling and stifling conditions. I posed a similar question to the women I interviewed: "As a woman who engages in feminist spirituality and activism and/or who promotes gender equality, how and why do you remain a member of the Roman Catholic Church, an institution that you yourself have referred to as patriarchal and hierarchical? How do you reconcile that?"

It was evidently a familiar question for the women with whom I spoke. Not only had they asked it of themselves countless times but, as Sister Corinne pointed out upon hearing the question in her interview, inquisitive relatives had also posed it: "Well, I've been asked that by ... members of my own family."

That the question has been raised over time and among diverse populations suggests that it remains a fundamental query that still resonates both within and outside women's religious life. The women's answers to this question reveal a range of reasons, feelings, and approaches, and they demonstrate how the sisters manage their membership within the Roman Catholic Church through various modes and degrees of acceptance, avoidance, and alternatives. Thus, in this chapter, I shed light not only on *why* they stay, but also on *how* they stay.

BY AVOIDING TENSIONS

For a small minority of sisters, the decision to stay within the Roman Catholic Church did not seem to cause them much stress. Some sisters did not appear overly concerned with the Church's patriarchal dimensions. For example, when I asked Sister Nellie, who held more conventional views, why she stayed and how she reconciled feminism and Catholicism, she replied with what Sisters Joan Chittister (1998) and Elizabeth Johnson (2003) would qualify as a patriarchal feminine response: "It's no big ... question for me I don't think. It's what I've grown up with." Yet when I asked her if she thought other women religious have a difficult time reconciling it, she replied, "Oh definitely I see it." Similarly, Sister Benita, who was very actively involved in providing community-based support for young women and single mothers, disclosed that she was less preoccupied with the gendered tensions: "It wasn't my biggest fight [laughs] ... I was just involved in other fights."[3]

For Sister Corinne, her decision to remain within the Church was related to how she felt less affected by patriarchy on a personal level:

> Well, for the Church ... there was uneasiness ... but I never found I was prevented from doing what I really wanted to do, you know, as a woman. I know that other women [pause] and I can understand how they feel ... but ... personally no.

When Sister Josephine reflected on why she stays, she emphasized both her tolerance of the institutional Church and her confidence in her own bond with God:

> I kind of dismiss it and live my life because it's not going to change ... [and] maybe I haven't found anything else that I would bother going to. You know, I live ... and I think this is happening even more, that you have a personal relationship with God and it doesn't matter what anybody else thinks or feels.

Similar to Sister Josephine's reluctant acceptance of the inevitability of the intransigence, Sister Edna also hinted at an uneasy acquiescence: "Well I guess ...

what more can you do? 'Cause it's kind of a resignation which is not the best but ... [pause]." While Sister Rita was concerned about gender inequality within the Church, she did not struggle with the decision to stay because she was preoccupied with more pragmatic matters: "Yeah, I mean I'm seventy-six and I can't go out ... I don't want to lose all I have gained [pension, health care, housing]." While some readers may interpret these outlooks by Sisters Nellie, Benita, Corinne, Josephine, Edna, and Rita as compromises suggestive of less liberal, and sometimes ambivalent stances, they are nevertheless indicative of the complex circumstances, including spiritual, psychological and practical tensions[4] that women religious must negotiate within the constraining context of their membership to the institutional Church.

BY ACKNOWLEDGING THE TENSIONS AND CONTRADICTIONS

Other sisters explained that their decision to stay within the Church was eased by their ability to acknowledge the tensions. As Sister Adele conveys, for most women religious, the first step entails recognizing the conflicts: "I think just by acknowledging all the contradictions, you know, and not pretending they're not there." However, as Sister Sarah reveals, the task is complex: "Well I think partly I deal with it through denial ... [but] most often I deal with it through constantly making that distinction for myself." Sister Noreen shed similar light on how challenging, yet worthwhile, it is to accept rather than to contest the contradictions:

> So what do you do? I started getting to the point where ... I didn't give up right away, but after a while I decided I'm wasting my time, and even in the congregation you come to a place of peace. You can bang your head against the wall or you can just decide, "Well, the train is leaving now; we're going with those on board," okay. You stop; you know you're not going to chug along. I think that has helped me a lot maintaining a certain serenity in the front of such absolute contradictions ... Yeah, I just see how far we can go, and then I just ... don't engage. Sometimes you can have a very constructive sharing. I read a lot and I read controversial books, you know, books that challenge things because I find myself in those, you know. I think okay I'm not odd here; this is okay, and I pass them on. I recommend a book and usually that's my strategy.

While Sister Noreen's account points to understandable phases of both frustration and defeat, it also demonstrates how she actively chooses tranquility, as well as knowledge acquisition and dissemination as coping mechanisms. While acknowledgement may not allow the sisters to completely resolve the tensions they encounter, their awareness of, and their eventually placid approaches to the strains do at least provide some degree of necessary relief.

BY ATTEMPTING TO CHANNEL THEIR ANGER

Contrary to the aforementioned sisters who were less stressed by the dilemma or at least eventually reached a place of peace with it, several other sisters revealed various experiences of tension as they reflected on the difficulties of being committed to both feminism and Catholicism. For example, in response to the question "Why stay?," Sister Clara recounted the considerable difficulty she experienced in trying to cope with her acute frustration over the male-dominated Church:

> I have a hard time with all of this 'cause I don't believe in patriarchy. It just drives me out of my mind ... I got so provoked; I just said I cannot waste anymore, I'm very passionate, anymore energy on this. I cannot do it ... I just remember decisively cleaning out my library [of feminist books] and just saying I can't cope with this. I put away all the books related to it, gave them away, put my English library in shape and that's where I find peace. So I had a hard time. I've always had a hard time with hierarchy.

As noted earlier, Sister Clara did not identify herself as a feminist. However, she claimed to have been "so strong" on gender equality even before she entered religious life – an actuality that is evidenced by her intense irritation. Disposing of her books on women's rights is a testament to the depth of her distress and inability to resolve the tensions between her feminist-oriented stance and the patriarchal structures of the Roman Catholic Church. However painful the experience was for Sister Clara, she was decisive in her action against expending further energy over patriarchy. Yet her abandonment of "feminist" books rather than "Catholic" rituals distinguishes her from many of her peers whom I interviewed, who have tended to do the opposite: abandon some Catholic traditions, while embracing feminist orientations (Schneiders 2004). In this sense, Sister Clara's reaction points to the complexity of multiple, overlapping, and occasionally contradictory choices and actions. Sister Clara's enduring anger resurfaced when she elaborated on why she remains within the conservative Catholic Church and attends Mass faithfully, while being a strong advocate for gender equality and a very outspoken critic of the patriarchal and hierarchical structures of the Church: "I go ahead and I try my very best, and, uh, they're not going to go away ... that still frustrated me greatly ... that's still frustrating."

When Sister Sophie reflected on why she stays, she too revealed the strong emotions associated with her choice; however, she is limited in her capacity to actively engage in reform due to ill-health: "I get very angry, you know, but ... I'm not in a position to do very much; but I certainly have my say." As I explore later in the chapter on moving beyond, despite her health constraints, Sister Sophie does engage in some forms of opposition whereby her dissonance is made known.

BY CONCENTRATING ON "JESUS" AND THEIR CATHOLIC ROOTS

It's me and Jesus; to hell with the rest! (Sister Mabel)

While Sister Mabel's words may seem terse, given her outspoken character, they do fittingly reflect why and how she remains within the Roman Catholic Church, and they echo those of Sister Joan Chittister (2004, 175) who also identified what had set her free from the constraints of the institutional Church: "It is God and I alone now." As I show below, other sisters expressed their emphasis on Jesus and God more joyously. Nevertheless, regardless of how they convey the point, for numerous feminist-oriented sisters, the reasons they have stayed within their Church has had a great deal to do with their adherence to the Catholic faith and, especially, with their loyalty to "Jesus" and his original gospel teachings which they recognized as being free of gendered stereotypes (Case 2016, 4). For example, when I asked her why she stayed, Sister Kelly emphasized Jesus and the Church's original simplicity that is distinct from the current institutionalized version:

> Oh that's a big question! Yeah. I guess because it's my roots ... when you talk about radical Christianity, you know, in the very beginning, the roots, I *believe* that can be lived again ... once the Greek and Roman power and pomp and circumstance goes, you know? I have said recently that I think Rome would excommunicate Jesus if he were around today.

As Sister Kelly continued with her explanation, her fondness toward the original foundation became more apparent: "I love the Church – what it's supposed to be. I love the heritage that Jesus left us."

Sister Ádele offered a similarly contextualized explanation for her favouring of Jesus-centredness and her disconnect from a Christian-imposing institutional Church (Chittister 2013, 2004):

> If you look back at Jesus and what he stood for because that's where I go back all the time. Once the Church became Romanized and identified with the Roman Empire and everybody had to be a Christian and all that stuff ... already there was such a movement away from Jesus and his way ... we have to keep coming back [to that].

"Coming back" to Jesus' teachings is indeed one of the key ways in which women religious have remained within the Church. As Schneiders (2004, 111) contends, the sisters have embraced "an image of a renewed church that is derived from the gospels rather than from imperial Rome."

Sister Theresa echoed Schneiders' assertion in her own words and as she did, the importance of the communal support for their approach was also made evident as it is something that cannot be overlooked because, as I show later in this chapter, the collective dimension represents one of the strongest reasons why the sisters have stayed within the Church: "the blessing of our community is that we continue to be lovers of Jesus ... because we base our reason for being far more on the gospels than we do on Rome or the Pope or the Vatican" (Sister Theresa). One may interpret the expression "lovers of Jesus" as related to the normative concept of "brides of Christ" whereby the sisters were cast in what may be perceived as a subservient role. However, it is clear here that the sisters are attempting to distinguish between the institutional authority of Rome and the portrayal of Jesus as someone who focused less on dogma and more on helping and respecting the marginalized, including women – the latter of which more closely resembles sisters' conception of "authentic" church practices (Gervais and Turenne Sjolander 2015).

While Sister Maureen also found solace by concentrating on Jesus, like Sister Kelly, she too continues to face enduring tension and has only partially resolved her dilemma:

> You know what? I could not reconcile that within myself. It was always a big question for me. What got me to reconcile that is what Father [priest's name removed] said, "We are foundationally one." So when the Church is founded on Jesus' vision, I still feel that, but I don't feel that all the things that have happened since are right, you know. But I'm at one with the Catholic Church because of that area but not with a lot of the other parts ... and, you know, I look at myself and I just, I just know I can't be a part of it.

Although she remains a member of her religious community and acknowledges her Catholic identity, the disconnect between Catholicism and feminism persists for Sister Maureen. As a way to cope with the enduring tension, Sister Maureen opts to pursue various alternatives including an intense exploration of what she refers to as "the feminine" and strongly encourages other women to do the same: "Any chance I get I say something [laughs] about the feminine, you know, and encourage them to look at the feminine part." While some feminist critics may perceive Sister Maureen's reference to the feminine as essentialist, her tactic is indicative of sisters' deliberate reclaiming of it, as well as of her own sagacious contemporary reconsideration of it (Adichie 2014; Case 2016).

Sister Loretta's response to the pivotal question of "Why stay?" also illustrates a loyalty to her Church but one that is perforated by distinctions and disagreements:

> Very good question but I'm not sure I have an answer for it. I just know that in my heart of hearts, I belong to this Church. I don't believe in all

the things that it does and it's doing. And I don't believe in patriarchy and all that stuff. But there is something in the Church that's for me. Whatever it is. I mean … I love the Church. I don't love all the things they're doing. It's like loving your child … and you don't like all the things they do! [laughs] It's something like that, and hopefully … we can make a change, you know, by plugging away little by little.

While Sister Marian was "fed up" with the Catholic Church, her attachment to it became evident when I asked her why she stayed:

Well the Catholic Church has made me who I am today … and out of gratitude … I respect that; I appreciate that. Like any other institution, it has its pros and its cons, and it just happens to have more cons than pros in my lifetime and … I stick with it because it fashioned me and groomed me … through my parents and the teachers I had … in school.

Despite her loyalty, similar to Sisters Maureen and Carmen, Sister Marian does attempt to counter the Church's entrenched patriarchal dimensions by using, for example, inclusive language (e.g., referring to "God" as "she" in conversation and in prayer). While such an oppositional tactic may appear to contradict Sister Marian's fidelity to the Church, it also illustrates how relations of domination, on the one hand, can construct and maintain religious affiliations, and on the other, are simultaneously denounced and resisted (Ammerman 2003; Griffith 1997).

BY REFUSING TO LEAVE THE INSTITUTIONAL CHURCH

Another way in which some sisters remain within the context of constraint is by standing their ground and refusing to leave the institutional Church – however frustrating staying within it may be. Despite her fervent feminist theological stance, Sister Edith remained strongly associated with Catholicism and with her identity as a woman religious but she did so with a tinge of resistance: "But it hasn't been a serious decision for me because I am a Sister [laughs] of [name of religious community]. I am a Roman Catholic and it's sort of like it's my Church [laughs]. Why should I abdicate?" Sister Edith's reply reflects the complex circumstances within which a woman religious finds herself when she readily identifies as both feminist and Catholic (Schneiders 2004). Despite her intense promotion of feminism and her enduring advocacy of women's ordination, Sister Edith's Catholic roots, like those of the sisters featured in the section above, remain firmly intact. While her claim of standing her ground within the Church may be interpreted as a defence of the Catholic faith, it must also be considered an indication of her refusal to accept the exclusion of women in "her" Church, which is an act of strategic resistance on her part (Gervais and Watson 2014).

Sister Loretta holds a similarly nuanced position. While she is strongly attached to the Church, and even "possessive" of it, she also conveyed her readiness to oppose injustice within it: "It's my Church ... and I will fight for it ... I wouldn't defend it. I'd fight for what is right." While Sister Loretta's courage and commitment are evident, she also recognizes the need to proceed with caution as words are spoken and actions are taken: "It's a fine line we're walking, you know [laughs], because we're still part of the Church, and I want to be part of the Church because ... it's my Church, and I believe in it. I believe in lots of things about it. It's just ... a very fine line ... we just have to be careful sometimes." While such caution may seem to undermine the potential of resistance, it nevertheless nuances the undeniable complexities associated with sisters' refusal to leave their Church.

By contrast, like many of their American counterparts (Kaylin 2000, 229), other sisters stand their ground more defiantly. Although they acknowledged the complexity related to the tension between their frustration with the Church's patriarchal constraints and their quests for gender equality, the following women religious confidently imparted a tone of resistance as they sought to remain within the Roman Catholic Church:

> The Church is very important to me because it is my Church, and I'm not going to let the turkeys [laughs], you know, exile me from my Church. (Sister Joelle)

> Yeah it's difficult. It's very difficult but they're not going to get rid of me and I am [laughs] not going to jump ship, you know. (Sister Kelly)

> I'm not about to leave my Church. It's my Church and I wish some of these people would get out of my Church! (Sister Ella)

Compared to Sisters Joelle's and Kelly's refusal to leave or be removed, Sister Ella's simultaneous unwillingness to withdraw and her hope that the patriarchal proponents would themselves depart is indicative of the extent of some women religious' frustration with the gendered domination and sexual apartheid in the institutional Church (Schneiders 2011, 25).

BY RECONCEPTUALIZING "CHURCH"

Just as the resistance by Sisters Edith, Joelle, Kelly, and Loretta has enabled them to remain within the Church, other sisters' reconceptualization of "church" has allowed them to maintain their membership within the Roman Catholic Church, albeit selectively. In response to the question "Why do you remain a member of the Roman Catholic Church?," many sisters, including Sister Theresa, immediately felt compelled to clarify how they do so by conceiving of "church" beyond the institutional structure: "Not that Church. We are the people. That's the church I represent." Similarly, Sister Sarah not only distinguished between the "institution" and the "people" but she also showed how disconnected she has been from the structural dimension: "There's a huge distinction between the Catholic Church as the institution and the Catholic Church as people of God ... I don't feel that it's something that ... I've gone beyond. I just don't know that the institutional Church has ever been really that important to me."

In distinguishing people from the hierarchical organization, Sister Mabel also emphasized them in her conception of "church":

> It depends on what I mean by Church. Church is the people of God. *That* I believe in ... [but] the bishop, the Vatican, the whole hierarchical structure I totally have absolutely no use for. I don't believe in it, and I don't feel it fits the modern day ... I don't believe in any of that but it doesn't affect my life and how I live it.

By criticizing the clergy-centredness of the institutional Church, Sister Ella also underscored the people-centredness of *her* Church: "The Church is *us* ... we are the Church! That's what I come back to. It's not the priests and the bishops ... they're part of us ... they lose their way and they lose their place!"

Despite having left her religious community, Naomi remains a practicing Catholic but she does so selectively through a broader understanding of "church" as community beyond the web of control:

> Well I think it's ... out of that conviction that the institutional Church is only that, it's the institutional Church and actually the church is the community of believers and so like my notion of church is just as valid; I'm just not on the power grid ... and ... I'm not about to lead the rebellion because I think it would fail and now I'm pretty mellow; I've gone through my angry stage for years and years ... I really tried hard and I was irritated for twenty years and after that I just thought, no, this is unproductive ... but I still grieve. I do. Even while I have chosen my particular tactic ... I really grieve. I grieve the loss of the wider community. I really grieve the loss of all those people who have had to leave because they cannot accommodate ... the existing situation.

While Naomi is confident with the choice of church that she has made, her emotionally charged struggles remain not only for her sake, but also for the well-being of others. While Carol's view is similar to Naomi's, including the concern over the widespread loss, she clarifies her complex affiliation with Catholicism and the institutional Church which further exemplifies how some faith-filled women maintain a loyalty to their original and sometimes deeply rooted religious identity, yet engage in alternative spiritual practices (Ammerman 2003; Griffith 1997). While Carol admits to having left the Church, her departure is not absolute: "I won't say officially. I mean I'm always going to be a Catholic. It's in my bones! But I'm less ... upset about what *that* hierarchical Church does ... I will always be part of the church beneath the Church."[5]

By deliberately emphasizing what "the Church" is and is not, and thus by laying claim to a church of their choosing (Barr Ebest 2003, 277; Schneiders 2004, xv), Naomi and Carol as well as Sisters Sarah, Mabel, and Ella have in some ways lessened the extent of the thwarting caused by the institutional dimensions of the Church of which they still remain a part (Gervais and Turenne Sjoldander 2015). At the very least, the openness afforded to them by their wider notions and other locations of church beyond the centralized Roman Catholic altar has helped to ease some of the tensions they still feel in relation to their decision to "stay" within "the Church" and, as I show in later chapters, it has made way for alternative forms of spiritual practice, as well as innovative forms of governance. Such a broadening on the part of women religious is further indicative of how their strategic negotiation between the centre and the margins of the Church reveal what they both accept and avoid, as well as how they are both productive and limited in doing so (Ammerman 2003; Nason-Clark & Fisher-Townsend 2005). By extension, it is also illustrative of how although powerful religious authorities might maintain dominant discourses and practices, deliberately innovative narratives and reconfigurations, however peripheral they may appear, inevitably emerge and often disrupt pre-existing and centralized arrangements (Ammerman 2003, 223).

BY SELECTIVELY WORKING BOTH WITHIN AND AGAINST THE CHURCH

Some sisters' emphases on both belonging to and changing the Church reinforces "reform from within" (Schneiders 2004). For example, Sister Theresa remained both a feminist and a member of the Roman Catholic Church by working toward change within the institution: "I don't think I just allow it [gender discrimination] to happen; I think I keep working against it and ... certainly don't accept it ... [but] I want to belong and change it." Similarly, while Sister Jeanette is very critical of the patriarchal aspects of the institutional Church, she stays within the Catholic tradition because she feels that "the gifts in the Church are very special" and therefore seeks to be "part of the renewal in the Church" by "contributing to ... bringing the Church forward." Although she accepts that she "may never live to see" the change, she is confident "that through perseverance and education" it will happen. Likewise, Sister Agnes is able to remain within the Church by focusing on her direct relationship with God and by drawing strength from the positive aspects:

Good question … I really believe that I am created by God and that I am answerable to God. Humans make a lot of mistakes, and one of the mistakes of the Catholic Church is its anti-women stance. So I try to do what I can to not be pulled down by it, but to be fully alive … I don't feel called to leave the Catholic Church.

Still others found it possible to stay because they were able to play a greater, albeit still limited, role within the Church. For example, despite her intense and lengthy grieving over the prohibited priesthood, Sister Carmen found solace in what proponents of full inclusivity may refer to as "the next best thing": "Part of that frustration was resolved by my community allowing me to go into pastoral work and being in pastoral work … I did everything; I was the pastor of that parish *de facto* rather than *de jure* in everything except the administration of the sacraments and offering of the Mass."[6] Sister Carmen's sense of resolution appears to fall within what many may perceive as a form of acquiescence to work only within the realm of possibilities that the Church's hierarchical and patriarchal structure afforded her. Yet the concrete ways in which she contributed to parish life brought her joy as they fulfilled her deep desire to minister to people. In addition, her accession should not be interpreted as a complete acquiescence because, as I illustrate in the chapter on feminist spirituality, she continues to advance and to thus model other changes including her commitment to always speak, pray and sing using gender inclusive language (Fischer 1988; Johnson 2002a; Schneiders 2004).

BY THRIVING ON THEIR COMMUNITY'S INCLUSIVITY AND INNOVATION

When asked why and how they stay within the Roman Catholic Church, many sisters referred immediately to the strength and support derived from the non-hierarchical and inclusive approaches of their religious communities. In doing so, many sisters distinguished very insistently between the conservativeness of the institutional Church and the forward-looking ways of their religious community. Such a distinction was made quite evident by Sister Theresa who clarified my use of the term "conservative" within my question. When I asked her why she, who believes so strongly in gender equality, belongs to what some might consider a "conservative religious institution" (meaning "the Roman Catholic Church"), in a raised voice she responded instantaneously and defensively: "I don't believe that I belong to a conservative institution if you're talking about my community!" Sister Theresa's definitive stance exemplifies women religious' pride in and protection of their renewed religious identities that they insist reflect their deinstitutionalized congregational arrangements, as well as their contemporary spiritual and societal priorities (Sullivan 2005). Sister Sophie, who is from the same community as Sister Theresa, elaborated on the encouraging context in which they find themselves: "I am just so glad that I am a member of this community because we are so, you know, with it! So alive! So aware! ... and we are! We're doing everything we can as a community, like our leaders are really with it ... I feel a part of it [Church] simply because I am in this community."

Similarly, as Sister Joelle explained why she stays, she underscored how her congregations' supportive model is liberating not only for her personally but also collectively because it allows the sisters in her community to manage the tensions together:

> Well there are a number of ways, you know. Number one is a certain understanding of church that is beyond the patriarchal structure. Another is that we have our own support network, with a lot of freedom ... financial, as well as freedom to be who we are and so that is very important. We have a community dimension, in which we have a shared understanding of who we are. And that encourages us to live up to our potential ... and, you know, not paying a whole lot of attention to what they are saying in Rome. [Laughs]

Sister Penelope echoed Sister Joelle's reasons for remaining in the institutional Roman Catholic Church, but she also added how their approach can serve as a model for others who are struggling with similar dilemmas:

> I stay within the Church because our congregation is within the Church. But on the other hand, I do what I believe to be right even though it's not always what the Church is thinking. I freely think the way I want and act the way I want as long as it's in accordance with my own constitution, and our own ... congregation, in a sense, is very liberal and it's very gospel-oriented, so as long as I feel I'm walking ... in line with what the gospels preach and with what ... our congregation is approving, I'm within my rights to be a member of the Catholic Church ... and I think my presence in believing and moving in those areas might, I would say, envision others to do the same ... and so in that sense hopefully be a role model for some people ... too.

Sister Penelope's attitude, particularly her alignment with gospel teachings, was also conveyed by Sister Helen Prejean, author of *Dead Man Walking*, who commented on the severity of the Vatican's critique against women religious via its early-twenty-first-century doctrinal assessment: "I know the road I'm on is the road of the gospel, so that's where my energies are" (Bradley Hagerty 2012). Such affirmation from such a renowned sister undoubtedly underlines how the inclusive and innovative Jesus-centred approaches by the congregations of Sisters Theresa, Sophie, Joelle, and Penelope do enable women religious not only to survive the tensions as they remain within the Church but also, as I show next, to thrive within their communities' atmosphere of support and solidarity.

BY FEELING EMPOWERED BY THEIR COMMUNITY'S INDEPENDENCE

While I elaborate upon the processes and outcomes of the sisters' new governance arrangements in a later chapter, it is instructive to briefly illustrate here how their innovative and independent contexts represent a central reason why many sisters remain affiliated with the Church. For example, Sister Agnes alluded to the benefits of her community's relative self-governing: "I think a reason I've been happy and fulfilled is I belong to a small autonomous congregation. Many congregations aren't autonomous as we are." As she elaborated on her deep frustration with the conservative and patriarchal characteristics of the Church and on the challenges associated with remaining with it, Sister Theresa's pride over her community's independence became evident:

> People don't realize ... the freedom we have as religious ... I guess we're very fortunate in being a pontifical community as opposed to a diocesan ... we're a small community. Our roots are here in Canada ... we're not jumping through the hoops that a lot of older communities have to tied in with Europe ... and the fact that we're small ... we know each other.

Both Sisters Theresa and Agnes are making reference to a governance structure that dates back to decisions made before the currently practised inclusive governance. Nevertheless, both the external affiliation and the internal governance structures are intentional because of the very independence that they facilitate for forward-thinking women religious who manoeuver beyond institutional constraints.

As Coburn and Smith (1999) and Mangion (2008) have shown in their respective feminist analyses of women's religious communities in the United States and in England and Wales, such autonomy was strategically secured by many groups of sisters. Rather than establishing themselves as diocesan congregations, which are under the constant control of the nearby bishop, many communities of women religious intentionally obtained papal approbation in order to avoid such invasive interference by local clerics (Mangion 2008, 215). Coburn and Smith (1999, 61) summed up the wider context and pointed to the "lesser of two evils" within the seemingly inescapable patriarchal structure: "... many Catholic sisterhoods felt the submission to male authority in Rome, thousands of miles away, was far preferable to subjugation to a local bishop who could closely monitor and control every aspect of community life."

While the autonomy to which Coburn and Smith refer has granted entire communities their relative sovereignty to govern their own internal affairs, it is precisely that independent internal governance, informed by inclusivity that has instilled a sense of individual independence. The resulting experiences of individual freedom, of which many sisters are particularly proud and grateful, are undoubtedly related to why they remain associated with the Church. For example, Sister Sophie feels safeguarded by her leadership team and community against the patriarchal power of the Church's male clerics: "I don't think they would have any influence, not while ... the administration that we have now [is still in place]."

Another pivotal and profound example came from Sister Agnes who exclaimed enthusiastically that she felt very well supported by her religious community and was therefore free to carry out her feminist projects. She then illustrated how such freedom was made more evident to her by other women outside of religious life:

> I really ache for laywomen who feel as I do about the Church ... I have more freedom as a religious woman than laywomen ... When [female colleague's name] ... would say even then in the '90s, "Oh Agnes, you're so fortunate to belong to a religious congregation and have the support for what you do ... I don't have that kind of support." At that time, I didn't quite know what she meant .. but she said it often.
>
> Then two events happened and I began to realize what she was talking about. As director of a spirituality centre she asked if we would bring our community-supported feminist play to her centre. We did so and she was thrilled with the positive response of the audience. The second event happened at our motherhouse. Our leadership team had invited an internationally known female retreat facilitator/speaker gifted in helping people grow into their best selves. Our general superior encouraged us to invite interested laywomen to the weekend as our guests. So I invited [this same woman] and when it was over she said, "Oh Agnes, that was such a wonderful weekend," and then she said it again ... "You women are so free ... you can invite in whoever you want to take part in these events ... I don't have that kind of support when I want to do something. You get an idea, Agnes, you can go to your leadership team and ... you support one another. You've got the money. You've got the power behind it. You've got the courage to go ahead even when your bishop would say you should be doing something else. We [laywomen] don't have that kind of support, you know." And I finally knew. God! This is what she's been trying to tell me for the last ten years, and it's finally sinking in.

Given how sisters' projects were firmly imposed on them under the past hierarchical system, as I show in chapter 8, the beneficial support illustrated by Sister Agnes must be understood as relatively unique to the recent governance model that embraces or at least considers more openly sisters' individual initiatives. Nevertheless, Sister Agnes' sense of fulfilment and happiness resulting from the support fostered by her community's independence is one of the key reasons why she remains part of the Church.[7]

As a member of a decentralized and democratically organized congregation, Sister Sarah also experienced a similar sense of support – one that she felt was unique to contemporary religious life and one that seemed strong enough to sustain her sense of belonging within a Church of which she was highly critical and thus did not necessarily feel as strongly affiliated:

> Sometimes I say if it wasn't for my religious community, I don't know if I would feel that I was still part of the Church ... but I'm also really aware ... of the fact that I am in a religious congregation. I have this kind of support and I have ways of expressing my faith that I have learned because of this, and I feel that my spirituality is able to flourish. But I'm really aware of ... other members of the Church ... who are really deprived of that.

It is significant to note that as they shed light on how their community's autonomy and support constitute central reasons why they remain within the Church, both Sisters Agnes and Sarah also expressed concern for the lay people who are unable to benefit from such backing and who thus may also inevitably struggle to stay within their Church. Such thoughtful consideration, including Sister Agnes' congregation's invitation to laywomen to attend the above-mentioned retreat is indicative of the ways in which women religious extend their inclusive initiatives and non-hierarchical approaches among lay people.

BY DRAWING ON THE SISTERS' ACCOMPLISHMENTS

As Sister Ella reflected on how she stayed in the Church by productively managing the tension between feminism and Catholicism, she referred to how she drew strength from the sisters' capacities to advance feminist-based ministries that are beneficial to others. Her explanation highlighted what others (Chittister 1995, 11–12; Kalven 2003, 35; Lux-Sterritt and Mangion 2011; Mangion 2008) have identified as historical indicators of feminism including how sisters have managed and financed their institutions and enterprises independently of male religious authorities for more than 1500 years:

> Well most times I don't feel conflicted by it because I've watched our women and other congregations too. We ran hospitals, and homes and schools and ... we didn't depend on the hierarchy ... So like we learned

how to manoeuvre around these kinds of things with our resourcefulness, and every now and again of course you come up against a stone wall, and it makes you angry ... but ... Joan Chittister is the one who mentioned that we're still finding ways to minister today and creative ways to help people that we wouldn't have thought of ten years ago even.

All the other sisters with whom I spoke echoed the same sentiments which demonstrate that the reasons they stay in the Church are due in large part to the strengths of the women's congregations that constitute the anchor that grounds them. At the same time, despite the patriarchal "stone wall[s]" they still encounter, they are sustained by the positive aspects and successes resulting from that grounding and stability. They are thus both anchored and buoyed by their congregation and their contemporary creativity.

CONCLUSION

The patriarchal and hierarchical authorities of the Roman Catholic Church have certainly constructed circumstances that are difficult to endure, leading to the obvious and persistent questions of why and how the sisters stay. These questions will undoubtedly remain relevant for the foreseeable future given the Vatican's twenty-first-century tactics (e.g., criminalization of women's ordination, investigation of women religious in the United States) to further entrench patriarchal power and given the Vatican's limited willingness to discuss women's leadership within the Roman Catholic Church.

Nevertheless, as I have shown in this chapter, a number of women religious are more than capable of circumnavigating such stifling contexts (Gervais and Turenne Sjolander 2015). Both questions (Why stay? How do you stay?) evoked a range of responses indicative of various degrees of acceptance, compromise, serenity, resistance, and even rejection. Many accounts exemplified how the women are "defecting in place" whereby those who feel alienated from the institutional Church remain within it because it represents their tradition, their roots, and their home and because they remain hopeful that they can effect change from within (Winter 2002, 30; Winter et al. 1994).

While in this chapter, I have shed light on both why and how current and former sisters remain affiliated with the institutional Roman Catholic Church, I have done so through examples flowing primarily from the women's internal negotiations and rationales. In the next chapter, I extend the focus on "how they stay" by concentrating more on the women's tactical strategies of critique and avoidance that allow them to not only survive the tensions associated with patriarchal constraints but to also thrive beyond them.

CHAPTER 4

Moving beyond patriarchal domination

[L]iving within patriarchal systems does forge among women recognizable experiences of suffering along with typical patterns of coping and victoriously resisting, strategies that enable women to survive. (Johnson 2002a, 61)

W hile sexist exclusions have undoubtedly thwarted the sisters' full participation in institutional Church activities, the women religious with whom I spoke have overtly and covertly resisted the controlling prohibitions by both action and inaction. Contrary to the sisters who *obediently* accept "the patriarchal ecclesiology that undergirds their own subordination" (Schneiders 2013, 530), the women I interviewed exercised their post–Vatican II autonomy-oriented and discernment-based notion of obedience[1] beyond their religious order and onto the terrain of the institutional Church (Ebaugh 1993; Wittberg 1994) and thus articulated both their refusal to accept patriarchal domination and their capacity to overcome it in confident and occasionally defiant manners. The women's accounts herein echo those of sisters who have both opposed and thwarted ecclesiastical, episcopal, and papal forms of "patriarchal absolutism" across the centuries including during medieval times (Gray 2007; Magray 1998; Mangion 2008; Schneiders 2013, 529; 2011; Wittberg 1994, 95). Yet, it is essential to recognize that, however beneficial and productive that opposition may have been, such feminist power within the context of patriarchal constraints was, and arguably still is, highly mediated and cautiously negotiated (Gray 2007).

In this light, by presenting the various ways in which contemporary sisters and former sisters disregard, disagree with, and dismiss the patriarchal constraints of the Roman Catholic Church, the complexity of their late-twentieth- and early-twenty-first-century strategies of avoidance, resistance, and divergence is made known.

SISTERS' DISREGARD OF THE CHURCH'S PATRIARCHAL DIMENSIONS

It always surprises me, given our experience, that we are so associated with the Church. (Sister Joelle)

While the testimonies in the previous chapter shed light on the sisters' frustration, disappointment, and concern over the patriarchal power of the Roman Catholic Church which poses particular challenges as they remain within it, some women religious' reactions conveyed their decisive disregard of Church authorities and practices. For example, sixty-eight-year-old Sister Adele's reaction revealed not only discomfort with, but also a disconnection from, the Church: "My predominant feeling is embarrassment. I'm embarrassed to identify with an institution that's moving backwards." Other sisters' sentiments consisted of anger and annoyance and are indicative of their capacity to decisively distance themselves from the Church's gendered positions and dated dimensions:

I get sick and tired of some of the things the pope [Pope Benedict XVI] is still pushing. (Sister Rita)

Well I'm fed up with the Catholic Church ... absolutely fed up with it! ... They are so far away from reality, you know, and I think if all the women in the Church presently withdrew their services, they'd have to put padlocks on the doors, do you know that? But women are not included ... the fact that women are not ... on an equal footing in the Church. I find it a sin ... I find it gross. (Sister Marian)

Comparatively, Sister Theresa's annoyance with the Church's male hierarchical authorities and their presumption of gendered obedience was so intense that about six hours after her early morning interview had ended, she returned to the interview room to share additional frustrations. As I was making notes on the day's interviews, while awaiting the supper for which the sisters insisted that I stay – a testament to their typically generous hospitality – I heard a knock on the door of the room that Sister Theresa herself had kindly set up for me to meet interviewees in her community's retirement residence. When I opened the door, there stood eighty-year-old Sister Theresa, hunched over and leaning with one hand on the walker that she had used to carefully shuffle her way across the considerable distance between her room and mine, with the index finger of the other hand shaking eagerly at me as she firmly, yet enthusiastically commanded: "Turn on your recorder, there is something else that I have to tell you!" For the next twenty minutes, I listened, awestruck, to Sister Theresa's captivating *cri de coeur* against the male-dominated Church hierarchy. While my original questions may have prompted her post-interview recollection, it was clearly Sister Theresa's own passionate views on the issues that propelled her to follow up so candidly and fervently. Here is some of what she had to say:

> I felt it was way behind the times as I still think the Church is ... I brought this thing [paper]. I subscribe to *Zenit* ... it comes out every day from the Vatican. I like to keep my eye on them to see what they're up to! ... But there was this thing that the Pope said last week. Oh! I couldn't believe it! ... "Pontiff says contemplatives give breath to the world." So he went to visit a contemplative order in Rome ... and he was complimenting them on being contemplative nuns. [Reading from the article:] "In this context the Pope stressed that also today 'Rome needs women who are all for God ... women who are able to obey their pastors'." Now that was *last week*! The Pope says, "Obey their pastors"! ... If I weren't on tape I'd say [pause and laughter] ... Like that kind of stuff, you know, I don't agree with. (Sister Theresa)[2]

The fact that Sister Theresa felt the need to keep her eye on the Vatican by monitoring one of its publications is a sign of how upsetting and worrisome the institution's sexist biases were for her, as they are for numerous women religious (Schneiders 2013). Unfortunately, the concern with the patronizing expectation of sisters' obedience to Church teachings and authorities recurred in my conversations with many sisters, including with Sister Joelle who shared two personal experiences that involved male clerics instructing women religious to obey Church authorities. Both instances occurred while she served as general superior of her community. The first incident happened within her local community:

> We had a new Bishop in [a city in Ontario], while I was in leadership ... so I invited him for dinner in the Chapter and then of course you have to give him the mic, eh, and so I introduced him and said, "Just say a few brief words," and he got up and didn't he give a talk on obedience [laughs]. So ... you see we have this kind of static, but we continue with our lives.

When I asked Sister Joelle how her community's sisters reacted to the bishop's speech on obedience, she relayed that their collective disregard of the "static" was clear: "Oh everybody was exactly the same. We've laughed about it ever since." The second incident occurred while she was in Rome:

> There's an organization called UISG [International Union of Superiors General] ... and we had a conference, we have one every three years in Rome. At this particular one in 2001, there were about 800 leaders from

all over the world ... and so we gathered in a round-table discussion ... we had ... really substantial discussions in a circular model. Then on the third day ... we had the obligatory courtesy call from the cardinal in charge of ... the Institutes of Consecrated Life, and ... [he said]: "You Sisters ... you see that your Sisters obey you, and you obey the Pope!" And I'm not exaggerating; this was literally on the big screens as we sat ...

Well ... at our table, particularly the western folks ... we were all making faces at each other. When he finished, we sat on our hands. There was scattered applause from some of ... the habited sisters, and then, in a wonderful moment of redemption, the president of our organization ... was on ... the stage with him. He had sat down and she was next to him, and she hands him the earphones so that he can hear in transla- tion what she is saying and she said: "We would like you to know, your Eminence, that we Sisters wish to be in obedient communion ... with all our brothers and sisters in the Church." Well, the whole place just erupted in applause.

Sister Joelle's accounts illustrate how both laughter and applause – both with- held and given – are part of nuns' repertoire of analytical tools and effective tactics that are sometimes subtly engaged in their handling of patronizing control and in their attempts to move beyond it, all the while maintaining their intersected identities as members of both the Church and a women-centred organization within it (Ammerman 2003, 223). Others point to further strat- egies through which they express their disregard. For example, Sister Sophie clarified how she discounted a priest's domination: "As a teacher, as a principal, I remember ... the pastor ... was the big chief ... he was the boss, but even at that time ... I remember I tended not to listen to him ... I let it go in one ear and out the other and usually it worked." Still others repelled patriarchal power with considerable confidence. For instance, when asked if her rights as a woman had been denied, Mildred responded assuredly: "I don't think so because I think it's only when you let it." In response to the same question, Sister Mabel gave a similar, yet more emphatic explanation about her ability to protect her own rights as a result of her strong personality: "No, I don't let it ... they [Church authorities] don't affect me at all."

The extent of the dissatisfaction expressed and the disregard relayed by Mildred as well as Sisters Rita, Marian, Theresa, Joelle, Sophie, and Mabel are indicative of the depth of their frustration over how patriarchal biases are manifested in Church discourse and action. Yet, their capacity to express such frustrations fearlessly demonstrates their noteworthy ability to detach themselves comfortably from the Church to which they belong[ed] (Chittister 2004; Schneiders 2004). Such an ability was enabled, at least in part, by wider conceptions of obedience that granted women religious in the post–Vatican II era greater degrees of choice, including the option to discern and disagree (Ebaugh 1993, 73; Wittberg 1994, 243), and evidently sisters have chosen to exercise their freedom not only within their religious community but also onto and in many ways against the treacherously patriarchal terrain of the institutional Church (Chittister 2004; Schneiders 2013).

THE SISTERS' DISAGREEMENT WITH CHURCH PRECEPTS

Women religious' disregard of the Roman Catholic Church has also been manifested through their disagreement with Church teachings and practices. Clearly, many sisters feel free to assert their dissent:

> I don't always agree with some of the statements that come out ... I don't always have to agree with what the Church is teaching. (Sister Jeanette)

> I don't agree with the structures. There's a lot of things I just don't agree with ... like there's no dialogue ... not listening to anybody and I find it very dogmatic. (Sister Loretta)

> I do what I believe to be right even though it's not always what the Church is thinking. I freely think the way I want and act the way I want as long as it's in accordance with my own constitution. (Sister Penelope)

> As for the teachings, what I go by is ... the creed, those are the teachings that I would hold. Apart from that ... I don't believe every word that the Holy Father says. (Sister Mabel)[3]

For most sisters, their disagreement is expressed by both words and actions. Yet for some sisters, like Sister Mabel, whose strengths lie in their oral abilities, their main and most effective strategy for resisting the Church's patriarchal power involves incisive verbal communication. Such also seemed to be the case for Sister Carmen who readily admitted how she tends to convey her disregard: "Maybe all I use is my mouth." Yet, while Sister Carmen is certainly regarded among her sister peers as a very "outspoken" advocate for gender equality within the Church, and she acknowledges that reputation herself, she also readily admits to not having acted in accordance with Church rules: "I didn't always conform to them." Sister Carmen's twofold tactics – words spoken and steps taken – point to the variety of both subtle and manifest ways in which they express their differing opinions.

THE SISTERS' DISMISSAL OF THE INSTITUTIONAL CHURCH

There is no doubt that women need to tell their stories. But at the same time, there comes a time when you are too tired of trying to be heard in a place like the church where no one wants to hear you. Then, you walk out of it, past it, beyond it. And often, invisibly. They think you're still there, because your body is, but your heart is long gone and your spirit free. I know. (Chittister 2004, 174)

Some of the women religious moved beyond disagreeing with the Church's precepts and daringly dismissed the Church's hierarchical dimensions. For example, Sister Mabel offered a sharp critique that sets her apart from the stereotypical image of passive nuns and points instead to her spunky refusal to conform:

> I bypass the other nonsense that goes on … the bishop, the Vatican, the whole hierarchical structure, I totally have absolutely no use for … I don't pay any attention to it. I haven't got time for that really you know … I just haven't got time for nonsense. I mean I haven't got time for craziness and like I said, it was craziness.

Sister Mabel's ability to confidently release herself from clerical constraints was also evident when she explained how she felt about the lack of recognition of and appreciation for women religious' contributions by Church authorities:

> I don't want it … it wouldn't mean a thing for me coming from the Church. It wouldn't mean a thing! … We know that in our hearts and that's the only place that matters. Like I know I get up each morning and I say, "Okay God, show me today how I have to live. Be with me in all my interactions that I show kindness and gentleness and compassion," and at the end of the day, I look back and say, "Yeah, I goofed there, goofed there." I mean it's so different, you know.

Just as Sister Mabel demonstrated her own self-sufficiency in terms of account-ability, Sister Sophie revealed her own self-reliance as she explained how she dismissed Church authorities:

> I just don't listen to the bishops … most of the time … the message that we get from our community to me … is real and when I hear something that the bishops have come out with, I just look at it very carefully. My first impression is just to ignore it really … I get very angry … but … I'm not in a position to do very much [due to illness] but I certainly

have my say ... and when we have chapter meetings, I'm right in there, expressing what I think.

Sister Sophie's twenty-first-century ignoring of bishops parallels the tactics engaged by European women religious in medieval times who dismissed epis-copal directives or delayed their implementation (Johnson 1991; McLaughlin 1989; Wittberg 1994, 95). That women religious have been "ignoring" or refusing bishops' demands for almost a thousand years speaks not only to their long-standing capacity to resist, but also to the fact that the reasons for their resistance – rooted primarily in patriarchal control – remain clearly entrenched and thus relatively unchanged. Imposed (and presumed) clerical authority over nuns constitutes one of the main enduring issues and Sister Noreen clarifies how she counters that hierarchical tradition by distinguishing between the Church and Catholicism: "I still identify as a Catholic, yes ... but that's not what the Catholic Church is ... see because ... I don't associate anyway, I don't go there ... I just don't waste energy there because ... my boss is not the parish priest."

Similarly, Naomi shared about her profound journey away from the insti-tutional Church: "For good or for ill, I have dismissed the institutional Church as the institution. I think it was Rosalie Bertell [a social justice activist nun] who said ... 'that's not my church' ... So, I have found a space and a community where I can be about a gospel way of life." Like their American and Euro-pean predecessors and counterparts, these Canadian sisters have purposefully repositioned themselves and refocused their attention beyond the clerical and hierarchical dimensions of the Church in order to overcome the potentially stifling patriarchal constraints (Chittister 2004; Lux-Sterritt and Mangion 2011; Magray 1998; Mangion 2008; Schneiders 2013; Wittberg 1994). As I exemplify below, their repositioning sometimes involves circumventing certain Church practices, even while they remain affiliated, to varying degrees, with the Catholic tradition (Ammerman 2003; Schneiders 2004).

THE SISTERS' AVOIDANCE OF CHURCH SACRAMENTS AND SPACES

I believe that's how the changes are going to come in the Church ... We find ways to work around it. (Sister Loretta)

The occasional or consistent avoidance of certain religious celebrations, sac-raments and Church spaces represented a popular strategy that the sisters employed to convey their disapproval of the patriarchal dimensions of the institutional Roman Catholic Church.

Avoiding Mass

As an expression of their frustration with the maleness of Church altars (Helman 2012), 60 percent of the women I interviewed chose not to attend Sunday or daily Mass either regularly or intermittently. Sister Sophie remarked, echoing sisters' comments on their gifts being rejected from male-dominated altars: "Well, I don't go every morning ... like everybody else does. Sometimes ... the reason why I go is for ... the community's sake. I really find that ... it is insulting [that there are no women at the altar] ... I mean. Glory! Any one of us could [celebrate Mass or give a homily] ... we have a lot to offer ..."

Sister Kelly acknowledged that she intentionally does not attend daily Mass regularly at her motherhouse and is aware that some of the more conservative sisters in her community may comment, "Well, she's not coming to Mass." Yet she is unapologetic about her absence from Mass because she sees value in the alternatives she practises which sometimes run concurrently with her congregation's daily Mass times: "I believe that we live and share Eucharist with others in our daily relationships. So when I am in relationship with another at the same time as Eucharist is being celebrated, I believe I share a living Eucharist with that person." Sister Loretta's reasons for avoiding Mass are located in what she finds limiting with the Mass and the preaching:

> A priest ... who comes to the motherhouse all the time and then they preach sin and sin and sin and sin! ... Holy cripes! ... I'm tired of hearing that! And yet we don't have any option. If you want to have Mass every day, you have to ... take whoever [available priest] and ... I would say, "Well, we don't have to have Mass every day." I do feel stifled in that we can't have other ways of celebrating sometimes ... and that has to do with the congregation too though because the congregation wants Mass all the time and I don't feel that we need to have Mass as such all the time ... But the whole Mass thing, it's just Mass, Mass, Mass. Every time you have a celebration, it's Mass, and I love the Mass ... There's nothing wrong with it. But it's not the only way to celebrate ... Sometimes when we're at a [partnership] meeting there's ... fifty, sixty women and you bring a man in to say Mass ... like you've got to bring somebody in for a Mass ... we could have a beautiful celebration ... we can go ahead and celebrate and we do. We do a lot more of that now.

Sister Loretta's personal preference to avoid Mass is also related to her frustration with her community's historical dependency on a male priest. Yet, as she alluded already and as I show later, not only does she replace the Mass with smaller women-led rituals that blend both liberal and radical religious feminist elements (Shih 2010), but her congregation has also recently started to host gatherings without the presence of a male cleric – a practice that is now more common among some Catholic communities.

Sister Mabel avoids routine Masses selectively after having positively experienced more progressive rituals facilitated by a broad-minded male priest:

> We had a retreat with Father [name]. Fabulous guy. Just fabulous ... We had the whole mother-god, father-god reading ... wonderful. Then we go back to having Father [name]. I couldn't go to Mass all last week! It shouldn't be torture. I can't take it. Sunday was bad enough! Isn't that awful?

Sister Mabel's experience and that of numerous current and former women religious suggest that some sisters' exposure to more diverse and encompassing rituals increases their inclination and ability to avoid routinized conventional Masses within their religious tradition (Ammerman 2003). While I explore the sisters' alternatives later, it is significant to note here that many of them are more readily able to avoid the male-dominated Mass because they substitute it with their own women-led rituals.

Boycotting chrism Mass

One of the particular ways in which the majority (78 percent) of the sisters and former sisters have been demonstrating their disapproval of the patriarchal Church is through their refusal to attend the annual chrism Mass. The Mass of Chrism is a Holy Week celebration held in a diocesan cathedral or basilica during which the chrism (e.g., oils) used only by the male clerics for sacraments (e.g., baptism, confirmation) is consecrated by the diocesan bishop in the presence of the presbyterium (body of priests).[4] A number of sisters expressed their frustration with this celebration, pointing particularly to its male-dominated nature as the key reason for their avoidance of it:

> I don't go to chrism Mass. I can't. I just hate it with all the male stuff there. (Sister Agnes)

> They'd be having a Mass about the chrism ... they expect you to be there ... I wouldn't go ... I'm not going to come to this because all I see is men up there and I'm part of this community ... it's just, all you can see is priests! (Sister Maureen)

> Well I haven't attended the chrism Mass for twenty years. (Sister Kelly)

Given that none of these sisters ever informed the diocesan bishop or priests of the reason for their absence, preferring instead to engage in a silent strike of sorts, it is not possible to assess if their non-attendance was even noticed by or had an impact on the male clerics. Nevertheless, such strategic boycotting in which the sisters actually forego a religious celebration, particularly a liturgy that is part of the Easter Triduum, serves as a testament to the intensity of their resolve against the male hierarchy of the institutional Church. It is also a significant example of "activism from within," whereby the sisters remain part of the institutional Church, yet abandon some aspects in order to engage their feminist orientations (Schneiders 2004, 95).

Yet, as Sister Ella explains, complete avoidance is challenging: "I have to make myself every other year go to the chrism Mass … just because it's such a wonderful celebration … [but] it's still a male bastion." Sister Ella's account reveals how her choices as a practising feminist Catholic remain filled with painful tensions (Schneiders 2004). While she boycotts one year, her biannual attendance reinforces how she will not be deterred by patriarchal domination and exclusion. As such, while alternating between her feminist and Catholic priorities, she attempts to uphold her forward-thinking principles.

Avoiding and reconsidering confession

For many other sisters, the resistance expressed against the maleness of Masses is also extended to other Church sacraments including confession.[5] Corresponding with shifting attitudes predominantly against confession among many lay Catholics over the past several decades (Cornwell 2014), the majority of sisters do not go to confession regularly, and many do not partake in the sacrament at all. Sixty-seven percent of the women I interviewed refuse to go to confession particularly because they no longer accept that the confessor is only and always a male cleric. While Sister Corinne was "a bit" frustrated with the male dominance of the sacrament of confession, Sister Penelope was much more emphatic with her response of "no" as she reflected on whether or not she felt obligated to go to confession to a male priest. Sister Sophie's position on the issue was also resolute: "I haven't been to confession in I don't know how many years … of course not. Why would I go to a man and tell him my sins?" Sister Ella shares a similar opinion on the patriarchal dimension of confession: "It's the same bag of tricks … the old boys' club that has … the authority to do that."

In addition to some theological misgivings associated with the sacrament, Sister Kelly's avoidance is related to very serious concerns regarding the priests' gendered mistreatment of women in the confessional[6] and their interest in the maintenance of patriarchal control:

> Well, I don't believe in confession anymore; that's number one … when
> I heard stories that women told me … of how [they] were treated in the
> confessional because they were not having children or because the doctor
> told them to take the pill or they would die if they would have another

child and how one woman was ordered out of the confessional [by the male priest] with that "mortal sin" out loudly. I just [sigh], those stories are real, you know. I think the love that Jesus … calls us to has been forgotten and what has taken its place is power and … control.

Sister Edith echoes Sister Kelly's position on the patriarchal domination evident within this sacrament and acts accordingly: "It's very much part of the male control so I don't go to confession much."

When reflecting on confession and the lower participation among Church members generally, and not just among women religious, Darlene also pointed to the male priests' interest in maintaining institutional control of the sacrament of reconciliation: "Which nobody goes to anymore! Like, I hear priests saying: 'I spent three hours there today and two people showed up' … Wow! They're not listening to the faithful on this. They're just holding onto clerical power." Darlene continued her critique of confession by pointing out that some priests are also not recognizing how women do not necessarily feel safe in a one-on-one meeting with a male priest in the confessional. She added emphatically: "Why would they?" In its entirety, Darlene's commentary serves as a reminder of how rather than adapting to parishioners' needs for more accessible, inclusive, comfortable, and safer practices of reconciliation which they had integrated in a group setting until a return to the original one-on-one format, male clerics tend instead to be latching on tighter to traditional customs in order to enforce their authority in the confessional.

While not wanting to miss the sacrament altogether, yet wanting to avoid an individual-based confession with a male priest, many women religious intentionally participate in it as rarely as possible and only attend what is known as general absolution, which consists of confession and reconciliation[7] administered to the entire parish congregation collectively and simultaneously. Many sisters preferred this option:

Well, to tell you the truth I probably go to confession once a year … when I do go it's to one of these public things … Not a one-on-one, no. (Sister Marian)

I prefer those [publicly shared general absolution], and I'm more comfortable with that; I haven't been to the confessional for a long time. (Sister Noreen)

Like a growing number of lay Catholics, some current and former sisters have distanced themselves from the formal sacrament as a whole, and while they are concerned about the gendered dimension of the Church, they did not relate it specifically to their general disconnection from confession. Such was the case for the following women, whose lighthearted words give a sense of its reduced centrality to their lives:

> I can hardly remember when the last time I went to confession was. (Judith)

> I don't go regularly to confession. [laughs] (Sister Maureen)

Still others have managed their experience of confession very strategically by selecting both the format and the person granting forgiveness. For example, Mildred noted that she did not feel frustrated or uncomfortable going to confession to a male confessor when she was a vowed religious because she chose the priests carefully: "Not much, because I always did it with my friends" [laughs]. Others are similarly careful about their contemporary choices:

> I only go when I feel it's necessary for me and I choose my confessor. (Sister Jeanette)

> I myself do not go to confession in the traditional way ... for years ... my relationship with my [female] spiritual director ... fulfills that need ... It used to be very negative and I would never want to return to that ... It's a sacrament of healing ... I've experienced some communal ways of that sacrament here at [progressive/forward-thinking church] where you can actually speak with a friend or a community member or someone else in the parish and then it's kind of a general absolution and that I find a very healing way of doing it ... It's a *very* different style. (Sister Sarah)

Carol, who has been very painfully marginalized by male parish priests due to her open identity as a lesbian, also shed light on the alternative she seeks for herself and for others outside of the institutional Church. Here she refers to how the therapy that she has been receiving after leaving both the sisterhood and the Church has been more helpful toward healing and holiness compared to the traditional Catholic confession:

> Yeah, [I went] when I was a sister ... I surely wouldn't now! ... But this bit about having to go one-on-one. You know, I go to analysis and pay a hundred bucks an hour ... that to me is my journey to try and become more *holy* ... Not the way we do it in a box privately. I mean if somebody wants to sit down and talk to a Christian who can say to them, "In God's name I forgive you." ... that's a *healing* experience in itself ... and if it's part of a journey ... toward wholeness again it's a *very* positive thing.

Not only have some sisters avoided going to confession themselves but in some instances they have actually discouraged others from going, or they have intentionally not informed others about the one-on-one meeting in the confessional. For example, Sister Penelope explained: "I've taught children, you know, to know what's right and wrong. To ask forgiveness of the person that they may have fought with or hurt, 'Say you're sorry,' that sort of thing, you know. But I never taught them they have to go tell the priest."

Given the weight that confession has carried historically as a sacrament, the fact that it is not of consequence or at least appears to be of lesser consequence in the sisters' lives points to the "weightlessness" they seem to have experienced as they have moved beyond it. These evolving attitudes among sisters are consistent with noticeable trends among lay Catholics who no longer go to confession and do not feel guilty about it (Cornwell 2014). Yet what is particularly significant in the case of women religious' boycott is that due to stereotypical assumptions of sisters as loyally compliant Church representatives which are also related to the vow of obedience, or at least to pre–Vatican II versions of it (Wittberg 1994), many onlookers would not expect *nuns* either to bypass or reconstitute a sacrament. Overall, these examples of avoidance illustrate that while current and former sisters come to their dismissals for various reasons and while they carry them out to various extents, many of the women disconnected themselves from Church sacraments in order to reconcile their Catholic values with their social justice, grassroots, and feminist principles. As I demonstrate in subsequent sections, similar rationales underlie the women's distancing from certain Church spaces.

Withdrawing from parish service

Similar to what their US predecessors and counterparts did in both schools and parishes in the nineteenth century and then again in the mid- to late twentieth century (Ebaugh, 1993, 144; Wittberg 1994, 93, 96), many of the contemporary women religious I interviewed resisted exploitive conditions at the hands of the male hierarchy by withdrawing their active support in parishes. Sister Kelly recounted how sisters from two religious communities in the same Ontario city, and thus within the same diocese, withdrew their domestic and secretarial services in parishes in the late 1960s after Vatican II. While they served as role models for other women in the struggle toward gender equality, they were treated harshly by the diocesan male hierarchy:

> All the anger [by the diocesan priests and bishop] when we decided we were not going to look after the altar boys anymore; we were not going to look after the churches anymore and choirs ... all of those kinds of things that kept the parish going, when we decided we were not going to do that, *oh my*! That was terrible! ... "Oh, the sisters. The sisters. *The* sisters!" ... Oh my! Oh my! (Sister Kelly)

After they withdrew, sisters from the diocese formed a group to meet with priests from the various regions of the diocese to explain their congregational renewal changes and the rationale behind them following Vatican II. Sister Kelly recalled a particularly troubling patriarchal response against them:

> We were told, "We don't like the way you are dressed." In other words, "You should be wearing a habit." The final confidential report of these meetings was sent to the bishop but was inadvertently seen by another priest who was heard to remark he "would put us in our place" and we "should put our veils back on our heads and get back into the convent where we belong."

Such a "backlash" type of reaction only exacerbated the controversy and it points to the repercussions that women religious face by male clerics when they withdraw from exploitive conditions. Yet it also reinforced the sisters' resolve to maintain their feminist position, and doing so through a collaboration between two communities, just as nineteenth-century women religious in the United States did for similar reasons (Wittberg 1994, 95), further enhanced their capacities to resist and, by extension, refuse diocesan demands. As I show in the chapter on inclusive spirituality, since that time many of the sisters involved in the withdrawal have remained outside of parish life altogether and have concentrated on welcoming people into their own spaces for retreats, counselling, Masses, and spiritual direction. Those who continued to be involved in parish life afterwards did so not through domestic service but rather by selectively contributing more fully to the enrichment of parishioners' spiritual experiences (e.g., leading prayer groups, sacramental preparation) and to the management of the parish by helping to include lay people more fully and fairly (e.g., committees).

Sidestepping the Vatican

Rome, Rome, well as far as I'm concerned Rome has to go! (Sister Kelly)

In my conversations with women religious, including Sister Kelly, I have frequently heard their condemning, and often bitterly spoken, references to "Rome" which has become synonymous with "the Vatican" and "the pope" all implying a patriarchal "faraway mission control" (Kaylin 2000, 11). Whether communally or individually, women religious have circumvented or simply disregarded Rome's control[8] in a variety of confident and creative ways. Yet, similar to their avoidance of some Masses and sacraments, sisters have chosen to elude the actual physical location of the Vatican itself because it is a space that constitutes the ultimate representation of the Roman Catholic Church's patriarchal and pompous power. For example, while displaying considerable agitation as she spoke, Sister Clara clarified the way in which she and another sister dodged the worship of male officials at the Vatican:

> We had an audience with the pope, and honest to God I nearly freaked out … in the Vatican and … poor John [Pope John Paul II], he wasn't well, and he had a cold and honest, Sister [name removed] was with me … and they [local sisters] were all lined up and this Italian sister pushed us out of the way to get in front … and they're all kneeling and kissing the cardinals' rings … and she [travel companion and sister-colleague] says, "Let's get out of here" [laughs], and I thought, "Oh God!" But … I was so disappointed with the Vatican … my highlight was Florence with Michelangelo … But anyway, like the Vatican, you know the signs, "No sleeveless" … I said, Where are the signs for the men? They get nothing. They can go in … wear what [they want] … See I get so worked up. But you see it's a waste of my energy. Who's going to change that?

As Sister Loretta shared a similar sentiment, she revealed the tension and even the disdain that she felt because she was obligated to be in Rome as part of her leadership team duties: "I was at a meeting in Rome some years ago there, and Rome is not my favourite place to be, but anyway I had to go to a meeting!" By contrast however, Sister Theresa, who also had Rome-bound leadership responsibilities, chose to avoid the place. She proudly, yet sadly, recalled her shunning strategies first against the pope and then later against the Vatican in its entirety:

> We were in St. Peter's Square [sigh] and they said that the Pope might be coming … and he was going to be up on the balcony … and that we could all see him up there. Our tour guide said that. The original plan was to go and visit some fountains up on a hillside there. Anyway I know I scandalized people by choosing to go see the fountains rather than stand there; even if the Pope did come out, it just didn't make sense to me to stand there and look at him from I don't know how far. That didn't impress me at all [circa 1980]. So I remember making that choice. It just didn't impress me to see him.
>
> But … the Vatican doesn't impress me. I … didn't go to the canon-ization. [A Canadian woman religious] was canonized when I was on the council during those eight years, and our community said … anyone who wanted to go could put their name in a hat and these lucky ten or fifteen sisters would be chosen to go over to accompany the four of us who were on the leadership team, and I said I've been to Rome twice and said I'd be glad to let someone else go in my place. Two of us did that on the leadership team. We just weren't impressed with all the goings-on. So

that's just an example of the way that I've acted ... just ... the pomp and pageantry and power and wealth! ... I've really been saddened the two times I've been there by the opulence. It just, it embarrasses me.

Sister Marian held a similar opinion regarding the grandeur of the Vatican: "I've been to the Vatican [laughs] ... Well you just go and take a look at that place and you'll know what I'm talking about ... we have to walk the talk. I don't mean that we should go around in rags; don't misunderstand me but I think there's a poverty of spirit [that] we need."

Taken together, these examples demonstrate the sisters' autonomy to formulate their own views on Church sacraments and settings, as well as their avoidance strategies in the face of painful experiences of patriarchy. As such, they are illustrative of Sister Ella's emphatic description of how her community of sisters circumnavigates the Church's patriarchal control: "We learned how to sidestep all of this stuff!" Renowned Sister-scholar Sandra Schneiders also used similar terminology as she explained how sisters have "stepped sideways, as it were – out of the pyramidal structure" for the past seven decades in order to free themselves from patriarchal control and to establish living and working arrangements based on equality and inclusivity (Schneiders 2011, 114). Although Sister Ella's and Sister Sandra Schneiders' mutual vocabulary is indicative of how aware and articulate women religious are of the tactics required to move beyond patriarchal domination, sisters' creative forms of navigating the oppressive structures, as well as their courageous capacities to maneuver around and beyond such impediments still go against the stereotypical reputation of passive and compliant women religious that is still common in the twenty-first century (Kristof 2010; Mangion 2008). Nevertheless, as I show next, their autonomy extends even further to other situations and settings.

THE SISTERS' INTREPID INDEPENDENCE

Sisters' spiritual and religious innovation, especially within the context of a controlling Church, has been largely contingent upon the sisters' independence on both individual and collective levels. The progressive changes they sought to bring about depended greatly on their confidence and resourcefulness in both thought and action. Sister Theresa exemplified such autonomy as she described a situation in which she maintained personal control over her own mobility. After she retired from teaching, she travelled to northern Canada to work among Indigenous peoples. She was tactical in her approach to remain independent and to thus avoid interference by male clerics: "I was very careful not to get in touch with a bishop or a priest. I didn't want anybody getting their hands on me or deciding that I was going to be with them. I just wanted the freedom to look around. My community was fine with that so I went up and looked around."

Sister Agnes echoed a similar sense of audacious autonomy: "A number of us just go ahead and do what we feel God is calling us to and aren't too hung up with rules." Sister Clara shared a comparable confidence when she emphasized how she did not allow the patriarchal Church to infringe upon her rights as a woman: "No, 'cause I do my own thing anyway." In a similar vein, Sister Mabel revealed her individual independence when she responded to my question about whether or not she had accomplished anything by her resistance against and disagreements with a parish priest when she defended one of the sisters in her community while she was general superior: "No! Other than he's not going to push me around … he's going to be more hesitant the next time talking to me I think." But when I asked her if she thought that anything had improved in light of the conversations, her response of "Nah" spoke volumes about the lack of fruitful dialogue and willingness on the part of some priests and their diocesan leadership to work toward improving the spiritual experiences of parishioners and, in this case, children.

Nevertheless, despite the inertia, sisters continue to exercise agency as they assert their autonomy within their conventional religious contexts (Ammerman 2003; Holtmann 2011b; Mahmood 2006). For example, when Sister Noreen reflected on how she was resourceful in overcoming the male domination of the Church, she exclaimed confidently, "It's easy." She went on to explain that her strategy is located outside of the institutional Church:

All human situations are a place to be church … to bring God and … love. All human situations are good for that. So if you operate out of this space, you can always fly under the radar all the time. I mean … you're working with other human beings and you carry something … that gives you life; you share it. That has nothing to do with like, you know, really, I wouldn't be able to teach the catechism of the Catholic Church, the book, you know … sometimes there is good stuff … but I don't need to do that you see. I can. I'm supposed to be about … love. I did all kinds of work in my life to this day because I always believe wherever the human situations are that's where the church is, okay.

Sister Noreen's account, along with the others presented above, point to how women religious' sense of independence is derived from their communal support, their courage to contest and their wider vision of faith and humanity beyond institutional rules – all of which have brought them onto more profound, and arguably, more fulfilling terrains.

CONCLUSION

Women ... go their own way ... (Chittister 2004, 156)

There is no doubt that the institutional Church's approach has been one of patriarchal domination, which "minimizes women in the name of God, trivializes the feminine, enshrines the male, [and] institutionalizes the masculine" (Chittister 1995, 149). Yet, like their predecessors[9] from earlier centuries, today's women religious are not completely powerless in their opposition against male clerics (Coburn and Smith 1999; Gray 2007; Magray 1998; Mangion 2008; Wittberg 1994). In fact, most of the current and former sisters herein are among a wider group of strong-minded women religious whose capacities to critically contest and counter the constraints convey courage and commitment (Gray 2007; Mangion 2008). As such, their accounts contribute to the growing recognition that women religious have "never totally accepted" patriarchal domination and institutionalized gender injustice (Schneiders 2013, 529; Ruether 2003, 5). In this regard, while it may have often appeared that "men won the argument because men framed the argument" (Chittister 1995, 149), the sisters have overcome such patriarchal manipulation, and as they have done so, they have not only moved past some constraining dimensions of their Church but have also demonstrated how they have exercised their own agency in order to move well beyond inhibiting assumptions associated with their religious identities and roles, particularly those that presume obedience (Ammerman 2003; Mahmood 2006).

As they have renounced their secondary status in the Roman Catholic Church (Schneiders 2013, 530), the women have simultaneously sidestepped many of the Church's institutional dimensions in both subtle and noticeable ways and often in particularly intersectional ways that point to how they strategically negotiate the (im)permeability of the Church's established boundaries (Ammerman 2003, 223; Schneiders 2011). While in this chapter I have shown that women religious both critique patriarchal power explicitly and strategize around institutional constraints creatively, in the next chapters I shed more specific light on the sisters' counter-institutional strategies in the areas of spirituality, governance, and activism.

CHAPTER 5

Practising inclusive spirituality

There's not only one image of God. We've done a lot on images of God and what is your image of God now? Has it changed? If it hasn't, where are you stuck? (Sister Mabel)

T he openness with which General Superior Sister Mabel encourages her sister-peers to consider God is indicative of many women religious' contemporary quests toward alternative spirituality. As the first of three chapters on the sisters' pursuit and protection of complementary spirituality, this one sheds light on the all-encompassing approaches that sisters have undertaken in order to generate inclusive spiritual experiences. In the next chapter, I illustrate the sisters' emphasis on feminist spirituality, while in the subsequent one, I draw attention to how the sisters overcome the backlash against their alternatives. Across all three chapters, I demonstrate how the women, like their counterparts across time and place, are not confining themselves to official boundaries and normative modes of religion but are instead making a-institutional choices toward greater spiritual freedom and inclusivity (Lux-Sterritt and Mangion 2011, 2). I begin this chapter with a reminder of the motivation behind sisters' search for alternate possibilities for worship and gathering. Then I present the sisters' all-inclusive spiritual practices which involve the integration of wider Christian and non-Christian traditions. The spaces and sites of sisters' spiritual innovations, including spirituality centres, are also highlighted.

BEYOND RELIGION AND BEYOND THE CATHOLIC ALTAR

It is this awareness of the universal God that we miss in life. Our God has always been a Catholic God – or at the very least a Christian God. We have, as a result, missed so much of God's revelation. (Chittister 2004, 15)

In an effort to overcome the broader patriarchal control of the Catholic Church, many sisters have adopted the approach articulated by Sister Mona, a mild-mannered and seemingly shy member of a leadership team who echoed Sister Joan Chittister's contention:

> We have to move beyond what is specifically Catholic to the reign of God, which is something much bigger, and that is where we will find our way.

The sisters and former sisters have been and, still are, moving beyond the mind-binding and heart-hardening of denominationalism (Chittister 2004, 13). While some remain devoted to Catholic doctrine, others reject doctrinal bureaucracy entirely. Sister Marian revealed that despite her gratitude to the Church, she could now more easily let go of the institutional Church based on how she has learned that God, not Rome, is at the helm: "I could *now*, but I've had a lot of teaching, you know, and grounding and ... opening up to an almighty God who is in charge of the world." Toward the end of our conversation, I asked Sister Marian if there was anything else that she wished to share; her response focused on wider spaces beyond the Catholic altar:

> You know ... as I get older, I think who needs it? [It was when] I was living out in the desert that I saw those old guys looking after their sheep, like Abraham. To walk in that land and think it's all God-given anyway ... we're God; we came from God and we're going back to God. It doesn't make any difference if we go to the United [church]. Now if the nuns heard me say that. [loudly] If we believe in a God and I do ... and I believe that I'm taken care of and loved in life and ... I'd like to live out that, then what am I clutching, you know?

Sister Marian's recognition is often cited by other sisters when they explain their departures from traditional Catholic doctrine, pointing to the undeniably dynamic and evolving process through which women religious reflect upon and renegotiate their religious identity at the intersection of the multiple religious narratives that are emerging as they explore and integrate other spiritual traditions (Ammerman 2003). While Sister Marian seems to depart further from Catholicism, Sister Joelle remains supportive of Catholicism as she rationalized the importance of a broader approach:

> I am firmly rooted ... in the Catholic tradition; it's such a rich tradition. I love it. But I also believe that ... God can be inclusive and ... I'm not of ... the conquering type, you know, where there is only the one true [religion] kind of thing. But I do believe in approaching an ecumenical dialogue ... from a sure knowledge of my own tradition and rootedness in it ... I think what's really important ... is wholeness, and human dignity.

Part of their awareness of the limitations is based on their childhood and early sisterhood memories of the divisiveness between religious traditions and the presumption of superiority on the part of Roman Catholic Church authorities. Similar to how Sister Joan Chittister (2004, 11) described her childhood confusion and current frustration with the way in which her Presbyterian stepfather was rejected because he was not Catholic, Judith recounted how such a widespread exclusionary mentality manifested itself within her experience as a young Catholic nun:

> Because my dad wasn't a Catholic, I remember someone telling me when I entered that if he were to die while I was a nun … that I wouldn't be allowed to go to the Church because at that time Catholics didn't go to anything in a Protestant Church. Even lay Catholics didn't, much less nuns, and that certainly seemed ridiculous to me.

Sisters and former sisters have long been aware and critical of the harmful divisiveness of such an assumption of religious superiority and segregation (Chittister 2004, 14) and, as I show later in this chapter, have thus worked extensively toward ecumenical initiatives. As Darlene explains, while they maintain some aspects of their Catholic faith and identity (Ammerman 2003), rather than trying to change a seemingly intractable institution, both current and former sisters are directing their energies elsewhere:

> The Church formed me … and gave me my desire for spirituality but even in the tradition of spirituality in the Church, it's not the main line … the mystical tradition was always on the fringe, and that's where I'm most comfortable in the Church, this day myself. I'm on the fringe. I'm Catholic, of course I'm Catholic; I'll always be Catholic, but I'm on the fringe. I don't work so hard at the renewal of the Church anymore; I leave that to God. It's going to come in God's time, in God's way, and perhaps the institutional part has to really flop. I can't see how it could flop much more than it has, with the scandals of the past years. (Darlene)

Darlene's Catholic identity parallels Sister Joelle's affirmation above and together they illustrate that while there is certainly a reticence expressed explicitly by some women to be disassociated with Catholicism in particular, others happily disconnect themselves as they bypass Church revitalization efforts and contribute to other initiatives beyond the Catholic sphere. These outlooks shed light on the innovative agency that women religious engage as they subvert some religious requirements while maintaining varying degrees of affiliation with their principal religious identity (Ammerman 2003; Griffith 1997; Holtmann 2011b).

Naomi is in a similar position as one who now embraces an eclectic variety of spiritual and New Age practices but recalled how her earlier relation to Catholicism was firm and taken for granted: "I grew up in an Irish Catholic family and ... we were all quite happy with Catholicism [laughs] ... it was culturally and personally appropriate I guess." Despite her fervent affiliation with Catholicism, her enduring frustration with the narrowness of the institutional Roman Catholic Church has meant that she no longer invests in it:

> At this point in my life, I have decided ... and this is true for many years now, I have spent little energy, time or money on reforming the Church. I've just decided that it's ... not worth it, both for the institution and for me because I don't think it's going to change and I would get worn down and angry and bitter; so I don't do a lot of that ... I worked for a good portion of my life to create something different and I don't think it's really possible so I've just decided it's not a wise use of my energy.

While Darlene's and Naomi's critiques may be somewhat expected from former sisters, their stances are echoed by many women religious. For example, Sister Joelle shared a similar view on selectively challenging the Church's male hierarchy: "I don't have a heck of a lot of energy to spend on protest. I mean there's a lot more important things to do and so I proceed with contributing where I think it's important and ... don't want to waste a lot of time on this to tell you the truth." A parallel opinion was held by leadership team member Sister Mona, who was inspired by a retreat director's message to take a different approach – one that she attempts to implement within her community: "not to spend energy fighting a system that is not going to change in our lifetime; go in directions where you can be effective."

Going in directions in order to be effective is precisely the tactic that many sisters and their religious orders have adopted. Such an approach is part of a broader attitude of avoidance among many women, vowed and non-vowed, who have decided that "there is no going back to any totalitarianism that calls itself religion" because religion is "prescriptive and defining" (Chittister 2004, 11, 20). As such, the sisters are "no longer being defined by the adversary" (Ganley 2007, 1) nor are they bogged down by "spiritual broodings" (Chittister 2004, 9). Instead, they are ensuring that they are less constrained by the institutional dogmatism, sexism, authoritarianism, and legalism that constitute the Roman Catholic religion (Chittister 2004, 9, 14; Schneiders 2013).

By extension, sisters and former sisters are not allowing their growth to be stunted by "religion" (Chittister 2004, 21). Rather, they have been moving beyond the religious certitudes of the institutional Church and journeying toward wholeness through a spirituality of search (Chittister 2004, 3, 16, 22–4).

Consequently, their spirituality has been evolving and, while for most their faith remains centred on Jesus and God, for others it also moves beyond Christian dimensions (Chittister 2004, 14, 24) and is shaped by a commitment to gender equity (Lux-Sterritt and Mangion 2011, 1). The distinction between religion and spirituality serves as part of the backdrop upon which the sisters' evolving spirituality emerges. Sister Sarah underscores the openness and richness of that approach to spirituality:

> If it wasn't for the spiritual aspect of it ... for me a real essential part of religious life is the spiritual expression of my life and ... the spiritual development of me ... of that dimension of myself as a person ... that's really key ... a big reason for me to enter and to stay in religious life is that my spirituality has grown and has taken all kinds of different shapes ... that's always remained a really important aspect for me.

Indeed, women religious' emphases on spirituality have remained steadfast, while at the same time, many sisters' spiritual trajectories have taken them far beyond the institutionalized and, therefore, formalized Catholic altars. In the next sections, I explore the "different shapes" (Sister Sarah) that the sisters ensure that their spirituality is taking.

Enrichment with other faith traditions and spiritualities

> *I still went to church after that ... But I ... tried to find a better church.*
> (Judith)

Here, Judith is referring to how, upon leaving her religious community, she searched for a more inclusive church experience that was far away from the male-domination of the Roman Catholic Church; her search ended in a Protestant church where she observed that all are welcome. While Judith's quest beyond Catholicism occurred when she was no longer a vowed religious, many women religious explore other religions while they remain Catholic nuns, further illustrating how they, along with many people of faith in the late twentieth and early twenty-first centuries, have embraced a non-static religious identity that is no longer bound by narratives of one denominational tradition (Ammerman 2003, 219). To varying degrees, the sisters and former sisters have either practised the spiritual customs of or collaborated with members of other traditions including, but not limited to, Native spirituality, Buddhism, Islam, Judaism, Hinduism, Mennonite, Anglican, Protestant/United, Pentecostal, and Baptist. Some sisters have collaborated with representatives from Christian and non-Christian traditions as part of ecumenical initiatives in Canada and, in some cases, as part of mission projects in economically developing countries. Many have also supplemented their Catholic faith with other spiritual traditions.

Buddhism. Several current and former sisters have explored what they refer to as "Eastern religions" including Buddhism. Many, like Darlene and Sister Joelle, have been inspired by renowned Buddhist monk and peace activist Thich Nhat Hanh. While Naomi is involved in a forward-thinking Roman Catholic parish and explores cosmology, she also draws upon the Buddhist tradition to enrich her faith experiences:

> My spirituality is heavily influenced by Buddhism and Thich Nhat Hanh; that whole spirituality. Buddhism has given me a real appreciation for being as opposed to doing. Buddhism has been very helpful in practices, breath practices that I just find really helpful ... and Buddhism integrates the body in a much healthier way for me than Catholicism and cosmology ... it's inclusive of the whole reality of life as opposed to, you know, the earlier, narrower interpretations.

Having been exposed to Buddhism in her younger years as a sister in a mission country and as one who has embraced it ever since and particularly again in recent years, ninety-one-year-old Sister Shannon conveyed with certitude her high esteem for that faith tradition: "I have great respect for the Buddhist way of life and their practice of Mindfulness." Sister Kelly has also observed how some of the people whom she supports in spiritual direction benefit considerably from embracing Buddhist principles and practising Buddhist rituals.

Similarly, when Sister Theresa was reflecting on how she does not feel contained within the Catholic faith, she explained how her spirituality was enriched by the Buddhist workshops that were offered at her community's spirituality centre and that underscored how Buddhism was not a religion per se: "Well ... it really deepened it and I really like their ... silence and quiet and just kinda getting back to point zero in your own." When asked if she thought that the Vatican would approve of her community's workshop facilitation and of her exploration of Buddhism, Sister Theresa's response was emphatic and confident: "Oh probably not, but I couldn't care less."

While most sisters referred to the distinct aspects of Buddhism that inspired them, Sister Kelly explained that her experience with Buddhism reminded her of the similarities across religious traditions: "Persons that I ... work with come from other denominations ... and the more that I work with persons who do hatha yoga or Zen Buddhism [the more I realize] ... it's all the same! There's no difference! Just different words, different names, you know, different titles. But it's the same flow of spirituality through it all." As I present later, Sister Kelly's perspective resonates with many sisters' and many religious communities' recent prioritization of unity, rather than disparity across religions.

Indigenous peoples' spiritual traditions. Many current and former sisters recalled how their spiritual development has been enhanced by what they referred to as "Native spirituality."[1] Such inspiration was particularly meaningful for Sister Jeanette, who did not self-identify as being of "Native" origin[2] until she was in her 40s because she feared that doing so earlier would have led to racial rejection: "For a long time I didn't recognize my Native culture because in those days, uh, if you were a person that [was] Native, they were like [pause]." She clarified that while she felt culturally ostracized within the wider society, she felt welcome within her religious community. She is now proud of and excited about what she calls "Native spirituality" and culture: "I had to claim it myself ... I ... embraced it and the gift it brings ... to ... humanity ... it's God's gift expressed in ... the Native culture and ... then I got really interested in it and really, you know, excited about it. But before that I would just put it on the back burner." For Sister Jeanette, the emphasis on nature became evident as she explained that she is now "interested in Native spirituality because ... I'm very earth-orientated ... the environment for me, it's really strong because of the respect Native peoples have for the earth and ... for ... what it nurtures in them. What it brings forth and the respect for it, you know ... that I really recognize in myself."

Sister Jeanette was also pleased to reveal that she has participated in Indigenous spiritual ceremonies hosted within the wider community, as well as by fellow sisters who also identify as Indigenous and who celebrate their cultural heritage and spiritual traditions: "[A]ny opportunity that came along I ... took advantage of it." She also enthusiastically explained how she shared some customs with her sister-peers: "In our cluster groups ... we each take our turn. So we prepare the prayer ... whatever the topic is we're going to share, you make it as creative as you want ... sisters recognize because of whatever way I create things, it's really earthy things so it really brings out ... that spirituality."

While some women religious embraced Indigenous peoples' spiritual traditions while participating in workshops[3] held within their community's spirituality centres, others, like Sisters Theresa and Sarah, followed them directly among Indigenous communities across Canada. As Sister Theresa explained how she encountered and enhanced her faith with "Native Spirituality," she also reflected on what she discovered while living in a mobile home in northern Canada among Indigenous peoples: "I never felt safer in my life than I was up there ... But these guys, their faith is so deep and strong. Oh my!" Sister Theresa also recalled how another aspect of her spiritual enhancement, namely earth-centredness, was intertwined with the Indigenous context in which she was living and it is one that she was especially excited about:

I read a lot of Thomas Berry and Brian Swimme and I watched, for some reason the Aboriginal channel had the twelve Brian Swimme's *Story of the Universe* ... Not the ones we're watching here but there was more nature and they showed them twice and I really, really enjoyed them! I got into it up there from that time period.

Many current and former sisters referred to renowned cosmologists Thomas Berry's and Brian Swimme's[4] positive influence on their spiritual growth as they have integrated a deeper respect for the earth and the universe within their spiritual practices. That Sister Theresa encountered this nature-oriented emphasis while living within an Indigenous context that affirmed that orientation was both timely and telling as it points to how various spiritual sources are often intertwined and sometimes unexpectedly so, yet women religious embrace those serendipitous opportunities constructively.

Like Sister Theresa, it was while she was living in a mobile home on a reservation in Western Canada that Sister Sarah developed a deep respect for Indigenous peoples' spiritual traditions. She recounted that while she has drawn on Buddhism, Hinduism, and Judaism, it was when she was embracing "Native spirituality" that she also formed an appreciation for, and became engaged with Celtic and earth-centred spiritualities:

That's where I really discovered ... my love for other cultures ... and I also felt very privileged in a sense because I was ... in a generation where there was a lot more listening happening of the culture that I was in. Like I was in the first generation really of that congregation who were experiencing sweat lodges and pipe ceremonies and the different types of rituals, whereas the sisters before me were really never invited into that and I was very much a part of that life ... It's been a huge influence on my prayer life; [it is] probably I would say the spirituality that has most influenced my prayer life ... I discovered a lot about myself when I was living ... with First Nations peoples ... I discovered my closeness to earth. I have a very earth-based spirituality ... I know that when I'm outside in the garden or just anywhere outside ... that's when I really ... just ... settle into myself. And I used to feel because I was living on reserves that were very rural it was very easy to go for a walk and be like immediately in the mountains, in the forest. It was like for me just walking through a door into another world all the time ... to be ... in this world just surrounded by nature. So I really learnt that about myself and that connection and I know that I long for that ... So ... definitely very earth-centred.

And then ... I discovered through my Celtic roots that is also very much a part of my ancestry. So I really felt that I learnt a lot about my own ancestry through Native spirituality. And I've never like studied

Celtic spirituality very much but what I have learnt about it, I find that there's a lot of similarities.

The ritual life of Native spirituality is very important to me. I still … smudge and although many Native peoples … and non-Native people frown on non-Native peoples doing ceremonies in public, it's not frowned upon in private … The people I lived with always told me … "Wherever you want to do this, it's fine" … But out of respect for those who don't understand that, I usually don't do that in public. But in private, I do like to smudge … I find that very centring … I like to listen to Native music … in my prayer.

Contrasting how many of the sisters reported a sense of the Catholic Church's rejection of the feminine, Sister Sarah explained that, "I never felt that with Native spirituality. There was always a place for feminine expression, for femininity, whether it was expressed by men or women." While I explore the integration of feminine gifts in the next chapter, Sister Sarah's comment is relevant here insofar as it points to how women religious have felt that their gendered contributions have been included and respected in other spiritual traditions and, ironically in this case, in one that the Roman Catholic Church had previously sought to destroy.

Islam and Judaism. While compared to Native spirituality, the religious tradition of Islam is a patriarchal one that is known to marginalize women on a variety of levels (Badran 2008; Jouili and Amir-Moazami 2008). Nevertheless, some current and former women religious are becoming informed about its rituals particularly from the perspective of Muslim women. As one who has enhanced her spiritual practices with both the Golden Rule and the Green Rule,[5] Sister Adele has also respectfully embraced other religious traditions, including Judaism through her collaboration with women of other faiths in their pursuit of peace throughout the world. More recently, however, she has especially been learning about Islam: "Personally I've had more to do with the Muslim community in the last number of years … it was a real privilege." She recalled how she and a fellow sister had been invited by a Muslim couple to break the fast with them during Ramadan. They felt privileged to be able to share in the prayers and gestures of the traditional ritual. Later, Sister Adele had gathered the women's prayer and peace group that she initiated for a retreat at her religious community's spirituality centre. She elaborated upon the experience:

We had deliberately chosen different forms of prayer like Christian and Muslim, several different traditions … so [our Muslim friend] led us in prayer and we went in the meditation room … and she explained the gestures and prayers and we all entered into that with her and I found that a real privilege and just important to me to honour others' ways of praying and just, like even within our own tradition, like we have so many ways that we pray as Christians and as Catholics. Lots of the ways that people pray as Catholics, I don't pray that way. Some of them I used to, some of them I never did. But … there needs to be that variety. I mean if we connect with our source [laughs] and if we connect with one another, I mean whatever helps to do that.

The sisters' interest in other religious traditions is not only apparent in their practising of some of their rituals, but it is also evident in their critiques against the institutional Church authorities' approaches and actions in relation to other religions and their followers. For example, Sister Theresa sharply criticized Pope Benedict XVI in 2009 for the presumption of religious superiority implied within his statements regarding Jewish people:

And then … the two … blunders that the Pope has made recently, number one with the Buddhists way back – 'member that fuss – and then the latest one offending the Jews by praying for them. Like okay pray for the Jews like you pray for anybody but that they come to Christ or something, like? … And then he wonders why, you know … there's a lot of unrest with the Pope and that kind of nonsense going on.

While their engagement with Judaism and Islam[6] may be nascent, both their collaboration and critique in their regard is a testament to the sisters' exemplary openness toward, and respect of other religious traditions that have historically been constructed in adversarial ways.

Earth-centred spirituality

Solidarity to me means being at one with all peoples and being at one with all of creation. It means touching the earth and all that is upon it with reverence and respect. (Sister Shannon)

While over the past decade, there have been increased interest and initiative on the part of communities of women religious to explore and promote earth-centred spirituality, nature has been a central part of many sisters' spirituality for a very long time, in some cases, since childhood. For example, Sister Mabel credits her father and the extensive "time [spent] outside with him" for her nature-informed spirituality: "My father taught me about God by looking at the stars and the earth … by walking through the fields … and he'd show me the blades of grass and how God was all loving, you know, and so I was free."

Sister Mabel still enriches her spiritual experiences by intentionally spending time in nature: "I go sit by the water. Just watch the tree."

Many sisters incorporate items from nature into the decorating of their spiritual spaces; some use leaves, branches, rocks, water, seeds, flowers, small animals, and insects as items upon which they base their reflections, either privately or collectively; some items are set as permanent decorative fixtures in prayer rooms, chapels, or retreat centres while others are integrated temporarily or seasonally within specific spiritual celebrations. While many sisters bring earth-based items indoors into their people-built spaces, others hold spiritual celebrations outside Church walls or buildings in nature settings in the midst of "God's creation," which are not necessarily Church-sanctioned spaces.[7] While such practices may not appear to be particularly novel to some readers, it is important to note that they are not typically incorporated into the Catholic ritual (traditional Mass), especially in an institutional sense. Thus, the ways in which the sisters are embracing items from nature as important symbols of spiritual ritual are indicative of significant shifts toward more genuine relationships with nature.

In addition, while some sisters ensure that the prayers and songs they include in their spiritual celebrations emphasize creation and the importance of respect and responsibility toward nature, still others are involved in developing and producing such music. For example, Judith has been part of a women's prayer and musical group that emphasizes the combined potential of women, land, and spirit. Her group records music and sells the CDs to raise funds for ecofeminist initiatives including awareness, advocacy and action toward the preservation and restoration of the earth, particularly land and water. As will become evident later in the chapter on activism, this example is one among many illustrative of the ways the current and former sisters blend their spirituality and activism.

While most sisters and former sisters blend nature-based themes or objects into their spiritual celebrations, some complement their liturgical rituals with intellectual and social justice awareness-oriented initiatives that further their own and their lay participants' understandings of earth-centredness. As such, some women religious and their communities seek to deepen understandings and practices of ecological justice as well as personal and planetary peace by exploring the possibilities opened up by connecting ecology and economy, and by blending science and religion.[8] The latter is understood within the new cosmology – an approach that has been profoundly inspiring current and former sisters in recent decades.

The new cosmology – universe-centred spirituality

Cosmology ... it's inclusive of the whole reality of life as opposed to ... the earlier, narrower interpretations. (Naomi)

The new cosmology[9] is a theological thread that interweaves scientific discoveries with mystical wisdom – which were, until recently, constructed in opposition to the Roman Catholic tradition – and emphasizes the sacredness and interconnectedness of all living beings within creation (Cannato 2006; Chittister 2004; O'Murchu 2008; Swimme and Berry 1992). Eighty-eight percent of both current and former sisters proudly claimed that the new cosmology has informed their spirituality. As Sister Adele excitedly explained how she and her colleagues feature the new cosmology within their spirituality centre's workshops, she shed light on the progress being made as a result of the innovative theology:

> What we can offer here is ... the focus ... on a spirituality that will sustain us. There's the new cosmology which we know now from science ... The old cosmology was ... there was heaven and the earth and under the earth ... that was the image anyway and so we based our theology on that cosmology and ... our spirituality, it came out of that ... and now the cosmology that we know of this evolving universe and beginning to find our place in that ... for me, it's a whole new basis and ... we're just beginning to have a new theology that's based on that ... and then ... comes ... a new way of looking at ourselves, and God and all of creation. So there's a whole new world view ... a whole new spirituality and that's growing up all over the place around the planet.
>
> I find it so hopeful because it is bringing us to that oneness ... and then to say, "Where are all those crazy divisions we ... put up ... and continue to institutionalize?" And then we have to have institutions like war ... to keep them going and an economy that's not fair and all that. So ... we've really been promoting that new cosmology and learning it together. We haven't been experts but we've been learning it together with others because we see it as a really important basis for new theology, a new spirituality ... a whole new world view, a whole new way of being in the world! ... So I think that's a way we can contribute to this equality and human rights and social justice.

The depth, popularity, and excitement to which Sister Adele refers also resonate with other women religious. Sister Theresa has been exploring the new cosmology for some time already and she is enjoying it "very much." She added that "it ties right into my spirituality and ... it's a big eye-opener for me."

Several other sisters enthusiastically explained the positive influence that the new cosmology has had on their spirituality and as they did so, much of what it emphasizes was revealed:

> My faith has grown like it's [sigh] [laughs], it's hard to put into words. Like it's not what it was when I was a child or a teenager or an early religious, and thank God! And that's what's supposed to happened to us! (Sister Kelly)

> I'm loving it ... my horizons are being broadened ... I'm such a part of the universe; I'm such a part of that little tree that's out there, all the baby trees and I have an appreciation for the Aboriginal people like I've never had before because they had that from the beginning, their connection with nature ... it's wonderful; it's a whole new thing for me with my spiritually. (Sister Rita)

> I love [it] ... like it has changed my whole way of thinking really ... it's changed my theology ... you know. Where is God? Where is heaven? What happens to us when we die? [laughs] Like all of those questions ... have changed for me. (Sister Loretta)[10]

> Yeah, yeah definitely ... I would say a big influence on our spirituality and my spirituality today is, yeah, our relationship to the cosmos, and that definitely informs the way that ... I even read scripture now. (Sister Sarah)

> I just find it so fascinating. It redefines ... your whole approach to God ... to what we are ... what's really important is to ... recognize the unconditional love of God for every ... part of creation; yeah ... the new theology out of the new cosmology really excites me; I've been doing a lot of reading in that area and it has very, very important ... understandings for ... approaches to social justice. (Sister Joelle)

> The big movement in theology today is the new cosmology and the new creation story and responding to that. You know, it's the oneness of all ... and absolute equality of all ... Yeah, I mean ... when I lived with my sister, I lived with a little dog; I discovered a whole personality ... the mystery of God's creation. All of us one in that great [pause] wow! (Darlene)

As these comments suggest, the women are undoubtedly encouraged and excited about the spiritual sustenance that they have found as they have expanded outward beyond their Catholic rituals and have considered more profoundly the ecological relationships of all beings. While the ideas generated through the new cosmology are not incompatible with Catholicism, they imply a decentring of the institutional Church in favour of organizing around a deep respect for all components of our shared ecosystem on earth and within the universe. In this light, the new cosmology has led to a major shift in spiritual focus among many of the women featured herein.[11]

However, it is that very institutional decentring and spiritual shifting that has led some sisters to proceed prudently. As Carol referred to the study groups on the new cosmology held at her former community's motherhouse, she recounted how both sisters and priests monitored and cautioned against the sister-facilitators' emphasis:

> There's a couple of them … that have been told, "Now be careful sisters. Be careful. The books now you're gettin' them into." You know, O'Murchu and … Brian Swimme and Berry and those guys. You know, "Be careful! You don't want to piss off the bishop." … Yeah. You kinda, you toe the line. You can go so far but not over, you know.

Despite the partial censoring, the sister-coordinators continued with the study sessions because they were convinced of their significance. Sister Adele who is from another religious community also considered the ongoing study of the new cosmology as essential. As she shed further light on the context and benefits of the evolving shift, she exemplified how women religious embrace emergent spiritual narratives (Ammerman 2003):

> Now … situating ourselves as … one group within the whole. I mean now my view of everything has changed or is changing because I now know the story of the universe … that's our history as Catholics, that's our history as Christians, as followers of Jesus. That's the history of all humanity. That's the history of all creation. So, for me it's most important that we situate ourselves in this huge story and find our place in it as followers of Jesus and really respect that … all the mainstream religions have their place in that story too. We're all one in that huge story … and we can't go backwards … focusing in on a lot of little rules as if they were really important. I can't do that. No. … I'm not interested in Church in a lot of little stuff. I think it's so unimportant, and I'd say our local in this universe is this planet [laughs] that we share with all life on this planet. So for me, how I live as a follower of Jesus, how we live as followers of Jesus on this planet in a really inclusive way is what counts now.

As I explore below, the sisters' spirituality centres represent the spaces where contemporary and inclusive orientations like the new cosmology are explored.

SPIRITUALITY CENTRES

Many communities of women religious have established spirituality and retreat centres where they have created spaces of enrichment and support for their own members as well as for a wider community of lay people with whom the sisters interact and whom they seek to assist. I highlight below some of the initiatives that are offered within such vibrant and leading edge centres.

Healing and reflecting through New Age practices

In comparison to the religious services provided by traditional parishes (largely sacramental preparation courses and traditional prayer groups), spirituality centres run by communities of women religious attend to the whole person. In various ways, the centres provide sources and spaces of support, healing, refuge, retreat, counselling, renewal, spiritual direction, and personal growth (Bruno-Jofré 2007). Moreover, the practical value of these spirituality centres cannot be overlooked given that they provide an effective use of convent space and much-needed revenue for the congregations, although the latter often subsidize the cost of the activities in order to ensure that their services are accessible to individuals with limited income – a further testament to women religious' efforts toward inclusivity and accessibility.

Sister Agnes proudly praised the retreat experiences that her community has offered over the years:

> I really enjoy those opportunities to develop more in those areas ... we get good people in for retreats ... our retreat program is quite good and has been! ... My first holistic retreat was *way* back! ... close to forty years ago ... at our camp ... an American nun who taught us *um* mantras and stuff. [softly] It was wonderful ... and these are the older nuns who organized that.

Spiritual direction also represents one of the sisters' major contributions to people's spiritual development. Seven current sisters and two former sisters still serve or have served as spiritual directors in a variety of settings, including their communities' spirituality centres. Sister Kelly referred to the diverse religious populations to whom she provides life-enhancing guidance through spiritual direction:

> I minister to a variety of people from differing faiths, Catholic and non-Catholic, Anglican, Lutheran, Mennonite, Quaker, some Anglican women priests, and lay ministers. I accompany persons who are painfully moving through the transition from the old theology, and how they were treated in the Church, to the new more holistic theology and spiritual cosmology. I meet people with whom I have worked in workshops, in

retreats, in spiritual direction and they'll say to me, "You've changed my life" and I think, "Oh! … It has made changes in persons."

As she critiqued the Church's lack of recognition of and appreciation for the support that sisters' spirituality centres provide, Sister Loretta shed light on the assistance that individuals receive through nuns' spiritual direction: "All the people that go to [Sister Ella's retreat centre] and it's never been recognized by the diocese at all that place … yeah and all the people that are helped there. That's just one place. I mean there's [spirituality centre] here in [city]."

The five spirituality centres, operated by communities represented by the women religious I interviewed, also offer restorative activities to varying degrees, including contemplative walking within or outside a labyrinth, dream therapy, massage therapy, psycho-therapy, meditation, mindfulness, peace dancing, reflexology, Reiki, Shibashi, therapeutic touch, yoga, and bioenergetics. Opportunities for the enhancement of spiritual development through these practices are also offered during spirituality retreats where in addition to following the retreat's routine, participants are encouraged to engage in these complementary activities in order to bring them peace, centredness, mindfulness, and insight. The locations where they occur are presented as "sacred spaces," but they include various milieus that are not confined to the chapel walls or to the labyrinths' perimeters. Several sisters also proudly mentioned that not only have healing opportunities developed from these offerings but their own spirituality has been enriched by them. Sister Maureen explains how she benefits from integrating practices that are new to her: "I pray every morning … by using a mantra … a centring prayer. I find that that has been … helpful for me." By their authentic embracing of such varied approaches, the sisters have been establishing meaningful alliances that are transforming their own spiritual and healing experiences and those of whom they serve through more inclusive and life-giving processes.

Such activities appear to be unique to sisters' spirituality centres and tend to be part of the "fringe" where Darlene works, as well as within the "underground church" where Sister Kelly operates. Darlene explained that she feels comfortable advocating gender equality in her spiritual direction practice within a retreat centre of a women's religious congregation:

> This is a kind of private ministry in a sense; it's not part of the officialdom … Even though I work here in a ministry that is supported by the sisters … They have a pretty open, justice-oriented kind of a thing anyway and I fit very well here, but I am on the fringe and I'm not very involved in the official Church out there. I don't go to parishes. I don't do any of that.

While Darlene's reference to the fringe illustrates a former nun's intentional positioning and initiative within a community of sisters' inclusive space, Sister Kelly's reference to the "underground church" sheds light on how a current nun maximizes another peripheral location. When Sister Kelly explained how she managed her dissatisfaction with the Church's male hierarchy by sidestepping it altogether, she revealed the strategic setting:

> I made up my mind that I was not going to work in the area of the clerical field at all, that I was going to work in the underground church so that's my focus ... a lot of my theology now has changed ... my focus again is women, human rights for women, and not only in the Church but all over.[12]

Sister Kelly's emphasis on the "underground church" entails her feminist writing, her involvement with women-church liturgies, and her alternative forms of counselling including dream therapy with both women religious and other laywomen.[13] While Sister Kelly has given countless dream workshops in women religious' spirituality centres across Canada "from coast to coast," neither they nor most of the activities offered in sisters' retreat centres have been advertised on the bulletin boards of traditional parishes nor promoted by neither priests nor lectors at the pulpit because they are not considered conventional Catholic content or legitimate Church practices. Thus, sisters' broader spiritual offerings are not reaching the wider community of Catholics, resulting unfortunately in lost opportunities and reminding us of how peripheral their status remains despite some critics' perception that sisters' spirituality centres are mere extensions of the institutional Church. Yet, although sisters themselves may view their spirituality centres as unique and independent of the institutional Church and while, in this regard, they may be constructed as alternative spaces compared to institutional Church locations, Darlene and Sister Kelly, as well as their progressive counterparts, adamantly contend that such activities and locations are not secondary but are rather central and therefore important and productive expressions of spirituality and "church" (Gervais and Turenne Sjolander 2015).

In addition to healing activities and spiritual direction, sisters' spirituality centres also offer workshops that blend spiritual contemplation with critical reflections on current social issues with emphases on non-violence, peace, social justice, and earth justice. Many of their workshops offer profound and critically oriented discussions and, in fact, sometimes revolutionary-based debates drawing on the ideas of renowned "radicals" such as Diarmuid O'Murchu, Edwina Gateley, Sister Joan Chittister, Brian Swimme, Thomas Berry, Bishop John S. Spong, and Hans Küng, among many others.[14] Such workshops are often offered at sisters' spirituality centres or at their smaller community outreach locations. Some communities of sisters not only offer ecologically mindful spiritual activities but they also do so in ecologically friendly spaces whereby they have ensured that their buildings are "green," particularly when they have constructed new facilities or have renovated existing ones. Thus, they ensure that both the space and the content of the spiritual experiences are earth-centred and eco-friendly.

Within the five spirituality centres represented by the current and for-mer women religious I interviewed, services are provided to Catholics and non-Catholics (including non-Christians) alike; specific faith backgrounds are not a prerequisite for participation at their spirituality centres. In fact, similar to the complementary practices carried out among American women religious (Kaylin 2000; Reed 2004, 299), the activities at the retreat centres draw their spiritual influences from a variety of faith traditions and alternative spiritualities, some of which were already illustrated above, including but not limited to Buddhism, Native spirituality, Islam, Judaism, Hinduism, the new cosmology, and feminisms.[15] Most of these activities place emphasis on spiri-tuality and not religion, and they are often non-denominational. In fact, one centre's welcome message specifically states: "Our emphasis is on spirituality rather than religion."

The diversity celebrated within sisters' spirituality centres is evident not only in the spiritual practices but also in many of the symbols that are either displayed throughout the buildings or integrated within the rituals. For exam-ple, one can still see the traditional symbols of Christianity and Catholicism, including crucifixes as well as statues, icons, and portraits of Jesus, the Virgin Mary, patron Saints, the Holy Family (Mary, Jesus and Joseph), the current pope, angels, and artwork depicting the Stations of the Cross. However, there now tends to be fewer of the traditional symbols, and those that remain have often been modernized to ensure that they are representative of racial, gender, and ecological justice. One can also see more contemporary images of peace, not only in the form of doves symbolizing the Holy Spirit and olive branches but also in the form of the internationally recognized peace sign, among others.

In these spaces, we also see evidence of non-Catholic and non-Christian spiritual traditions, including images of Buddha and Gandhi, yoga mats, golden rule and green rule posters, social justice posters including Buddhist-based ones,[16] pottery globes of the earth to symbolize earth-centredness, as well as statuettes symbolizing interconnectedness and solidarity, etc. The assortment of books, cards, and CDs on display in their libraries also reflects various spiritual teachings, ecological awareness, current social issues as well as self-help and healing strategies based on a range of perspectives. While ecumenical symbols and efforts are not new or unique among women religious or among some inclusively oriented laypeople and priests, the sites and spaces where they are situated and rendered visible are indicative of genuine expressions of inclusive spirituality and thus provide evidence of actual ecumenical practice beyond the promises of ecumenical dialogue and collaboration.

Sisters' spirituality centres and retreat spaces are also often decorated with symbols of other cultural traditions from Latin America, Africa, Asia, and Europe. While in many instances, they are souvenirs from locations of mission projects, they are not just made visible as colourful décor; rather, they are set up intentionally and meaningfully by the sisters to express inclusivity and respect of multiple religious and cultural approaches. In this light, such décor reflects sisters' instilling of sacred objects in alternative symbols.

SELECTIVE, CREATIVE, AND INCLUSIVE INVOLVEMENT IN PARISHES

Women religious have contributed to parishes for decades in both creative and inclusive ways. As I have shown elsewhere (Gervais and Turenne Sjolander 2015, 385), the women I interviewed, including Sisters Theresa and Ella, have practised a horizontal diffusion of power that has empowered lay people to participate more fully and take on leadership roles in parishes. In various forms of parish ministry, other sisters have offered spiritual direction (Sister Adele), innovative liturgical preparation (Sister Rita), advanced scriptural preparation (Sister Maureen), and have performed baptisms (Sister Theresa) or heard confessions (Sister Loretta) – initiatives or sacraments that are not typically allowed to be carried out by nuns but ones that were approved by male clerics.[17]

Yet more recently, having been inspired and strengthened by the spiritual enrichment they have gained from the aforementioned opportunities with other religious orientations and within their retreat centres, some sisters have attempted to engage in parishes in more profound, theological, and intellectual ways. In an effort to rise above the exclusionary Catholic altars, many women religious have been strategically selecting Church spaces that are more inclusive because they now expect more from and wish to contribute more to their church experiences. For example, Sister Adele emphasized her tactic: "I choose the circles I travel in the Church … I choose to be where there's that freedom." Sister Agnes clarified that her approach is to be selective of the spaces she occupies: "I seek out parts of the Church that are not hung up on patriarchy and hierarchy. I seek out the parish where they welcome female homilists … who are not ordained." Although homilies by lay people are not officially permitted, in addition to two sisters who have given homilies during retreats and celebrations in their own chapels, six other participants disclosed that they give homilies because they have intentionally become and have remained parishioners in forward-thinking and inclusive parishes that enable both vowed and non-vowed women to give the sermons. It should be noted, however, that their parishes are considered unique and are often subject to scrutiny by diocesan bishops, but Sister Adele's proud assertion of "We do it anyway" signals how forward-looking women religious sometimes subvert religious requisites not only individually or within their own orders but also collectively across a wider spiritual community (Ammerman 2003; Griffith 1997).

In one such progressive parish where several current and former women religious with whom I spoke are members and thus experience "that freedom," the priest rarely gives the homily. Instead, many women religious have been instrumental in sharing profoundly inspiring and theologically enriching homilies. Some sisters are also writers, producers, and directors of children's and adults' re-enactments of the Christmas and Easter stories. It is within these initiatives that women religious, like Sister Agnes, ensure that cultural and spiritual diversity are represented. For example, in 2009, Sister Agnes ensured that the children acting the parts of Mary and Joseph, as well as the doll representing Jesus during the Christmas pageant were of African origin in order to be more culturally inclusive. She made the same effort during the Easter celebrations in 2010 and 2013. On another Christmas Eve, Sister Agnes and other parish leaders ensured that Canadian Indigenous peoples' spiritual traditions and their historical contexts were integrated within the pageant carried out by the children and in the songs sung by the choir during the play; such attentiveness are indicative of some sisters' efforts to offer deeper and social justice-infused "church" experiences by annexing new spiritual representations with canonically constrained Roman Catholic Church customs.[18]

CONCLUSION: "BEING CHURCH" BEYOND "THE CHURCH"

More women worldwide will continue to put Christ-like values ahead of Catholic Church laws. (Sister Shannon)

Given their dissatisfaction with Church-defined normative modes of spirituality, contemporary women religious, like their historical counterparts, have courageously moved ahead and are living what they believe (Lux-Sterritt and Mangion 2011, 16; Schneiders 2004, 107). Their encompassing spirituality is shaped not only by their openness to other religious orientations and New Age practices beyond the Catholic tradition but also by their broader conceptions of "church" (Gervais and Turenne Sjolander 2015; Winter 2002). The current and former sisters have ensured that their living out of the Jesus-centred gospel teachings is not mediated by and through Rome – the ultimate epicentre of the institutional Church. Thus, their courageous approach has provided them with a considerable degree of autonomy and freedom through which it has become possible for them to imagine and practise a broader spirituality within a wider and more inclusive sense of "church" (Chittister 2004, 16; Ebaugh 1993), all the while retaining, and for some more selectively than others, affiliations with their original religious identity as Roman Catholics (Ammerman 2003).

Regardless of the proximity to the institutional Church through which they have either led or followed spiritual and liturgical innovations, the sisters have been "busy *being* church" (Schneiders 2004, 106) by thinking and living both within and beyond the institutional setting. They have strategically recreated spaces in order to not only survive the dogmatic constraints but to thrive through their all-encompassing and all-inclusive spiritual practices (Gervais and Turenne Sjolander 2015). In other words, by looking and living beyond the boundaries of the Catholic tradition, the current and former sisters have renewed and reinforced their earnest dedication to carrying out their ministry by becoming more deeply reflexive and inclusively interconnected. As such, by extending the scholarly gaze on lived religion beyond the conventional domains of male clerics, public religion, and institutional Church spaces and instead onto terrains involving women's experiences, I have, in this chapter, revealed the complex nuances of sisters' spiritual intersectionality and innovation (Neitz 2003, 289).

CHAPTER 6

Engendering feminist spirituality

Religious ... must now make cause with the very essence of feminist thought –
for the sake of their own spiritual liberation, the liberation of men, and the
emancipation of God from sexist and patriarchal definitions. (Chittister
1995, 154)

In this second chapter on women religious' spiritual innovations, I illustrate current and former sisters' emphasis on feminist spirituality, which
is another, and arguably a more contentious, approach through which some
women religious choose to overcome traditional and exclusionary religious
boundaries. I begin the chapter by presenting examples that are illustrative of
the reasons underlying the sisters' alternatives. I then shed light on the dynamics of their women-led and women-centred celebrations.

IMPETUS FOR FEMINIST SPIRITUALITY

[W]omen religious have begun to question the very theology upon which past
models of womanhood have been based. (Chittister 1995, 14)

The sisters' spiritual innovations are partly attributable to the freedom afforded
to religious orders since the implementation of Vatican II when rigidly regi-
mented rituals were allowed to evolve into more inclusive and creative practices
(Peddigrew 2008). Yet despite the progress made since the mid-1960s, it is
the institutional Church's intractability on the issue of gender equality that
also serves as part of the impetus for women religious and other laywomen to
pursue spiritual alternatives.

Many post–Vatican II improvements have been made in terms of gender
inclusivity within the Roman Catholic Church through the "allowance" of girls
as altar servers and of women as readers, communion servers, committee chairs,

collection counters, and secretarial staff in parishes.[1] To varying degrees, women also work or volunteer in various positions at the diocesan, national, and international levels of Church administration and, in recent decades, they have also been permitted to serve as chaplains in hospitals, high schools, universities, and prisons. Yet, as the aforementioned Church texts (e.g., General Instruction of the Roman Missal, *Redemptionis Sacramentum*) make clear, some of these gains, especially at the altars and in the sanctuary, remain partial, temporary, and at the discretion of male clerics (Morrill and Roll 2007; Roll 2015b).

Furthermore, as some sisters have noted, the involvement of females, particularly at the leadership level, continue to be severely limited. For example, although women have also been "authorized" to study and teach theology, such experiences constitute both inclusivity and exclusivity within the Church. Women as both students and professors were finally permitted in academic theology programs in the 1940s in the United States and in the 1960s and 1970s in Canada (Fox 2016; Leonard 2007). Since women, including women religious, were deprived of ordination, many like Sister Edith turned to the study of theology as an alternative and "loved it … as a passion." Yet, regardless of their advanced studies, including at the doctoral level, women are still forbidden to more fully apply their theological proficiency as priests or as church leaders.

Moreover, many sisters contend that the patriarchal control in some dioceses and parishes has increased rather than decreased since the renewal-oriented changes resulting from Vatican II. Sister Benita sheds light on the current constraints: "They're allowing you to do communion … They think they're doing wonderful things [by allowing girls and women to participate], but they're not giving any power." In this sense, the priests may be transferring labour to the sisters – something one might question as a form of offloading responsibility rather than as a form of genuine power sharing. Sister Kelly insists that such limitations are attributable to the issue of women being ignored by what she regards as an errant institution: "I really believe that right now we are living in a sinful Church … and how the Church in the face of what [progress] … has happened in societies … around … equality … of women, it has fallen on deaf ears in our Church."

In recognizing women's unique approaches to both the form and content of liturgical celebrations, Sister Shannon remains concerned over the exclusion that she has observed for more than seventy-two years in religious life: "Isn't it a pity that the Church has not accepted women?" Sister Noreen's lament over the losses resulting from the gendered limitations specified what Sister Shannon implied – that churchgoers' spirituality could be enriched if women were allowed to give sermons and interpret biblical teachings: "I'm listening [to homilies] sometimes and think what a shame; people are being deprived here …

I could cry; you know, like some stories are narrowly interpreted; they're so much richer, like our faith is rich, it's just that we don't give it the full ... it's so limited."

In light of the limitations and their stifling consequences, Sister Marian reiterated the significance of women's prerogative: "women taking their part in liturgy ... that's what I mean more than anything; we have a *right* to be there, you know." As I illustrate in the subsequent sections, women religious have taken that right seriously, and while some have exercised it within church or chapel walls, others have embodied it in alternative spaces far beyond the institutional Church's parameters and certainly well beyond the Church's patriarchal altars – in spaces that can be variously understood as the women's own altars.

SISTERS' INNOVATIONS IN SPIRITUALITY

By no longer "aspiring to the goals and definitions of the male world" and "rather than trying to reform the male establishment which is usually regarded as church" (Chittister 2004, 175), Sister Joelle explained that sisters' encompassing practices of spirituality are possible because there is "a certain understanding of church that is beyond the patriarchal structure." Through their accounts and my participant observation, it is evident that sisters lead and follow a variety of rituals. While some women religious remain uncritically supportive of solely traditional and dogmatic male-led religious rituals, all the sisters I interviewed were involved in celebrations that are open and adaptable, yet still Jesus-centred and Gospel-based, the latter of which they mentioned frequently during interviews. They consider Jesus-centred and Gospel-based approaches to be more genuinely faithful to the fundamental teachings of Christian traditions because they are not constrained by man-made dogmatic rules. The sisters emphasize and practise them intentionally as ways to counter highly institutionalized, routinized, and regulated Church doctrine that they view as contradicting Jesus' alleged messages and examples of inclusivity, reconciliation, and peace.

Still others plan gatherings that are non-traditional, women-led and women-centred. While the two extremes sometimes coexist among sisters of the same communities, given their own personal preferences, the majority of the current and former sisters – in fact all except perhaps for conventional-leaning Sister Nellie – have tended to move beyond the traditional status quo rituals and have opted for the more encompassing Gospel-based and/or women-oriented celebrations; in some cases, they blend elements of various approaches (Gervais 2012). Before I present concrete examples of their women-centred practices, for the sake of understanding, I briefly explain one of the main inspirational sources of their gender-sensitive innovations.

FEMINIST SPIRITUALITY

Curiously, while not all of the women religious identified as feminists, their religious communities represented herein have either prioritized feminist spirituality or have at the very least opened their chapels and spirituality centres to its exploration. Consequently, either by choice or by collective circumstance, most of the sisters interviewed, with the exception of Sister Nellie and to a certain degree Sister Edna, have participated in some form of feminist spiritual rituals. In some cases where sisters have either not identified as feminists and/or hold primarily liberal feminist views, they have nevertheless sometimes participated in feminist spiritual initiatives that are aligned with more radical religious feminist tenets (e.g., women-church, Goddess images) and/or in those that have perhaps combined both liberal (e.g., inclusive language) and radical feminist religious practices (Shih 2010). Such an actuality points not only to the sometimes unbeknownst disconnect between one's feminist religious identities and one's feminist religious practices but also to the intersectional ways in which the practices may be shared and experienced simultaneously (Ammerman 2003; Shih 2010).

In order to more fully appreciate the sisters' embracing of feminist spirituality, regardless of the extent and complexity of their engagement, it is essential to first understand both what it is and what it is not. Feminist spirituality is not about femaleness; it is about gender justice and freeing all of life from domination (Chittister 1995, 151). Feminist spirituality certainly "calls to conscience" male-only and male-oriented interpretations and governance of the world, as well as "solely male-defined theology" (Chittister 1995, 152) and thus seeks "the emancipation of God from sexist and patriarchal definitions" (Chittister 1995, 154). But contrary to common misconceptions, feminist spirituality is not intended primarily for women to have a church of their own because it "is not a movement for women only" (Winter 2002, 28).

Moreover, while feminist spirituality is built on "the gifts of women, the respect for the feminine, and the awareness of the feminine," being an inclusive approach, it does not deny the masculine nature of God (Chittister 1995, 155). Rather, the purpose is to articulate a new vision of "church" – one that allows for the restoration of an intuitive and imaginative reinterpretation of Catholic tradition (Winter 2002, 28). By extension, feminist spirituality seeks to advance a new spirituality in all of us that is integrated and inclusive, as well as humble and oriented toward human equality (Chittister 1995, 154–5). Furthermore, feminist spiritual rituals and practices inspire models of community which make it possible for the women religious to experience their "own way of being and behaving" (Chittister 1995; Kalven 2003, 44). As a result, these practices permit the flourishing of a spirituality that is more life-affirming.

In contradistinction to Roman Catholic religious rituals, feminist spirituality embraces the sacred feminine[2] and brings to light new and more inclusive images of God (Winter 2002, 24–6). The sacred feminine refers generally to worship, practices, and scholarship that honour a sacred female life-force or deity and that emphasizes the sacred gifts of femininity and women's spirituality. Such inclusive imagery is part of and contributes to "the church [that many] women want" (Johnson 2002b). Winter expands on what is desired in such a church:

> [W]hat women really long for is a just church, not just a church. We want a living liturgy, not just a re-enactment of a designated rite. When I say a living liturgy, I mean more than a liturgy that is alive. I mean a paradigm shift in perspective. We need to comprehend that God's word cannot be bound by a book or rules and regulations, but is revealed primarily in life, in and through you and me. We are the word, you and I … We want a truly catholic church, one universally open to the Spirit, less vindictive, not so narrow. We must all work together to shape a church inclusive of all sorts of people, even radical feminists. (Winter 2002, 30–1)

In other words, for women religious, feminist spiritual practice is not a catechism to be memorized; rather, it is a process to be lived and experienced as people evolve (Gervais and Turenne Sjolander 2015).

LITURGICAL INNOVATIONS WITHIN THEIR OWN SPACES

We're called to be … midwives of new ways … I feel called to … new things and moving forward. (Sister Adele)

The sisters' prioritization of innovative spiritual practice is evident in spaces both within and outside the traditional Church. It is, however, within their own communal spaces – residences, motherhouses,[3] retreat centres – spaces that they own and govern, where women religious have the most freedom to be courageous as they infuse their creative talents into novel spiritual initiatives that enrich their Masses, anniversary celebrations, retreats, and prayers. By way of concrete examples, the sections that follow build on what I already alluded to regarding the sisters' reconceptualization of "church" in the chapter on why they stay.

Women-led and women-centred celebrations

The sisters have been leading and experiencing church "creatively as women" as a result of their dedication to women-led liturgies and spiritual celebrations that involve, but are not limited to, women-led homilies, inclusive language, liturgical dances, and the integration of all participants including lay people.

The gatherings they lead are a testament to the sisters' genuine intentions to celebrate and contribute what they refer to as their "gifts" as women.

For many, their efforts involve the practice of feminist spirituality, which encompasses women's worship, where women play a central, and sometimes exclusive, leadership role. It also emphasizes circular leadership forged on a relational understanding of interconnectedness that is shared among all participants who take on specific tasks in the celebrations (Winter 2002). Sister Jeanette, along with some of her sister peers, integrate feminist spirituality within their traditional Catholic rituals: "Whenever the opportunity arises, we do it ... [in] any of our . . . celebrations we have or liturgies or prayer service or any way we can, we try to include that ... creativity and ... the role of women in the Church." The blending of feminist spirituality with the Catholic celebrations to which Sister Jeanette refers was reported by 69 percent of the sisters and former sisters.

Many of these new rituals occur within the sisters' own motherhouses and spirituality centres where the entire communities of sisters gather for chapter meetings, anniversary celebrations, holidays, Masses, and retreats. For these ceremonies, the sisters prepare extensively to ensure that the prayers, readings, songs, homilies, dances, and all the language used are inclusive, women-centred and, in many cases, women-led. In recent years, some communities of sisters have organized gatherings that are led solely by women and to which clerics are intentionally not invited.

Such exclusive leadership enables the women to manage all the components of the celebrations, including the reading of the Gospel and the sharing of the homily, which in official Masses, are roles reserved only for the male priest. Often times, the general superior serves as the main presider and other members of the leadership team take on leading roles in the celebrations, but many other sisters contribute with readings, words of remembrance, and expressions of encouragement, as well as with music. While there is no official Mass and thus Eucharist is neither prepared nor shared, the celebrations do integrate some aspects of the Mass, including similar prayers, psalms, readings from the Bible, a gospel reading, a homily or reflection, intercessions, the Lord's Prayer, as well as the sign of peace, among others.

Such celebrations are also enriched with contemporary and non-traditional ideas that would not likely be approved by bishops or priests, who are intentionally absent as a result of the sisters' own planning. For example, during the reflections and tributes, all shared by women religious at one of the Jubilee celebrations that I attended, I heard inspirational references to Teresa of Avila,[4] Joyce Rupp,[5] Macrina Wiederkehr,[6] and Diarmuid O'Murchu.[7] Prayers also referred to a "Creator God" which is a testament to the sisters' emphasis on both inclusive language and earth-centredness. While such women-led gatherings may be more common today among sisters, Sister Agnes recalled participating in a retreat led by an American woman religious over four decades ago and she reminisced positively about the alternatives offered then: "A woman doing a retreat so we didn't have Mass everyday ... It was wonderful." All of the current and former sisters with whom I spoke felt the same way about both past and present women-led gatherings.

Another way in which feminist principles are embedded within the sisters' spiritual services is through the new wording in the statement that sisters use to renew their vows and thus their religious commitment, particularly during their jubilees when they celebrate the anniversaries of religious life. While some sisters choose to renew their original and thus traditional vows, many sisters opt to use the new wording at their jubilees – in which they refer to "living a proper relationship with God's creation," to living "compassionately and non-violently" as they respond to "injustices in our world," to caring particularly for the "dignity of women," and to "embracing with joy and hope our brothers and sisters, especially the most vulnerable" among them.[8] In contrast to the wording of original vows that emphasized compliance to Church dogma and to the vows of obedience, poverty, and chastity, the new vocabulary is indicative of contemporary emphases on inclusivity, earth-centredness and gender equality – all of which are feminist principles and priorities that are also reflected in many of their congregations updated constitutions (Ebaugh 1993, 147).

While more recently many communities of women religious have attempted to ensure that their rituals have been led and attended exclusively by women, some of their celebrations have been and continue to be "feminist Catholic"[9] and thus liberal feminist in form insofar as they may occur within a conventional Mass that is officially led by a male priest whose presence sometimes curtails their feminist efforts (Gervais 2015, 2012; Schneiders 2004; Shih 2010). Despite the prevalence of clerical disapproval against some aspects of sisters' creative contributions to liturgies, women religious continue to strive for more equal, and thus liberal feminist, opportunities for inclusion in all areas of Masses, including homilies, and some priests do "allow" for modifications to the traditional Mass. For example, as Sister Kelly reflected on how she created openings in order to overcome the stifling of her feminine and feminist orientations by the Catholic Church, she related how she strategically positioned herself to not only give a homily but to also read the Gospel – both "privileges" traditionally reserved only for male priests[10] (Helman 2012; Kaylin 2000):

> I'll give you a little incident ... we were celebrating our eightieth anniversary and I was asked to give the homily. A priest friend of mine was to be the celebrant, and I said to him that if I were to give the homily

I would like to read the gospel on which the homily was based. And he replied, "But don't tell anyone that you are going to do that." So I read the gospel and gave the homily. After the celebration he congratulated me and said, "We couldn't do that, you know. The Church is missing so much, so much!"

Sister Ella also reinforced how some priests are simultaneously impressed and intimidated by women religious because of their resourcefulness and advanced capacities: "One of the priests ... told me straight out one day, 'We're afraid of you gals, you've been renewed ... you have had all kinds of help in your renewal,' and he said, 'you know, we haven't had that.'" Depending on the priests' and bishops' attitudes toward the sisters' renewal, women religious were either supported or placed at greater risk of being reprimanded for their advancement efforts.

Many sisters also referred to liturgical dance as a meaningful example of feminist spiritual expression within liturgical celebrations that they hold within their retreat centres. Liturgical dance involves dance movements as expressions of worship. Several sisters were delighted to have the dancing integrated within their special anniversary Masses but were met with disapproval[11] by priests or bishops in attendance. For example, when asked if she struggled against the Church's stance on particular issues, Sister Maureen responded emphatically: "Liturgical dance!" [laughs] ... I like it ... at the Edwina Gateley [retreat held at the sisters' spirituality centre], we had ... the dance and ... she was excellent at it! ... and we also had a dance at the beginning ... but the ... poor priest put his stuff [papers] on his face so he couldn't see!" [laughs]

Sister Agnes observed a similar reaction at one of her community's events:

He [the bishop] was at a Jubilee celebration ... he experienced things probably which he didn't like ... there was liturgical dance ... there was singing of ... stuff from scripture and things that he wouldn't have liked ... We had put so much work into the celebration, it was celebratory! He was up there like this [arms folded] and ... some of the priests were mad ... the sanctuary was all male and mad, you know!

As I expand upon later, while liturgical dance seems to enrich and energize many women religious' spiritual celebrations, the clerical resistance against it appears symbolic of the priestly backlash against the sisters' alternative theologies and forms of worship.

It is essential to note that not all women-led celebrations are "feminist" in nature or based solely on feminist spirituality. Some sisters lead traditional or Jesus-centred liturgies and incorporate some broader aspects that are reflective of New Age, gender-inclusive, and earth-centred dimensions, pointing again to their overlapping religious practices and ones that integrate varying degrees of feminism, Catholicism, femininity, and creation-centredness (Ammerman 2003; Shih 2010). Such blended celebrations are also illustrative of the ways in which sisters avoid potentially conflicting situations in which religious rituals may exist either in complete opposition to certain traditions or as intended only to conserve them; rather, the sisters can be seen as sometimes doing both – upholding some traditions while exposing their limitations by revising them through the integration of alternatives (Ammerman 2003; Griffith 1997). They often also enhance their ritual or prayer space with soothing and inspiring décor that include colourful tapestries, paintings or photos, and non-traditional statues (e.g., figurines that are not symbols of Catholicism). Sister Ella is one such woman religious who proudly leads a retreat centre: "Here we have wonderful celebrations … we don't have a priest come."[12] On a daily basis, Sister Ella facilitates circular-based gatherings in which she typically identifies a theme, reads a gospel-based passage, offers a reflection that is often Jesus-centred, and invites participants to read prayers and to share their thoughts on the topic. Prior to each gathering, Sister Ella decorates the space within a pre-existing chapel and adds various combinations of traditional and non-traditional images, tapestries, ornaments, sculptures, or carvings that represent the daily theme. To suggest that such practices are indicative of sisters' efforts to feminize prayer sites may open up an unresolvable debate on gendered divisions of labour and space. Nevertheless, at the very least, one may recognize that such practices reflect the sisters' values beyond what is typically represented in a church or chapel whose architectural design and décor have been historically created and controlled by men.

As Sister Ella's efforts illustrate, while many of the sisters' late-twentieth- and early-twenty-first-century celebrations have integrated feminist spirituality, some of their rituals do maintain a traditional basis that is Jesus-centred and gospel-based. Nevertheless, the majority of their gatherings are led exclusively by women and are thus, to various degrees, feministed[13] and/or feminized. Given the array of dimensions involved, it is apparent that these sisters have developed their spiritual innovations at the crossroad of their multiple identities, including their religious identities as Catholics, and in many instances as non-institutional Catholics and their gender identities as women representing diverse and often non-conflictual affiliations with feminism and femininity (Adichie 2014; Ammerman 2003; Neitz 2003).

Spiritual celebrations outside church and chapel walls

I love the Mass ... There's nothing wrong with it. But it's not the only way to celebrate. (Sister Loretta)

While most sisters attend Mass regularly in either parish churches or in their own chapels and while they also participate in officially planned women-led and women-centred celebrations within their own motherhouses or spirituality centres, some sisters prefer informal small group and spontaneous alternatives. In order to avoid scrutiny while attempting to carry out more fully their women-led and women-centred spiritual practices, the majority (66 percent) of sisters and former sisters organize small and intimate "underground" gatherings[14] in which they lead their own liturgies, Eucharistic celebrations or prayers and reflections among other women religious and laywomen with whom they feel they can share these pursuits safely (Schneiders 2004; Winter 2002). In these gatherings, the sisters and former sisters ensure that the preparation, language, participation, prayers, and reflections are authentically inclusive and attentive to women's experiences. While some engage in them irregularly, others follow organized schedules whereby they substitute Church services in order to celebrate privately in small women-led groups.[15]

Such unofficial initiatives, often located in private spaces and not within church or chapel walls, are for many sisters, expressions of "women-church" which participants find both liberating and life-giving (Winter 2002). Sister Penelope clarified the context:

[A lot of women are] moving onto other areas outside the Church walls, outside the hierarchy where they feel the freedom to be able to do, well, let's say not services as much as prayers and bring the community together in different settings for celebrating life.

Similar to their American counterparts (Kaylin 2000), Sister Penelope's explanation is indicative of how some sisters intentionally avoid Catholic canonical constraints in the celebrations they carry out in smaller clusters of like-minded sisters who may forego a Sunday Mass in order to practise both Catholic feminist rituals simultaneously. Sister Penelope, who did not actually identify as feminist, proudly explained how she practised the outside-the-norm and off-the-record women-led spiritual initiatives:

Oh yeah ... we often do ... if we want to have ... a Eucharist celebration of life as I say, we will, and if we want to have a ... penitential service ourselves, we will ... we don't need a priest to be present for it ... and you just don't inform the ... hierarchy that those kinds of things are happening ...

> What they don't know doesn't hurt them ... we don't need to inform because we ... have the freedom to do so.

Sister Loretta's experience resonated with Sister Penelope's: "We do a lot of our own prayer services ... often times when we have a cluster meeting, we'll share bread and wine ... we do a lot. We do all kinds of things but we don't do them too publicly." Sister Loretta shed further light on how she, and the like-minded sisters who join her, view their practices as genuine: "I mean we're not doing all the things that you say as a Mass. But I believe it's Eucharist ... but I don't think the Church would recognize it as Eucharist ... But we believe it's Eucharist."

In contrast to Sister Loretta's cautious qualification about her gatherings not being fully "a Mass," Sister Kelly believes somewhat similarly but feels even less constrained by or loyal to the official "Mass" being presided over by an ordained male priest. Sister Kelly insisted that "we can celebrate Eucharist. We do not need ordination and I'm convinced of that." In an effort to move beyond the "painful" theology that is "preached" in traditional churches, Sister Kelly justifies her selective attendance of Masses and her involvement with private small group celebrations infused with feminist and other approaches to spirituality, by emphasizing a broader conception of "the Eucharist." In doing so and in echoing renowned theologian and songwriter Miriam Winter (2002), Sister Kelly presents an informed rationale for unofficial gatherings:

> Even, you know, the Eucharist, the understanding of what Eucharist is, I know that [sigh] the rite is one thing but then the Eucharist of solidarity ... *we* give Eucharist to one another. *We* are to be the bread. *We!* ... if we ever come as a church to realize that God dwells within us, not out there. As Morwood says, "not an elsewhere God." God is here, and so, as Jesus said, you know, "I'm bread for you. I'm giving my life for you." [softly] I do that ... That's what Eucharist is.[16]

While Sisters Penelope, Loretta, and Kelly referred to a specific sacrament that is central to the Catholic Mass and is thus associated with rituals within Church walls, they themselves are promoting and practising variations of it in other spaces outside of the confines of Catholic Churches. Furthermore, while alternative forms of Eucharistic and penitential services may appear to imitate Catholic traditions, as already noted above, the sisters work hard, and through a primarily liberal religious feminist lens (Shih 2010), to both feminize and "feminist" the rituals in order to ensure that they are non-patriarchal and thereby, non-oppressive and non-exclusionary (Schneiders 2004, 105–6). Moreover, as previously shown, many current and former sisters avoid replicating the Eucharist altogether and establish their own forms of communal sharing in which women's experiences are central (Schneiders 2004).

Confession outside the confessional

Outside of institutional Church walls, sisters and former sisters have not only been organizing and experiencing spiritual and liturgical celebrations, but they have also been involved unofficially in the practise of some sacraments, one of which is reconciliation, also popularly known as confession. Historically, confessions have commonly occurred in an enclosed booth within the church (called a "confessional"), most often with the priest and the parishioner separated by a screened partition for privacy (Cornwell 2014). However, several sisters and former sisters recounted how they have heard confessions outside of the confessional and are not concerned about the institutional legality of their actions. For example, Darlene placed importance in sacraments and she admitted to hearing confessions often as a pastoral counsellor and spiritual director. For her, "there is a small-'s' sacrament …" that she knows is legitimately "Sacramental" because she feels God's presence: "I think they are Sacramental because I know God is there."

Others reinforce this idea of how confessions are happening outside of the traditional sacrament and sisters reveal divergent ideas about the importance of confession to their ministries. For example, as Sister Loretta reflected on her right to administer sacraments, her comment was emphatic and revealed the non-church space where she supports others through confession: "Why not?! [laughs] … I don't believe in confession, mind you … in my work in spiritual direction I hear lots of confessions." Although Sister Josephine herself only goes "once in a while," she would like to hear confessions more regularly; she was nevertheless pleased that she has heard at least two confessions so far, both having occurred outside of church walls, one in a residential setting and the other in a spirituality centre: "A kid went to confession to me in [country name] and when I was doing retreat, a sister said she would not confess to a priest." In the latter case, the sister's intentional avoidance of a male priest is indicative of the wider gender-based discomfort felt among many women religious beyond the ones with whom I spoke. But, as Sister Agnes explains, women religious have not been the only people from whom sisters have been hearing confessions in non-Church contexts: "I have heard confession, not often but on occasion, where the teenager was more comfortable saying it to me."

The sisters above reflect on how confessions seem worthwhile for those with whom they are working, and so they take on the role of holding the space for these confessions. While it may appear that sisters are breaking Church rules by administering the sacrament of reconciliation when they are not officially qualified to do so as non-ordained females, the application of Church rules pertaining to the administration of some sacraments, including confession, seems to be muddled. For example, as Sisters Loretta and Theresa have noted, some sisters who have worked in remote regions of northern Canada have been authorized to administer sacraments, such as confession and baptism, due to the absence of male priests in these areas. In these cases, women are not being entrusted with extra responsibility or power as a means of gender justice, rather it would seem that this is an example of women being expected to take on excess labour to make up for a shortage of male clergy in remote areas. While rare, exceptions to the rules are officially made by bishops. As such, the Church is sending a mixed message by condoning women's involvement with sacraments only when it is convenient for Church purposes, yet all the while continuing to officially ban their role in administering the sacred rituals of the sacraments. Nevertheless, whether it is "allowed" or not, what is of particular interest here are the sisters' practices outside the confines of the Church and what is accomplished as a result – namely a source of support for parishioners and other women religious who do not receive spiritual sustenance from the traditional, male-centric rituals of the Sacrament of Reconciliation as they currently stand.

Feminine images of God and inclusive language

God is a girl and Jesus is a boy. (Author's three-year-old son)

One evening in 2010, as my then three-year-old son laid his head on his pillow at bedtime after we had shared our nightly words of gratitude, he announced prophetically and with much conviction that "God is a girl and Jesus is a boy." It was not articulated as a question as one may expect from a child of his age; it was expressed as a matter-of-fact statement. Many traditional Catholic or Christian parents may have "corrected" him and reminded him that "God" is a male because he is the "father." Instead, I smiled as I acknowledged and affirmed his belief, one that I too had come to appreciate and embrace as I had been learning from the current and former sisters about feminist spirituality. A week later, I shared his comment at a retreat centre with women religious and they were delighted that such a young child had a broad view of God. After one sister repeated the statement upon hearing it, she smiled and said, "What a wise little boy."[17]

The gendered imaging implied in my son's statement is certainly not a twenty-first-century realization. While archaeologists have found evidence of the worship of "the Great Goddess" during the earlier part of the Neolithic period dating back to approximately 7000 BCE, some experts trace it as far back as the Upper Palaeolithic Age of about 25,000 BCE (Stone 1976, xii, 10). Since at least the mid-twentieth century, feminist theologians and scholars, as well as vowed and non-vowed women, have been exploring and embracing the concept of female deities, as well as women preachers in early Christianity (Schenk 2017). While sister-scholars like Joan Chittister (2004, 1995), Elizabeth Johnson (2002a,b), and Sandra Schneiders (2004) have been advocating for gender inclusive images and languages, others, including Mary Daly (1973; 1968), Rosemary Radford Ruether (1983), and Miriam Winter (2002), have also been explaining and practising the sacred feminine and women-church uninhibitedly. Still other writers and journalists, including Kaylin (2000) and Reed (2004), have presented experiential accounts of sisters and their active choices in support of the feminine image of God.[18] Renowned yet theologically flawed fictional books adapted into screenplays (Schenk 2004), like *The Shack* (Young 2007) and *The Da Vinci Code* (Brown 2003), as well as experiential accounts, like *The Dance of the Dissident Daughter* (Monk Kidd 1996), have also drawn attention to either feminine images of God or the sacred feminine.

Such emphases on feminine images of God are born out of the contention and concern that the long-held and unidimensional portrayal of God as "the Father" has diminished the spiritual status of femaleness and, by extension, the social status of women (Chittister 2004, 33). Goddess imagery, and thus the recognition of "God our Mother," has undeniably been validating for countless women who embrace a fuller image of a "God of Being," inclusive of both "Father" and "Mother" (Bloch 1997; Chittister 2004, 32–6). Yet, attempts to move beyond the invisibility of women, femaleness, and femininity in the Roman Catholic Church have been met with serious challenges. As Chittister (2004, 33) has noted, "To confront the heresy of God the Father, I discovered quickly, is to be called a heretic." Anyone who does not consider "God" as male is considered "a radical, an iconoclast, some sort of ecclesiastical anarchist" in the eyes of Church authorities (Chittister 2004, 34).

Sister Kelly experienced first-hand that to which Chittister has referred; she herself has been called a heretic by local Church authorities because of her promotion of both masculine and feminine images of God and of inclusive language in a book that she authored: "Oh yes! And even inclusive language, God image, you know who God is; if it doesn't comply with a masculine God, you know, uh, beware!" Yet, the feminist dimensions of Sister Kelly's views in this regard are rather convoluted given how the religious identities and the religious practices that inform her staunch spiritual stance are not as synchronized as one may expect. Recall how Sister Kelly does not self-identify as a "radical" feminist; yet her embracing of feminine images of God and of female Goddess wisdoms are actually associated with "radical" religious feminist precepts (Shih 2010). Thus, similar to many of her peers, while it may be unbeknownst to her eighty-year-old self, there appears to be a simultaneous connection and disconnection, however puzzling that may be, between the feminist identity to which she does not relate and the feminist religious practices that she actually carries out. What is further perplexing is how the radical feminist identity that she herself rejects is one that has in fact been used against her by the male Church authorities who have criticized her above-mentioned book.

Despite the inevitability of critiques by patriarchal Church authorities, many sisters and former sisters insist on embracing feminine images of God and expressing gender equality within their spirituality through the use of inclusive language. Many sisters who participate in traditional or parish-based Masses use gender-neutral language in the liturgy, or they use the feminine pronoun in preference to the male. For example, Sisters Carmen and Marian relayed how they intentionally use inclusive language during Mass or in their prayers:

> Oh yeah where it can be changed to "everybody" and "everyone" yes … like for example when we say the Creed, [I was at Mass] this morning and they were saying "for all men"; I just say "for all people." I do what I want. But I can say "people." I go ahead but I'm not going to fight over it. (Sister Carmen)

> Well I refer to Her, to God as She because of the attributes of the feminine … I think that's what the world needs and the Church needs … I wouldn't go to the wall over whether God is He or She I can tell you that, but, uh, in my prayer I do … 'cause it's only prolonging that division or separation. (Sister Marian)

While Sisters Carmen and Marian were not prepared to clash over the wording, their quiet resistance is nevertheless indicative of their willingness to model inclusive language through their firm liberal feminist belief in gender equality (Shih 2010) and to thus oppose some problematic aspects of the traditional Mass while they simultaneously conserve the main dimensions of it (Griffith 1997). Sister Agnes also feels certain and well justified in her gender inclusive approach to language and action: "[Saint] Irenaeus says … 'The glory of God is *man* fully alive.' But I believe the glory of God is also *woman* fully alive … so I am the glory of God when I am fully alive … I'm confident with that."

While many sisters have been feminizing and feministing the wording of prayers for decades and have thus been moving in a more inclusive direction (Woligrosky et al. 2011), the male hierarchy at the Vatican has been working just as hard to entrench the masculinization of the wording of the prayers and to thus further the exclusionary discourses and practices of the Mass. Rather than the Vatican rendering the Mass prayers more inclusive, as had been done in a 1992 revision, when linguistics reforms were undertaken in the twenty-first century, Church officials actually cemented the masculinization of the text even further in the revised 2011 English version of the *New Roman Missal* by using antiquated and "deliberately sexist English" vocabulary including "man" as a generic (Roll 2015a, 74; 2011, 6). Thus, while sisters' use of inclusive language within their own spiritual spaces may be increasing positively, their similar attempts within institutional Church walls may be met with even more resistance in years to come – a context that will inevitably exacerbate tensions on the one hand, yet potentially lead to the pursuit of further, and arguably more fruitful, alternatives on the other.

Further feminist initiatives through other outlets

Sister Kelly claims that some of the work "in spirituality centres was about ... the resurrection ... of the feminine ... and the integration ... of those [masculine and feminine] opposites." One of the most pivotal ways in which such a "resurrection" was accomplished in the early twenty-first century in some of the sisters' spirituality centres was through a play presented by a team of sisters from another religious community. Sister Agnes was one of the key members who co-produced and co-directed a play[19] that featured the stories of silenced and forgotten women who were related to well-known men within the Christian tradition. The play was staged in a variety of community and spirituality centres operated by women religious in Ontario. She justified her involvement with the play by drawing attention to the importance of overcoming gender inequality and promoting the worthiness of all, both of which are emphasized within her religious community's mandate: "I feel very much called to that aspect of our charism, the dignity of women, the dignity of all people. But men have a better chance at it in society and especially in the Church."[20]

Sister Agnes' religious community has been highly supportive of the play. In fact, they have provided much of the infrastructure required to produce and stage the play. The community supported the creation of a theatre company[21] of which Sister Agnes and some other sisters from her community were a part; the community provided financial, as well as promotional support to the group because the theatre company sought to give voice to marginalized people within society, and it emphasized innovative visions intended to inspire new relationships among people and the earth. In this light and in keeping with the commonly held view that the play raises more questions than answers, Sister Agnes elaborated on the significance of the play: "I believe it is a vehicle for transformation. As the members of the audience – mainly women but also some open-minded men – experience the unfolding of the various stories on stage, they begin to ask themselves questions that they had never thought about before."

Moreover, Sister Agnes provided further testament to her own, as well as the theatre group's feminist orientation. During her interview when she first identified herself as the director of the play, she immediately corrected herself and the theatre company's inclusive approach came to light: "Ah, I shouldn't say director, we were all directing it ... we were all kinda working at it." Taken together – Sister Agnes' prioritization of a play featuring forgotten women, her religious community's generous support of it, and the theatre group's shared directing – are testaments not only to women religious' creative expressions of feminist spirituality but also to the mutually supportive ways in which they engage in it. They are further reflective of how the sisters ensure that their religious narratives and experiences are the product of informed, yet open-ended interactions that embrace the diversity of all those who are involved (Ammerman 2003, 224).

CONCLUSION

The sisters' priorities and practices of feminist spirituality represent firm departures from patriarchal Church traditions and, as such, reflect the a-institutional choices they are willing to make toward greater spiritual freedom (Lux-Sterritt and Mangion 2011, 2). Whether or not the sisters explicitly identify as feminists, their focus on prayer rituals and spiritual celebrations that are achieved through women-led, women-centred, inclusive, and integrative approaches reflect how their spaces and practices are feminist in their orientation. Yet, the sisters' constructions and customs of feminist spirituality should not be perceived as only and always in opposition to the Church. Women religious have not generated such advancements only in order to overcome gender-based discrimination within the Roman Catholic Church. Their innovations should be recognized as a testament to their own ingenuity. Along similar lines, their priorities and practices of feminist spirituality should also not always be considered as absolute dismissals of the institutional Church because many of their rituals do still take place within a strong commitment to the Catholic traditions and Christian gospel values (Barr Ebest 2003; Kaylin 2000). There is thus no doubt that both continuity and fluidity are evident in the sisters' spiritual endeavours (Ammerman 2003). In this way, and especially in an intersectional sense, their spiritual practices, along with their corresponding religious identities, are at once both structured and emergent (Ammerman 2003, 224). In this light, sisters' spiritual journeys should not be characterized as either feminist or faithful as such identities or orientations are not necessarily divergent or dichotomous but rather dialogic ones that are mutually enhancing, and arguably co-productive (Gervais 2012).

Regardless of the specific or multiple orientations guiding their spiritual pursuits, their experiential accounts have drawn our attention to the spaces within their community and Church that women religious have decided belong to them – spaces over which they have authorship and control (Kalven 2003; Kaylin 2000; Reed 2004). It is within those spaces that women religious are showing that there is more than one way and more than one location, beyond the one institutionally authorized way and beyond the one officially sanctioned Church altar, to be spiritual and to practise the gospels (Gervais and Turenne Sjolander 2015). For the sake of their own spiritual liberation, they have drawn on a multiplicity of perspectives and realities diversely shaped by gender, culture, and ethnicity and have thus advanced transformative rituals rooted in earlier traditions (Ammerman 2003; Chittister 1995; Winter 2002, 27–8). The sisters' examples have demonstrated empirically how women religious are shifting their own understandings, priorities, practices, and locations of Church and are thus enhancing and improving their own and others' spiritual experiences by integrating feminist orientations with the gospel teachings in very practical, progressive, and therefore productive ways (Chittister 2013; Winter 2002), and they are often doing so far beyond the officially sanctioned Church altars.

CHAPTER 7

Defending their alternative altars

There is another world out there waiting to be heard, and they are not going to wait any longer for permission to speak their own truths. (Chittister 1998, 171)

In this chapter, I shed light on the defence tactics that the sisters have engaged in order to protect and promote their spiritual innovations. The chapter proceeds in five stages. First, I draw attention to the Church's constraints against women religious' spiritual innovations, particularly against their promotion of gender inclusivity. Second, I illustrate how sisters manage clerical resistance against their feminist spirituality initiatives. Third, I show how women religious must also contend with the reluctance of both sisters and other laywomen to embrace feminist spiritual initiatives. Fourth, I present how sisters overcome the resistance by "doing it anyway" and how such an intrepid attitude is supported by women religious' communities' inclusive governance. Finally, the conclusion underscores the worthiness of defending feminist spiritual orientations.

REJECTION OF SISTERS' PROMOTION OF GENDER EQUALITY

Of all the issues facing religious life, feminism is surely ... the most danger-ous because it brings us most in conflict with the flow of history. (Chittister 1995, 166)

As current and former sisters have countered the traditional patriarchal dimen-sions of the Church, the dangerousness to which Chittister refers has often surfaced in the form of backlash by the Church's male hierarchy. In addition to the pervasive disrespect and manifest exclusions that sisters have faced gener-ally, some women religious have also experienced negative repercussions when attempting specifically to advance gender equality and feminine spirituality within Church activities. For example, Sister Kelly who published a feminist-oriented book that advocated for greater inclusiveness in the Catholic Church, was "branded a heretic" by local priests, accused of "disrupting people" by a canon lawyer, and questioned by an apostolic delegate[1] as to whether or not she was "a sister in good standing" in her congregation.

As a condemned feminist author, Sister Kelly is not alone. Other world-renowned feminist-oriented sister-authors, such as Sisters Joan Chittister and Elizabeth Johnson, have also been subjected to harsh criticism by Church officials. Together, their twentieth- and twenty-first-century efforts bear similarity to the works of Sister Marguerite Porete, who was a fourteenth-century nun whose writings and speeches challenged the gendered teachings and limitations of the Church. Since Sister Porete refused to be silenced and she adamantly defended her right as a woman to speak in public, she was burned alive at the stake (Lahav 2011). While Sisters Kelly, Joan Chittister and Elizabeth Johnson have not met such a fatal fate, the condemnation they have faced from Church officials is indicative of the Church's incessant intolerance against women's displays of leadership.

Relatedly, Sister Carmen's attempts to draw attention to women's right to the diaconate and ordination fell on deaf ears: "Oh, I've spoken to two bishops about deacons. One of them said to me once 'We know how you stand!" [laughs]. Not only was Sister Carmen reminded of the male hierarchy's intractability but she was also ridiculed by priests and bishops; yet the outspoken women's rights advocate was not deterred: "I was named as a radical [and called] names ... sometimes laughed at ... [but] it just made me to be more definite."

Comparably, Sister Sarah remembered a degrading instance that transpired after she advocated for gender-sensitive language:

> I did have an experience when working with one priest in particular on a mission ... [there was] an issue around inclusive language that I was publically reprimanded for ... and that was very humiliating ... it was somebody who really worked out of a very patriarchal model.

Sister Agnes has also felt this dejection personally. As an outspoken, passionate, and energetic seventy-two-year-old, she has also encountered a considerable amount of resistance and criticism against her feminist efforts. She has been censured by school-based priests for integrating inclusive and invigorating rituals in both liturgies and theatrical plays in high schools. One of Sister Agnes' earlier experiences of rejection occurred after she completed graduate studies at the Jesuit School of Theology at Berkeley in California when she enthusiastically shared about her feminist-based experience with a long-time male priest friend with whom she had forward-thinking conversations just a year earlier. As she explains, his reaction involved an unexpected anti-feminist criticism coupled with an explicit pro-violence stance:

> So I'm telling him … something … on feminism from Berkeley and I didn't catch on fast enough. He really wasn't all that comfortable with it, but I went a little bit further, and I realized that I had gone too far. He put up his hands and he said, "Agnes, I want you to know I'm from a country where it's a right and proper thing for a husband to slap a wife for a happy marriage." Verbatim! I could hardly eat … we went ahead with the meal. But the pleasantness, the fun was all gone. I had pushed it a little too far … But he'd been away from me for a while. So he had not heard any of that stuff … [whispering]. But those words, I couldn't believe what I was hearing … he was factual. I had pushed too far. He made it very clear. I was not to mention that, at least that's what I picked up; I didn't want to ever talk feminism or women with him, you know.

Whereas Sisters Kelly, Carmen, Sarah, and Agnes referred to individually based incidents of patriarchal critique, Sister Loretta recalled an instance of gendered backlash that affected her entire congregation when they tried to advance and defend their initiatives within their diocese. According to Sister Loretta, the belittling produced a collective sense of defeat among the sisters:

> Well, a few years ago, we were very vociferous about things and … we got into trouble. I'm talking, we as a congregation … and it was like you're hitting your head against a stone wall. So we didn't seem to be accomplishing anything by that. All they did say was "They're just angry women" … and that's not true. So we kind of pulled back … I'm talking now from what I think … from my point of view. I think we kind of gave up on that and said it's not worth it.

These troubling accounts of reprimands reveal how religious institutions, in this case the Roman Catholic Church and its male clerical officials, exercise their self-legitimated patriarchal authority in order to control whose voices and which narratives are privileged and which ones are not only ignored but are also disparaged as religious identities and practices are both shaped and contested (Ammerman 2003, 223; Nason-Clark 1997).

While the above-mentioned sisters' feminist orientations were dismissed directly, Darlene's sense of rejection stemmed less directly from Church officials and more from her own self-reflection. When asked whether she had ever been dismissed or excluded on the basis of gender, Darlene explained how her positive reputation within her diocese and province had both privileged and paralysed her:

> No ... because ... I was prominent enough to be the token woman so
> in itself, in a way, I was self-exiled ... But I felt the disconnection ... By
> my faithfulness to God in my life ... I got more ... to the fringe ... The
> hardest part was knowing that it wasn't very healthy, that I needed to be
> more honest and that I ... couldn't have both. So I, again, I self-exiled
> out of that situation.

While on the one hand, her prominent role in her diocese, and arguably
her confident personality, likely spared her from patriarchal-based disrespect,
that very same reputation constrained her ability to speak out openly about
feminism and her concerns regarding gender inequality in the Church and in
society. As a result, Darlene struggled in silence for a long time because she felt
that she could not be her true feminist self in a Church that was so blatantly
sexist and in a women's religious community that was at the time not ready
to embrace feminism fully. Yet while she herself did not experience specific
moments of dismissal and disregard, she was well aware that other sisters had:

> I didn't work in a parish ... and I think those who have, have been much
> more wounded. Like there's one of our sisters in my former community,
> for example, who has written in her will that she does not want a priest
> to officiate at her funeral ... because she was a pastoral worker and she
> was very disrespected by the Church, the official Church.

The statement is undeniably compelling. A nun who refuses to have a priest
preside over her funeral speaks volumes about the depth of the wounds resulting from patriarchal attitudes and actions in the Church. Part of that hurt has
derived from the Church's intolerance of feminism.

Facing clerical disapproval of their feminist inclusivity and spirituality

> *But if we women do not question the contorting of God into maleness, do not
> share their own notions of God, then we doom ourselves to nonidentity and
> men to heterodoxical arrogance.* (Chittister 2004, 172)

Current and former sisters confidently consider their alternative healing and
spiritual initiatives as essential elements of personal and spiritual growth. The
sisters themselves, as well as the lay people who participate in their innovative activities report benefiting profoundly from their life-giving and uplifting
initiatives. Yet, some of their practices have come into direct conflict with the
hierarchy of the Catholic Church and, as a result, have been subject to questioning and critique. Consequently, sisters have often had to defend and protect
their endeavours on their very own properties, and sometimes confrontationally
against clerics (including priests, bishops, diocesan, and Vatican officials) who

have refused to embrace their ideas and activities that support gender equality and women-centred spirituality.

Former general superiors and current leadership team members recounted numerous occasions when they had to resist the bishop's or the priest's interference with their liturgical and retreat programs. Some sisters have actually been reprimanded for employing world-renowned feminist speakers for retreats. For example, when Sister Mabel was the general superior of her community, the local bishop questioned her about having invited prominent feminist speaker Edwina Gateley[2] to lead a retreat. He stated that had he known in advance about the plans to have her facilitate, "it wouldn't have happened." Sister Mabel explained her reaction:

> I said, "You gotta be kidding me … what's your problem with Edwina Gateley? … I just don't understand with all the … poor people right in this area and you're concerned about Edwina Gateley? … Obviously we're not going to agree, Bishop, and we never will because I think that Edwina Gateley could put a lot of us to shame, a lot of the priests and you to shame …" and he didn't like it. The other thing he said to me which is very telling, he said, "You're an apostolic congregation," and he said, "As bishop I cannot tell you who to bring in; I can't do anything if you bring someone in that I don't approve of. But if you have one layperson there then I step in to protect the Church." I said, "Bishop I cannot believe what I'm hearing," and I told him he was disrespectful … One layperson! He has to protect the laity from what? Edwina Gateley?!

Similarly, when Sister Joelle was general superior, she too had to defend various feminist, New Age, and non-Christian activities that were being offered at her religious community's retreat centre. She confidently and successfully challenged the inquiring bishop:

> I'll give you an example: when I was leader, we had a spirituality centre connected to our motherhouse, very, very thriving, and it was interfaith; we had Buddhists making retreat there, we had yoga classes, and so on. I don't know if you remember, a few years ago Rome published a document … condemning a whole lot of New Age stuff … even twelve steps … It's right in there. So our bishop was one of the signatories to that document and he came to see me and raised some concerns, and I had been prepared; I knew he was coming; I had met with the staff, and we … got our act together and … I was prepared so when he began to raise these questions, I very directly said, "Bishop … we are very much in the Catholic tradition, but we also believe that our mission … embraces these particular facets that we're dealing with." Well, he dropped it.

Sister Kelly also encountered criticism by male priests regarding the dream therapy that she offered at her community's spiritual direction centre: "When I started to do dream work [sigh] ... the chaplain here told one of our sisters that it was the work of the devil ... and got out his theology books to prove it ... and so when I started to do the dream workshops in the area with lay people and others ... the clergy were quite up in arms about that ... it was heresy."

After decades, and arguably centuries, of experiences like those recounted by Sisters Mabel, Joelle, and Kelly, women's religious orders have felt compelled to formally address such clerical interference. To this end, in a document intended to draw Canadian Catholic bishops' attention to what nuns viewed as a wide range of problematic policies within the institutional Church, one of the religious communities represented in this study included the following statement, among an extensive list of messages and recommendations, in order to express their disagreement with how activities within their own spaces have been obstructed: "We deplore the control of some bishops who require communities to cancel programs in spirituality centres, even though these programs offer education in aspects of life in harmony with the teachings of the Church." Such a document, which contributed to an official message sent to the Canadian Catholic bishops by the Canadian Religious Conference during the first decade of the twenty-first century but which remains anonymous in order to protect the identity of the women and their communities, is indicative of the organized and determined ways in which sisters are defending their initiatives. Such a direct critique against the Church hierarchy also represents an unusual and thus significant form of resistance on the part of the sisters.

Yet, despite their intervention, women religious' initiatives continue to be thwarted. For example, Sister Kelly experienced further consequences when her feminist-oriented[3] book on Church and spiritual reform fell into the hands of a canon lawyer who reprimanded her for writing the book and for her unconventional work in general. But she stood her ground:

> The canon lawyer told me that I was a Marxist; that I was disturbing and disrupting people by what I had written. I replied, "You are now doing exactly what I am addressing in that book." Oh, he did not like that! It is important for me to say that I had previously given a copy to the local bishop at that time and he had congratulated and affirmed me for the writing of the book.

Notwithstanding the supportive bishop, the involvement of a canon lawyer in Sister Kelly's case is a reflection of the Roman Catholic Church's systematic tactics "to delegitimate the feminist endeavor" (Schneiders 2004, xvi; see also Chittister 1998; Manning 2006). Still, Sister Kelly was not deterred; in fact, her fearless disregard may come as a surprise to many who view nuns as loyally compliant to the Church: "I could have been excommunicated but I don't care. It doesn't mean a thing." While formal repercussions or the risk thereof may have applied to sisters' own retreat centres and publications, as I show next, similar, albeit less formal tensions have arisen in parishes where sisters have led ministries.

Sister Mabel recounted a negative incident in a parish that occurred in the latter half of the first decade of the twenty-first century and that involved one of the members of her community:

> We had a struggle with Father [name] at [a local parish church] last year. [Sister Hilda] and he had a big fight and he wrote the bishop; he wrote to everybody. But we've pulled out of [that church] … we don't go there at all. We don't have our jubilees there … He's too biased … [Sister Hilda] had a … church choir and he did everything possible … In the winter … he'd turn the heat off for their practice. He'd lock up things so she couldn't get them … [so she was concerned for] these little kids … and she finally pulled out.

As one can see, Sister Hilda[4] and her religious community responded to the tensions by withdrawing their services from the parish and by hosting their jubilee celebrations elsewhere. While some observers may consider these responses cowardly because it appears that the nuns abandoned the parishioners, others may view them as strategic because they have enabled the sisters to hold their gatherings uninhibitedly outside the institutional and intractable confines of the parish building. Sister Hilda's tactics certainly parallel those of women religious of earlier eras who defied clerical control by removing resources that were highly valued by lay people (Wittberg 1994, 96). While women religious across time and place have sometimes used their withdrawal from parish work as a bargaining tool to protect themselves against interference by bishops (Wittberg 1994, 96), Sister Hilda and her community concentrated instead on ensuring that they did not turn their backs on the parishioners. As Sister Mabel explained, through an inclusive approach, Sister Hilda did dialogue about the concerns with the parishioners: "she called the whole group of lay people together and they met here [at the motherhouse]."

Whereas Sister Hilda's experience appears to have resulted in a loss for her parish, a similar tension encountered by Sister Theresa seemed to have produced a gain for both her and the parishioners in a Church setting among Indigenous peoples in northern Canada. Recall from chapter 2 the priest who was not pleased with her involvement in liturgical preparation and who had told parishioners that she was not really a nun because she did not wear a habit; the fallout worked in her favour:

> A Polish priest … just over from Poland, who they sent in … to say Mass
> and be with us there [laughs] … He was so annoyed with me, I guess with
> the way I was running the parish that he … went to the bishop and he
> said to the bishop, "Either she goes or I go." So guess who went! [laughs][5]

In the end, it was the priest who went. But, Sister Theresa's case was rare insofar as she was disrespected by a priest yet defended by a bishop who chose to support and maintain her contributions to the remote northern parish. By contrast, many other sisters recounted having been further dismissed by bishops when priests have complained about or critiqued their work. Such was certainly the case for Sister Agnes as she defended her innovative and inclusive approach to high-school Masses, as well as her direction of a feminist-oriented play.

As Sister Agnes recalled examples of when she protested against injustices within the Church, she shared about a particularly challenging incident that occurred while she was a beloved high-school chaplain. She identified the example as "significant" because "it's got to do with hierarchical … patriarchal" structures. Upon using the term "chaplain" she immediately clarified that it was not the official title that she held because the Archbishop at that time "reminded us all [that it was] not chaplain. In fact, he didn't even like the word chaplaincy in any form, adjective or anything else … for women."

She went on to explain how she encountered backlash from a newly ordained priest who had been assigned to the parish where the high school students attended Mass as part of the school's religion activities. She stated proudly that various school departments were involved in making the Mass experience effective for the students and the collective efforts clearly produced results because her school was known to have the highest percentage of students attending Masses in their city. Such popular success is attributable to the enthusiastically shared effort under Sister Agnes' chaplaincy leadership that encouraged the young people to participate and to do "things they hadn't done before."

Given that the theme of the first Mass of that school year revolved around building community, Sister Agnes, along with the students and other teachers, had planned to have the first reading acted out through music – "beautiful and lovely, gracious music and praise" according to Sister Agnes; it was to also involve liturgical dance. After she sent the plan for the readings and for the Mass as a whole to the newly ordained and recently assigned priest, he refused to let the young students into the church to rehearse. When Sister Agnes confronted the priest, not only did he claim that the proposal was unacceptable, but he also questioned why she had sent him the readings in the first place. When she explained that she thought he needed the material in advance so that he could prepare the homily in accordance with the school's selected theme of community building, he replied harshly: "I don't have to be told how to prepare a homily. I know what they have to hear!" As Sister Agnes relayed the response, she whispered as she repeated the words emphatically and derisively: "I know what they have to hear!"

According to Sister Agnes, the principal was "really upset 'cause he loves our liturgy. He knows the kids love going there and he loves the way they all get involved and the liturgy means something to them." Thus, the principal organized a lunch meeting with Sister Agnes and the new priest. Sister Agnes recalled that at the gathering she had explained to the priest how up until then "some movement" had always been choreographed into the liturgy and that it was especially fitting because they felt it was necessary to show that they were building community in light of the racial tension surfacing at that time. As Sister Agnes recounted, the priest's stance on her initiatives was intransigent:

> The line ... that sticks with me ... and he said verbatim, "There will be no bodily stimulation to take away from the purity of the Eucharist" ... I'm sure Augustine would have been proud of him! ... So [the principal] couldn't believe what he was hearing and he tried to support me. But he was getting no place by saying, "Agnes' liturgies are really alive." And so he [the priest] wasn't budging ... I never have trouble eating, but I couldn't get that salad down. So anyway ... it's not over yet. So [at] the Mass ... he allows those readings, but they're just read. And then, when it comes to the homily ... the homily is all on sex, masturbation, and hell. When I got back to school and walked into the ... teacher's room, staff – men and women – hugged me ... I could almost cry when I think of this young whippersnapper priest ... [the principal] was just so angry! Everybody was! Like, like he didn't even do it well. It was just so horrible ... it was just out of the 1500s ... just givin' everybody hell for kids watching dirty ... videos, you know. And what happens? Hell! What a way to begin the [school year].[6]

According to Sister Agnes, the school principal, who had been "a strong Catholic leader in schools ... building community ... for years and years and years," organized a second meeting in support of Sister Agnes' approach. When the principal questioned the new priest about why his homily did not tie into either the readings or the community-building theme which they viewed as so pivotal at the beginning of the school year, "[the priest] just said 'I am the priest' ... So the priest's power comes from the ... bishop's power which comes from God ... and he says 'I am God's representative and God speaks directly to me. I have been ordained the priest. I have been ordained to give the homily. God speaks to me and I listen to God to tell people what God has said to me.'" In light of such a hierarchical and impudent attitude, several school officials brought the matter to the attention of the archbishop, and while they were "stuck with him [the priest]," their efforts seemed to yield some progress because "he toned down a little bit … he was never as bad as he had been when God spoke directly to him that first day!"

Sister Agnes' account of the stifling of her chaplaincy initiatives provides important evidence of how patriarchal power impacts the worship experiences of not only women religious but also of the adult educators and young people whom they serve. However, school is not the only space where Sister Agnes felt the centralized male authority of the Church manifested against her.

While Sister Agnes was duly praised by fellow sisters and by other women and pro-feminist men for the play on biblical women that she co-led, she was heavily criticized for it by her diocesan bishop, local priests, and even a male cousin known for his loyalty to the local bishop. On two different occasions when the play was about to be performed, she proactively informed the diocesan bishop and a monsignor so that they would be aware of it in case concerns were brought to their attention: "I wanted him to know why I was doing it and I wanted him to hear it from me, the instigator." As she noted, she was not seeking their approval: "I wasn't asking his permission to do it. I just said we were doing it." Both declined her offer of tickets and refused to attend the performance. While the monsignor sarcastically wished her good luck, the bishop questioned the purpose of the theatrical production by asking her: "Why are you doing a play on that?" He apparently did not understand her response. She related that he assumed the audience would be angry and in disagreement, but she effectively clarified that their reaction toward the play and the characters was rather considerate. Sister Agnes explained to the bishop that the audience was "not angry so much as they were crying" and that "they felt very compassionate" because the author's intention was "not to promote anger. She's a compassionate playwright … and all these women [characters in the play] speak compassionately, questioningly, but compassionately about the [biblical] men in their lives." In fact, the positive responses from the audiences in the numerous spirituality centres where the play was staged actually inspired the creation of a social-justice-oriented theatre company, which was financed and promoted by Sister Agnes' religious community.

The critiques were certainly not unique to the bishop or monsignor. Sister Agnes also stated that, "one of his [bishop's] top men … has spoken against [our religious community] on a number of occasions … and against the play." Interestingly however, Sister Agnes felt that the most direct critique came not from the Church hierarchy but from one of her male cousins, who is known in the community for his religious and political involvement. He reluctantly attended the play, and while he congratulated Sister Agnes, he appeared, at least to her, to be shocked by it and questioned her later by asking, "What would your mother think of this?" She happily explained how her mother, prior to her passing, was very supportive of her feminist initiatives. Sister Agnes also reported that her cousin criticized her later in relation to the play by telling her: "I kinda wish you were doing some ministry that the Bishop wants you to do." But Sister Agnes was not dissuaded. In fact, she takes pride in her change-provoking tactics:

> Now some people would say, "Agnes, for God's sake, you're a real trou-
> blemaker!" ... I'm a quiet troublemaker. I'm not a Joanna Manning trou-
> blemaker. But I'm glad there's a Joanna Manning! ... I'm proud to be
> that kind of troublemaker! Oh God! Our Church needs some trouble! [7]

While Sister Agnes is both willing and able to stir things up on her own, she draws strength and courage from the support and freedom offered by her religious community's leader:

> I remember going to our general superior and saying, "I have been asked
> to bring our play to [another city in Ontario], but I don't want to get us ...
> into trouble with bishops or get us into added trouble with bishops." She
> said, "Agnes, I'm tired of being aware of what bishops want or don't want.
> Let's go ahead and do what God is calling us to and not worry about bish-
> ops." So that really helped me to get that kind of support from our leader.

Sister Agnes' experience with multiple sources of critique is certainly not unique. Many other women religious, including Sisters Adele, Clara, Ella, Joelle, Loretta, Maureen, and Sarah, as well as former Sisters Carol, Darlene, Judith, and Mildred, have also recounted how, in addition to the backlash they encountered by priests and bishops, it has often been male relatives (e.g., fathers, brothers, cousins, uncles) who have posed the greatest challenge against women religious' anti-patriarchal stances and pro-social justice opinions. Yet, as the next section illustrates, some critiques do stem from female counterparts.

Sisters facing reluctance by other women for gender equality

Isn't it sad to think what's been lost ... with the male language and every-thing. (Judith)

It would be inaccurate to portray the antifeminist critiques as stemming solely from males who are either part of or supportive of the male hierarchy of the institutional Church. Many current and former sisters recounted instances of both women religious and other laywomen favouring patriarchal traditions and resisting feminist-oriented progress – an occurrence that is relatively common given the enduring effects of the symptomatic internalization of patriarchy (Chittister 1998; hooks 2007) and one that points to the importance of understanding religious identities and initiatives within all of their institutional and relational contexts (Ammerman 2003, 224). For example, during her interview in 2009, when Sister Benita was explaining that femininity is not regarded positively by the official Church, she also added that some women themselves are part of the intractability: "It's … a traditional thing … the person I was with today is so conservative. She won't go back to [church name] if they continue to have women altar girls. I said, "What?" [laughs] That's how far back she goes."

Sisters have also encountered reluctance on the part of women within their own religious communities. For instance, Sister Sophie relayed how some sisters are not yet comfortable with women-only liturgical gatherings: "we have a lot to offer … but there are so many who … [believe that] father has to be here so we're up against it." Sister Mabel also relayed the individual and collective resistance she faces against her gender-inclusive preferences:

> The congregation, that's where you're bound. I'd speak out a lot more …
> and have more mother-god readings … if I did not belong to the [name
> of congregation]. So community is a barrier. We have one very strong
> one in the congregation … who is resisting changes completely … it's
> fundamentalism … so there are some struggles.

Similarly, when referring to expressing feminist ideas, Sister Joelle shed light on her efforts and on the disappointing reactions and results: "I did a study and gave a talk to … some of the leading superiors about inclusive language and we made a real attempt in the congregation to use it during the liturgy … but it slipped back, and there was quite a resistance to it on the part of some [sisters]." Sister Adele faced comparable opposition by both laywomen in her parish and by sisters from her religious community:

> Oh resistance at times … to a lot of different things from different …
> places within the Church … language for instance … that was probably
> the first [initiative] … trying to change the language and be inclusive …
> there was certainly resistance within the community, there was resistance
> with … some of the women in the parish … a lot of people just said, Well,
> you know, "man" includes woman … and yet I remember reading early
> on, you know, language is formative and that really helped me and … even
> the resistance was an expression of that. Language had been formative; I
> never questioned it. I just began to question that in '77, '78, when I was
> a student in [a US city] and I lived with very strong feminist women …
> and then coming home and wanting to change language … But I mean
> when I was on the leadership team … two of us worked a lot with liturgy

and did lots of changes with language and … lots of that got reversed after we left! … But then I've been on the liturgy committee, and so I just keep coming back and so do others and we just keep whatever we've planned; we are careful with the language … the people are where they're at with stuff … but … when I'm planning anything, I have to continue to do that, and will continue and do continue and have for years and so do others. So gradually … others have picked up. But I mean … when I came back from [the US city] fresh from that experience the other people hadn't had that.

These accounts reveal how, despite the collective identity and momentum that had moved some gender-inclusive practices forward within their religious communities, individual opinions entrenched in tradition proved to be predictable, yet unavoidable obstacles. While the circumstances were frustrating, Sister Adele's consideration of the sisters who may not agree with her approach is in itself an exemplary testament to her sense of inclusivity. What is similarly impressive is her perseverance: she remains undeterred and thus still forges ahead, as do many other feminist-oriented sisters who, as I show next, just do it anyhow.

OVERCOMING CONSTRAINTS BY "DOING IT ANYWAY"

We've just been so used to … doing our own thing. (Sister Joelle)

In light of the constraints with which current and former sisters have had to contend, and as a testament to their own creativity, many of them have learned to firmly maintain their positions and to develop alternatives accordingly. Their corresponding courage, confidence, and conviction come to light in their individual and collective tactics, which are illustrated below.

Standing their ground

Sister Agnes recounted a time when she had to stand her ground against an adult male altar server who dismissed her because she was a woman and who attempted to prevent her from serving communion during a funeral Mass:

When I had journeyed with a [friend] … whose little baby died at age four … [my friend] asked me to be Eucharistic minister … and [in] that conservative Church … I could tell when I went up to be Eucharistic minister I got the evil eye from … a senior altar server … he came to me and whispered in my ear, "We have enough Eucharistic ministers," and I just stood there. Then he said again a little louder [whispers]: "We have enough Eucharistic ministers." I still stood there. I didn't even look at him. The third time … I just stood there … and honest to God … I said after I would have joggled him. I think I would have made a fool of myself

if he had tried to get away [with it] … and so that was another time where
I just stood my ground.

Sister Agnes and her fellow sisters' efforts to integrate women in all aspects
of liturgical rituals in their convent and community celebrations have been
continuously thwarted by bishops and priests who have presided over them
in the past and who have sought to preserve the altar as the Church's ultimate
patriarchal space (Helman 2012). Many sisters clarified that in the end, they
had stood their ground whether it was in person, by phone, or via email. Sister
Kelly explained how in the case of liturgical dance, despite the overall clerical
disapproval as well as the specific critiques of it being "too long," her religious
community has kept the movement as part of their creative liturgies at jubilee
celebrations held within their own motherhouses: "They [the clergy] don't like
it but we do [it]." Sister Loretta also underscored her community's intrepid
independence: "We just do what we believe in and we forge ahead."

Secretive and selective schemes

In some cases, as Sister Mabel stated, forging ahead implies selectively avoiding
the bishop's scrutiny altogether: "We don't show him the program … We don't
show him anything! We just go ahead and celebrate and we get a priest that
we like." Sister Agnes elaborated on another secretive and selective scheme
that her religious community employs in order to evade the diocesan bishop:
"We just stopped inviting him … We try to arrange things when he's away if
possible … We plan our Jubilee when he's busy, out of the country … at least
out of the province." Sister Penelope revealed another avoidance tactic: "We
don't ask permission [anymore] so we don't have consequences [from Church
authorities]."

The sisters' schemes extend beyond their liturgies and also apply to the
New Age practices that they offer in their retreat centres. Darlene, who works
at a spirituality centre operated by a community of sisters, reflected on the
sisters' secretly strategic tactics to overcome Church-imposed restrictions. In
reference to the 2009 ban against Reiki[8] by the US Conference of Catholic
Bishops, Darlene explained that "We have one person who does Reiki here. But
it's off of our brochure now because … the bishops … banned it … [but] we
still offer it during retreats." Sister Mabel, a Reiki master, who at the time of her
interview was too busy to offer it herself due her employment responsibilities,
also critiqued the ban and proudly stated how it continued to be practised
within her community's motherhouse:

I studied Reiki ... I taught Reiki ... I did a lot with the dying ... and now that's condemned by the Holy Father. I laughed out loud that no one can do Reiki ... it's a healing art that goes way back to the thirteenth century; I mean [the ban] it's crazy ... We have Reiki tables though and Sister Hilda [still] does Reiki too.

While such assertive reactions and clandestine approaches on the part of women religious encountering prohibitions and exclusions have been documented elsewhere and over time (Chittister 1995; Coburn and Smith 1999; Schneiders 2013; Wittberg 1994), they nevertheless point to the previously unknown lengths to which Ontario-based Canadian women religious have gone to uphold their eclectic and creative spiritual enterprises.

Notwithstanding how impressively one may regard the sisters' intentionally surreptitious tactics, the corresponding losses are disconcerting. Given that so many of the sisters' feminist New Age endeavours are deliberately covert in order to be kept hidden from the Church's male hierarchy, many of them consequently remain unnoticed by, and thus unavailable to, the wider public. This secretiveness, albeit necessary, results in a lost opportunity for sisters to serve openly as models among other like-minded laywomen, as well as secular women and men who would otherwise be interested in and/or benefit from not only their spiritual innovations but also their organizational improvements and activist advancements. Consequently, many of their novel and life-enriching practices remain internal to their religious communities and thus relatively insular. In this light, while the sisters' position "on the margins" of the Church may be productive and beneficial in some regards, it undoubtedly restricts their reach across certain spheres, and it may limit their ability to help individuals enrich their religious experiences, as well as to influence broader Church practices regarding women and other marginalized populations.

Sisters' "do it anyway" attitude supported by religious communities

The courage with which most[9] sisters have been advancing their spiritual innovations has undoubtedly been bolstered by the support of their leadership teams and their communities of women religious. For example, at the time of her interview, Sister Mabel was a general superior; in that capacity, she lent her unconditional support to Sister Kelly, one of the sisters in her community who had to defend her feminist-oriented book, "I expected the flack and I told her I'll stand by [her] no matter what happens, if that becomes an issue because that's freedom of expression. I'll get expelled. I don't care ... it would be a privilege!" Sister Mabel's willingness to risk her membership in the institutional Church is indicative of the extent to which some women religious are prepared to circumvent the Church's patriarchal constraints.[10] Such tenacity can also be understood within the context of many sisters' contentment with their alternative spiritual and community pursuits through which they thrive beyond the institutional Church.

Even for former sisters, the benefits of communal solidarity remain significant to them. Many women who no longer have the infrastructural backing of a religious order have been resourceful in finding other sources of collective support that have helped them enhance their wide-ranging spiritual growth. For example, Judith explained how she has deepened her spirituality outside of both the Roman Catholic Church and her former religious order: "I take advantage of things ... through the community of women ... our singing group, which is a *very* spiritual group." Judith's spirituality is also enriched by her continued involvement with the sisters of her former religious community because she partakes in anniversaries and other celebrations.[11] The fact that Judith, along with another former sister who left the congregation at the same time that she did, are still invited back to the religious community's gatherings is a testament to their community's inclusive and reconciliatory approach. The group dimension has also been important for former sisters Carol, Darlene, and Naomi. While all three have remained involved in Church choirs to varying degrees,[12] Darlene has gained solidarity-based strength after joining a dispersed ecumenical community, which focuses on promoting and living peace and justice.

CONCLUSION

Sophia-God's participation ... empowers the praxis of freedom ... A more inclusive way ... can come about that bears the ancient wisdom with a new justice. (Johnson 2002a, 273)

As I have shown in these three chapters on feminist and inclusive spiritualities, the sisters' persistent practices, while seemingly peripheral, represent pivotal pursuits aimed at transforming androcentric religious traditions (Schneiders 2004, 111) and reveal the centre-periphery productivity generated by women religious on the margins of the Roman Catholic Church. There is no doubt that the landscape of the institutional Church is shifting as a result of feminist spirituality (Winter 2002, 27) and it is communities of women religious that have been one of the organized outlets for inclusive language and the modelling of female spiritual leaders (Chittister 1995,13). As such, like that of their predecessors across the ages, the former and current sisters' expressions of faith have both resisted and bypassed the institutional forms set by their male counterparts (Lux-Sterritt and Mangion 2011, 6), and in so doing, they have subverted expectations and modelled innovations simultaneously (Griffith 1997).

In this way, as the critiques and constraints against it illustrated herein have shown, "feminist spirituality [has] indeed [become] dangerous for the ortho-doxies that categorize and control" (Chittister 1995, 155). It thus remains an approach that is in continual need of safeguarding.

The sisters' defence of their integration efforts must be recognized as cou-rageous especially given the well-known repercussions against women religious who openly contest and seek to transform the Roman Catholic Church (Chit-tister 2004; Johnson 2002a; Schneiders 2013). As sisters continue to defend their alternatives, they draw strength from their past victories, as they have over-come male domination and have contested inequality successfully on numerous occasions in the past (Magray 1998; Mangion 2008). As I demonstrate in the next chapter, the sisters' capacities to resist patriarchal interference against their feminist spirituality have also been facilitated by their communities' recently created organizational inclusivity.

CHAPTER 8

Generating circular governance

We have changed, oh yes! Ever more democratically! (Sister Carmen)

n order to illustrate what Sister Carmen underscored emphatically, I shed light in this chapter on the contemporary governance models that the sisters' communities have engendered since the mid-1960s. Their most recent manifestations of governance which embody inclusive, circular, and democratic decision-making and task-sharing are juxtaposed with the hyper-institutionalized hierarchical structure through which communities and convents of women religious were ruled authoritatively for centuries prior to the post-1960s transformational shifts (Ebaugh 1993; Lux-Sterritt and Mangion 2011; Schneiders 2013; Wittberg 1994).

Understandings of institutional changes are not new among those who are familiar with Vatican II–based reforms in women's religious congregations. Such organizational shifts have been documented among women's religious orders in the United States (Ebaugh 1993, 1977; Wittberg 1994) and in Canada (Anthony 1997a,b; Bruno-Jofré 2007; Dumont 1995; Laurin, Juteau and Duchesne 1991; Leonard 2007; Smyth 2007, 2000). However, in-depth perspectives of current or former women religious on the advancements, nuances, and challenges associated with the transition and particularly its twenty-first-century manifestations in Canada are not as well known. Thus, I also draw attention to the sisters' contemporary management practices.

After briefly highlighting the hierarchical dimensions of the sisters' former institutions, including the strict control of obedience, I illustrate the influences that led to the transition away from institutionalized structures. I then present various components and processes that characterize women religious' contemporary governance models through which more autonomous and inclusive conceptions and practices of obedience have evolved.[1] Lastly, I draw attention to the benefits and the limitations of the sisters' decentralized leadership and organizational arrangements.

PAST HIERARCHICAL GOVERNANCE STRUCTURE

As I have illustrated elsewhere (Gervais and Watson 2014), the sisters themselves are well aware and highly critical of the constraining contexts in which they lived and worked prior to the mid-1960s. Many viewed the intense institutionalization – structured hierarchically and ruled by absolute authority – as "militaristic"[2] and "verbally abusive" (Sister Marian), "childish" (Sister Kelly) and a "religious boot-camp" (Naomi). Within this "total institution" lifestyle common to pre-1960s convent settings (Schneiders 2011, 211), nuns were bound by the strict monitoring of the vow of obedience which "was often codified into minute rules governing every aspect of daily life" and inextricably intertwined with the religious orders' hierarchical governance structure as it was intended "to fulfill all of the commands of the superior" (Wittberg 1994, 126, 241 respectively). As one of the three vows (e.g., poverty and chastity) that women religious professed, obedience and its absolute acquiescence to religious (e.g., both Church and religious orders) authority remained unquestioned until the more liberating conditions fostered by the Second Vatican Council, at which time sisters' choices were, and continue to be considered through dialogue and negotiation.

Sister Penelope explained that while the past expectation of complete compliance to obedience was made very clear, the understanding of it was not: "Obedience was almost like a blind obedience ... what was rule was to be obeyed and that's what your obedience is." As has been found among women religious in the United States and England, the excessive control of, as well as the lack of both clarity and consultation in relation to obedience in the pre–Vatican II era and during the initial transition period beyond it, often had very debilitating consequences on sisters' mental health (Armstrong 1981; Wittberg 1994, 242). Many of the women religious I interviewed felt that the "autocratic" regimentation had "crushed" them (Naomi) or they had observed how others like former Sister Charlotte "really broke under the strictness of it" (Sister Loretta).

The same hierarchical and "hyper-institutionalized" structure that led to the strict and sometimes abusive control of women religious (Gervais and Watson 2014) was also imposed against the people under the sisters' supervision, many of whom suffered traumatically as a result. According to the women I interviewed, neither they nor their religious communities were implicated in cases of abuse against children; however, it is essential to acknowledge and to be critical of the systematic abuse that children have suffered at the hands of nuns in orphanages, industrial and residential schools, as well as workhouses in North America, Europe, and throughout the world.[3] The hierarchical control that regulated sisters' own communal arrangements also permeated the establishments they operated. Yet such institutional domination by sisters must be understood as having been manipulated by the "institutional awe" that was designed to ensure the absolute reverence of, and thus obedience to, the Church's male hierarchy to which women religious, and by extension the lay-people they oversaw, were strictly subjected (Ebaugh 1993, 66).

TRANSITION TOWARD NEW GOVERNANCE

In the mid-1960s, after having identified the problematic aspects of their own hierarchical and patriarchal structures, the sisters' religious communities began to replace their authoritative arrangements with governance models based on shared leadership and inclusive decision-making. While this major shift evolved over several decades following the Second Vatican Council, the overall transformation had been years in the making prior to it for two main reasons. First, the Church appeared to be adapting to mounting pressure inspired by increasing democratic governance in Western societies and was thus called to transform its authoritative structure, and therefore its hierarchical image, into one of collegiality and subsidiarity in which Church authorities were to work in consultation with the laity – "the people of God" (Ebaugh 1993, 67).[4] This transition within the Church and among women's religious orders is also set against the 1960s backdrop of broader transformations, namely the decentralization and deinstitutionalization movements, that were occurring simultaneously across many societal spheres including the criminal justice, social work, and health care systems (Cohen 1985; Ebaugh 2003, vi). The renewal of governance practices within the sisters' communities, and arguably in most sectors at that time, also coincided with observable shifts in which the individual was becoming a more pronounced societal focus compared to the family and community (Sullivan 2005, 21).

Second, and relatedly, having long been frustrated by centralized communal control on the one hand and inspired by calls toward decentralization and individual autonomy on the other, women religious were involved in revitalization efforts on their own long before Vatican II. But they recognize that the Second Vatican Council offered both freedom and new motivation to move ever more forward (Leonard 2012).

Influence of Vatican II on new governance

Echoing findings in Canadian scholarly literature (Bruno-Jofré 2007; Leonard 2007; Smyth 2007), the sisters themselves attributed the major shifts in their governance models, at least in part, to the calls for renewal established by the Second Vatican Council and particularly by *Perfectae Caritatis*, the Council's 1965 Decree on the Adaptation and Renewal of Religious Life (Pope Paul VI, 1965). Sisters Adele and Shannon not only credited Vatican II with having inspired changes in relations and processes but they also showed how their community, like most women's religious congregations of the day, worked fervently and methodically at the renewal of Religious Life (Chittister 1995, 1983; Ebaugh 1993; Schneiders 2013):

> We didn't do it all on our own. It changed the way we … went about our chapters … it changed the way we'd have small discussion groups and then we'd speak to the large group and … it changed … everything really about our life … and opened up doors … to new possibilities. (Sister Adele)

> Transformative changes in all aspects of the life and ministry of the […] sisters were made: – rewriting the constitutions – changes in apostolates and institutional ministries – the living out of the vows, prayer life, convent living – modification of the traditional habit. These changes were inspired by the Vatican Council and were reflected in the life of women's congregations worldwide. They led to a greater understanding of the meaning of "apostolic vocation," giving witness in the world to the Gospel imperative to create a more just and social order and to cherish all of God's creation in the globalized economy of the twenty-first century. (Sister Shannon)

As Sister Shannon shed light on the long-term implications of Vatican II, she also emphasized how fully embracing the openness at the outset enabled her community to address complex contexts over time and even into the next century. Among the women I interviewed, and especially for those who stayed,[5] the changes to religious life prompted by Vatican II were met with considerable enthusiasm, despite the inertia and inefficiency that may have slowed their implementation in some instances and locations (Leonard 2012, 2007):

> We ate up Vatican II. That was a watershed moment, no question, and that's where we learned … I remember distinctly … being so impressed by … the revelation … that religious were a part of the laity. (Sister Joelle)

> That was the beginning of so many things. Now, not near fast enough and it didn't work in some places. But on the whole … (Sister Clara)

> It changed it radically … we had been coming up to that gradually … But Vatican II just, I remember … it was at the same time … in the '60s when … Apollo was going off to the moon, the first one … and … the Major Superior at that time … the theme that she had chosen was "onward and upward" … and it's been that way ever since. Onward and upward! … Opening our minds … understanding … who we are as Sisters … who we're called to be. (Sister Kelly)

Rediscovering who they were "called to be" involved, as Sister Joelle noted, women religious accepting their new Vatican II–based classification as part of the laity. While critics may have perceived this new status, which was clearly outside and in all ways beneath the Church's official authoritative control, as a demotion, various examples throughout this book illustrate how many women religious embraced it and exercised it strategically in order to more fully pursue their renewal plans aimed at working in solidarity with other lay members of the Church and with marginalized populations.

Following who they were "called to be" also involved sisters studying seriously their religious orders' foundations and then drawing upon their pre-institutional arrangements in order to infuse historically and spiritually meaningful aspects in the development of their new governance models. Sister Ella conveyed the related excitement and effort:

> Oh! We really took to it and worked ... well, of course Rome said you have twelve years to look into ... your roots and ... come up with a new constitution ... So we got going! Did we have meetings! Did we do research! ... A team went to the source ... an international team went to [the European country where the order was founded] twice to work there ... with the origins ... Oh! ... [it was] very, uh, rich. (Sister Ella)

A testament to the seriousness with which women's religious congregations embraced governmental change is evident in how they carefully complemented their constitutional reforms with expert advice from renowned canonists and chapter facilitators in order to more judiciously shape their evolving governance structures so that they reflected renewal as authentically and as inclusively as possible.

Managing Vatican II changes through evolving and effective leadership

Like Sister Clara, although Sisters Ella and Kelly happily recalled the exciting context, they also recognized the challenges that impeded the full and immediate implementation of Vatican II principles, which serve as further reminders of the multiplicity of women's narratives and experiences within religious institutional contexts (Ammerman 2003; Nason-Clark and Fisher-Townsend 2005; Neitz 2003; Shih 2010):

> It was too fast for some of them ...'course there was a whole spectrum of all of us: It's going too quickly. It's not going quickly enough. (Sister Ella)

> People were all at different stages and I think that's important to remember within Church and within community ... we're all at different stages of personal growth and faith growth. (Sister Kelly)

As Sisters Noreen and Adele clarified, such challenges were as true for leaders as they were for members:

> I entered in '63 and ... the Vatican Council was in full swing and our novice mistress ... she was a woman on the edge too; she was way ahead of her time ... of course the general superior, she was not there [yet]. So she [mistress] was between us, the young ones coming up ... full of ideas, and the general superior, and she would open the door and sometimes she would have to shut it a bit because it was too much. But that's where I grew up. That was the kind of space I found myself in and it was quite an interesting spot because I could become extremely frustrated; I could see what [the novice mistress] was trying to do and I figured sooner or later she's going to do it ... She was under great stress and ... the general superior was in turn pressured by someone else, like, you know, the chain of the institution line. (Sister Noreen)

> The general superior ... her personal preferences would have been not to change but she was a really faithful woman and she went beyond her personal preferences and really encouraged us to open up. I really admired her! ... For her personally, it was a challenge and, uh, she took up that challenge because it was the thing to do. (Sister Adele)

While the sisters are aware of their limitations, they are equally cognizant of how their strengths propelled their momentum toward newer forms of governance. While the rate at which Vatican II–related changes within women's religious orders were embraced was affected by institutional inertia and leaders' personal preferences, many sisters attributed their communities' post–Vatican II advancements to the fortitude and foresight of their leaders who, as Sisters Noreen and Adele pointed out above, had to negotiate change on various levels. Sister Agnes shared the same opinion as she reflected on her community's post–Vatican II renewal: "We were able to progress well ... we've been blessed with really good leaders on the whole ... we've elected really good women."

Similarly, speaking about her own experience with shared leadership in more recent decades, Sister Ella proudly underscored her team's aptitude: "as ... general superior ... [in] my second term, we were very talented ladies, the five of us ... Oh boy! Oh! We knew it! ... I tell ya!" Some may perceive Sister Ella's comment as lacking in modesty, particularly for a nun who has pledged a life of humble service, like Sister Corinne reminded us: "We were trained to be modest, you know. Don't forget that [laughs]!" However, in the broader context of the Roman Catholic Church where women religious' contributions have been undervalued for far too long, such a statement reveals the sense of empowerment that sisters value for themselves and that they encourage among other women. Furthermore, sisters' leadership is considered exemplary in many regards because their centuries-long women-led social and financial stewardship has sustained their survival and renewal into the twenty-first century (Chittister 2004; Ebaugh 1993, 137; Reed 2004; Smyth 2007). As I discuss in the ensuing section, sisters' empowerment and leadership are also attributable in part to the feminist lenses that many women religious were espousing at the same time that they were implementing Vatican II–based changes.

Influence of feminism on new governance

While Vatican II provided women religious with the institutional freedom required to transform their organizational arrangements, the feminist ideologies emerging with increased intensity in the 1960s also had considerable influence on both why and how sisters undertook their governmental renewal (Anthony 1997b; Ebaugh 1993; Peddigrew 2008). Although in the 1960s and 1970s, women religious engaged in feminist critiques against the gendered oppression inherent within the institutional Roman Catholic Church, they also applied a feminist analysis "in and to their own lives" – an exercise through which they realized that the structures of their own communities were also "deeply impregnated with the principles and practices of patriarchy" (Schneiders 2013, 564).

While the emerging feminist lenses led sisters to integrate more inclusive approaches within the inner workings of their own administration, they also strengthened women religious' capacity to resist patriarchal interference in the management of their convents and congregations. Such interference, whose intensity and rigidity for more than eight centuries often eroded "the powers of female governance," led to countless consequences for women religious including stricter stifling in cloistered convents, congregational foundresses, and superiors being tried and convicted of heresy, as well as the disbanding or relocation of religious orders (Lux-Sterritt and Mangion 2011, 3–5; see also Gray 2007; Lux-Sterritt 2005; Magray 1998; Wittberg 1994). Thus, the mid-twentieth-century context of renewal, infused with feminist-based stirrings, provided an opportunity for women religious to reclaim their independence and restore sovereignty over their own governmental affairs. Many orders faced serious opposition to their feminist-informed renewal efforts, which were cast in terms of [dis]obedience by the Church's male hierarchy for having "gone too far" (Schneiders 2011, 112–13). Yet most maintained their resolve on feminist terms and thus carried out their organizational restructuring strategically and, in some instances, dramatically with some controversial cases in the United States having been highly publicized (Ebaugh 1993, 139). It is for these reasons that women religious' management of institutional transformations must be recognized as not only having been informed by feminism but also for actually having modelled governmental modernization in undeniably feminist ways (Sullivan 2005, 3).

NEW LEADERSHIP MODELS

> *Our little community ... has done very well! And it has let go of structures and set up small ... networks like clusters and ... life circles and ... cut down on superiors, you know, some of those hierarchical structures ... So it was done gradually and got the sisters to take on a personal ... responsibility and ownership ... and they presented us with opportunities to learn more ... so that we're better prepared.* (Sister Edna)

Sister Edna's explanation captures the essence of the steps and benefits of the renewal process. A major part of the revitalization involved considerable changes in the governance framework that regulated the sisters' lives over "a very long period of hyper-institutionalization and over-identification with the hierarchical-clerical element of the Church" (Schneiders 2013, 638). The sisters' determination to move far beyond such constraints was voiced unreservedly by all the women I interviewed. Sister Ella's enthusiasm for inclusive governance and the sisters' propelling of it was first revealed when she critiqued the hierarchical nature of the institutional Church: "It's a pyramid structure and it's wrong. It's outdated and ... it soon needs to become a circular model, which we sisters have been working at for so long! ... and it's so wonderful ... it itself is healing." Sister Ella illustrates how sisters, having long ago recognized the dysfunction of the pyramidal nature of both Church and convent structures, worked tirelessly in their own congregational spaces to bring about change wherever and however they could within the confines of the hierarchical Church. The next sections shed light on the changes that the sisters advanced.

TOWARD A "FEMININE CIRCULAR FORM OF GOVERNMENT"[6]

After having long recognized that their own institutional structure was also hierarchical and authoritative (Ebaugh 1993; Gervais and Watson 2014; Schneiders 2013), it is interesting to observe how and how much the sisters have changed those structures and what they have accomplished through the major transformations in their governance frameworks.

When Sister Theresa described the transformation toward inclusive leadership, she commented that one of the major changes she had observed was the shift from a one-person controlled hierarchy to a group-led management configuration. As soon as I mentioned the terms "leadership team" she interrupted immediately and stated emphatically: "Which we didn't have! That would be one change right there!" She continued to explain:

When I entered there was the superior general, her assistant, and two councillors ... Now we have ... changed her name; she signs "general superior" rather than "superior general" [because] superior general ... to me is more masculine; general superior is more feminine ... So now we have a general superior and a leadership team as opposed to a superior general, an assistant, and two councillors.

As Sister Agnes referred to similar shifts in her community's governance, her vocabulary was also reflective of her feminist-based distinction between patri-archal pyramidal patterns and women-centred circularity:

We have really been working at that throughout the last years gradually moving away from the superior general ... to more of a circle type thing, moving away from the hierarchical ladder of the male to the female circle ... and on the whole I think very successfully in our little congregation.

Sister Sarah also used language indicative of the non-hierarchical practices that her community carries out; yet, as she did so, she pointed to how the terminology seemed unique to religious life: "I find that we often do need to use it [former title of 'superior'] outside of religious life. Within religious life, people understand the word 'leadership team' ... But outside of religious life, people don't know what that means." Sister Sarah's interpretation suggests that old stereotypes of rigid mother superiors may still be prevalent among members of the wider public who may not be aware of the extent to which nuns are practising inclusive governance.

One way in which five congregations practised circular governance was through changes in the selection and inclusion of delegates at meetings (Anthony 1997b). In the past, a limited number of sisters would be appointed as delegates to chapter meetings. Over the years, participation became open to all sisters. As Sister Clara passionately explained the progress, she simultane-ously emphasized the rationale behind the "big shift" while she lamented the gradual evolution and celebrated what the change represented:

I've *always* had a hard time with hierarchy ... I was on the council for eight years and I tried desperately ... to get delegated authority ... Any-way, we got there, but it took all my eight years in office ... This delegated authority finally ... makes a big difference. That's an adult model. (Sister Clara)

Sister Kelly also clarified the implications for delegates as she elaborated on their shift away from the exclusionary and pyramidal processes and toward the inclusive and non-hierarchical practices:

[T]hat happened right after Vatican II and when we rewrote our constitution … it was from the understanding that leadership and membership go hand in hand and we stopped having … [appointed] delegates! You know, everyone was a delegate … so that has evolved to what … the team … is … now … we call them teams now …they're talking about … [a] feminine circular form of government, which is basically what we applied for ourselves after Vatican II in our new constitution. So it is not meant to be [sigh] hierarchical.

Sister Marian elaborated on the now cherished decentralized and democratic model:

[T]he opening up of chapters … everybody's involved in that … and if they're not involved it's their own [choice] … everything is so well explained … the communication I think has exploded … that's … what is good about it and the fact that we are all involved and can go and put our X on whoever we want to … nominate … and listen to the women who have agreed to let their names stand and … question them … It's a very open process … I am pleased … because … when I entered, it was all so silent; everybody went around … like it was the tombs or something … but this is more life-giving.

While Sister Joelle was also pleased with her community's democratic orientation, she alluded to how their process is a relatively recent one – "in the last … twenty-five years" – and is still in progress, pointing to the varied stages of evolvement among the religious orders represented herein. Regardless of the phase of development at which they may be, such democratic processes involve greater and highly valued consultation among the members (Wittberg 1994).

Decentralized and circular governance

It's … a communal discernment thing … we all belong to clusters and … we're there as equals. (Sister Mabel)

In order to maximize their consultation-filled decision-making processes, women religious have also established other leadership-sharing arrangements that support the daily management of both their communal living and their collective engagement. While the titles of the groups and processes vary, they share a common thread of inclusively oriented decentralized delegation.

Round tables. In Sister Sarah's community, round tables foster shared leadership that is respectful of each woman's voice, and by extension their choice:

We … function on what we call a round table model of governance and basically this means that every person … is part of one aspect; she chooses which aspect of governance she would like to be involved in ... whether that's finance, social justice ... The round tables ... change so ... we've had ... different ones around education, spirituality ... so that's kind of the model that we use. It's something where everybody, *everybody* is able to have a voice ... in the leadership in one dimension.

While in Sister Sarah's community, the round tables encourage opportunities for women religious to contribute to the congregation's broader vision and its engagement priorities, groupings in other religious communities assist with various aspects of communal living.

Clusters. As Sister Edna noted above, one of the ways that women religious practice decentralized governance is through clusters.[7] As the co-initiator of clusters in her own community in the 1980s, Sister Ella is well positioned to explain what they entail:

In my time as ... general superior ... we did ... a very smart thing ... We started to encourage our sisters to belong to clusters ... and that was a big move ... We didn't have a superior in our [local] houses. We clustered ... and it was because we found we didn't have ... enough sisters with leadership qualities to go around ... in the different houses, and so why name somebody who didn't want it or who didn't have the gifts for it? ... So we ... got ... on to this clustering which was a certain way of ... living out our way of life.

It was very important that you chose women that you felt that you could share and care about. That was the idea of the clusters: sharing and caring ... So for instance if somebody gets very sick in your cluster, well, everybody, you know, four or five people, are all concerned about her and gets her to the hospital and does all of this. Well, a superior would have done those kinds of things you see [laughs]. Well now ... it was *wonderful!* For us, it was an answer and *everybody* had to belong to a cluster! A cluster ... had to be three or more ... I think it opened us up to the responsibility for each other and it broke down that we leave the responsibility to one person.

While Sister Ella was candid about the pragmatic reason for initiating clusters in her community, she and other former leaders also emphasized how the new approach was intentional because it reflected the inclusive circular governance model that they had been refining since the 1960s and, as their own accounts suggest, the decades-long efforts have been worthwhile.

While one leadership team member explained that such clusters function as "circular government where it [is] shared responsibility," Sister Noreen, a former general superior from the early 1990s, emphasized how clusters enable the sisters to "come together by choice" with women of their "choosing." By extension, Sister Jeanette highlighted the inclusivity and creativity made possible in a cluster setting; she clarified that unlike how she feels limited in a priest-controlled parish church, "in our cluster groups ... we each take our turn. So we prepare the prayer ... whatever the topic is we're going to share, you make it as creative as you want." Sister Josephine conveyed similar aspects of both the interactions within, and the benefits of the clusters, all the while being candid about the challenges posed by members with differing opinions:

> We do have a little community of seven sisters, which we get together ... once a month. Especially this year since chapter's coming up ... they've sent us with all kinds of papers to discuss ... I think we're individuals ... we have one ... who often brings up topics that ... we're okay with but she's not and that's all right. So it's not ... [perfect but] they would help ... if you had a medical crisis or something. Sister [Joy] for instance when I had [surgery], she came and stayed two nights with me.

Whereas clusters foster mutual support through companionship regardless of diverse and sometimes conflicting personalities and preferences, life circles encourage an additional layer of solidarity that facilitates individual care, spiritual growth, and household upkeep.

Life circles. In six[8] of the eight communities of women religious, the hierarchical structure maintained for hundreds of years by the authority of the "superior" was also replaced by the inception of life circles in the early twenty-first century. While clusters consist of groupings of sisters who may live in close proximity to each other but not necessarily together for the purpose of fellowship and care, life circles are units of women religious who live together in larger settings, like community or retirement residences, and who assume the leadership of certain dimensions which assist in the governance of communal living. Sister Mabel explained how the life circles were established, how they operate, and how they are beneficial in her congregation:

> Clusters go way back ... but life circles ... I did. We wanted the sisters at the motherhouse to take ownership of their environment. They always had a superior and so we decided ... there's no superior inside the house. The life circles, there's one [for] hospitality, one is spirituality, one is community living, and one is transportation, and the sisters are in one of those and they totally take care of all that ... they meet every week. Ordinarily I wouldn't be involved at all but they asked if once a month we could meet with them. So once a month we meet. But ... they chair the meeting, and I only give input if they ask me ... But they feel much

freer … It's been working wonderfully … they feel responsible; they feel involved; they feel it's their home. The quality of life has changed to a much more peaceful process.

As Sister Mabel's community officially described their life circles, the terminology that they used was indicative of the conceptual and practical shifts resulting from their new leadership approaches. For example, the sisters explained that life circles are specifically part of a "circular governance model" that fosters "a holistic approach" to caring for the sisters and their residence. Similarly, as Sister Maureen echoed Sister Mabel's account, her vocabulary was illustrative of the gender-based priorities and practices that characterize their new era of governance which they seek to share with other groups: "I'm with the pastoral and spiritual life circle and we meet and … share and then we get into a large group once a month and we all share about that … So … we're trying to live … a feminine model of leadership. We're working on that in the community too."

As is evident by their titles, each life circle is responsible for a particular aspect of communal living. For example, in Sisters Mabel and Maureen's community, the Pastoral Circle organizes various elements involved in liturgical preparation, pastoral care, chapel maintenance, spiritual development, communion service, and the scheduling of Mass. The Hospitality Circle ensures that visitors to the residence receive a hospitable welcome and that their needs are met throughout the duration of their stay. The Transportation Circle coordinates sisters' travel to and from appointments and outings. The Community Living Circle facilitates social gatherings and recreational opportunities, and it manages the sisters' allowances and other needs. Such decentralized management is in stark contrast to the superior's authoritative direction over all of these logistical aspects in the past, all of which were administered by way of sisters' submission to obedience under the superior's control (Ebaugh 1993; Wittberg 1994). As will become evident next, the sisters' pride in the membership to a life circle and their enthusiasm toward their responsibilities therein has resulted in noticeably favourable outcomes.

BENEFITS OF NEW GOVERNANCE

It's time consuming, but it's liberating at the same time. (Sister Nellie)

The changes to the sisters' governance frameworks have yielded numerous benefits both inwardly and outwardly. After illustrating the internal advantages, I shed light on the external ones which involve their modelling of inclusive leadership among others.

Internal benefits

The women identified significant and meaningful benefits to their evolving governance arrangements that have impacted them internally, including for them personally and collectively within their own religious community.

Personal freedom and mutual respect

> *It freed people up.* (Sister Mabel)

When discussing the overall advantages of the reforms in governance practices, most sisters concentrated on the collective progress they have made. But a few sisters also pointed to how the changes benefitted them personally, especially since they were able to move beyond the constraints of both blind and strict obedience (Wittberg 1994, 242):

> Well, yeah, [it was] easier … More easily I could do what I wanted to. (Sister Carmen)

> It certainly has been a very pleasant experience … of growth … It has facilitated … personal growth among our members, and as a community, a certain amount of freedom … to just think on our own and to make judgments and to express ourselves, to express … what we think of … our chapter meetings … There used to be … just a small group of people who … had the nerve … to stand up and give their opinions and now … sometimes it surprises you, people give their opinion; they're not afraid anymore. They used to be … afraid of … superiors. (Sister Sophie)

While Sister Marian echoed such emphasis on personal freedom, she also admitted that the evolving governance led to considerable changes in her own way of dealing with others more thoughtfully:

> Now it's independence in a healthier way … independence of person and of thought … and of awareness that God is present in all of us and … when the going gets tough, I choose … to respond to the God in the person before me … and not be saying, "I told you that fourteen times!," which I'd be used to saying … My temperament is not the sweetest in the world … it's toned down and it's more meaningful and more respectful of the person opposite me. (Sister Marian)

By openly admitting to having learned to be more considerate of others, in part as a result of the less authoritative context, Sister Marian illustrates how the evolving governance led to personal transformations which, by extension, gave rise to more peaceful interactions within the wider group of sisters.

Increased consultation and dialogue

> *Certainly in my congregation, I'm very proud! I think we have worked very hard at moving away from the [hierarchical structure]. I think we have excelled in that, really! ... We're not set up ... apart. This was ... a major shift! And the decisions being taken, being shared with a sister's consultation, a whole consultation process. An incredible thing!* (Sister Noreen)

Paralleling Sister Noreen's enthusiasm, other women referred readily to the new opportunities for consultation resulting from the changes in their governance practices, which are indicative of the additional gains achieved as the locus of power shifted in their communities (Wittberg 1994, 246). Sister Mabel shed light on the process from a leader's perspective: "We bring everything to them [sister-members] in a community day ... share about it ... so there's a lot of dialogue." As two members of Sister Mabel's community substantiated her explanation, they elaborated on the circular process and their appreciation of it, and as they did so, they illustrated how the renewed notion of obedience involving both collective contemplation and individual freedom, was indeed as consultative as it had been intended through the Vatican II–based reforms (Ebaugh 1993, 73; Wittberg 1994, 243):

> It's like the circle thing ... it's not dictated onto us. We share and talk about it and then we come to consensus ... It's good ... I wouldn't have said that ... before but [I feel] much more validated in the community because of that. (Sister Maureen)

> In the last chapter, we implemented the concept of feminine ... leadership ... a circular model ... We have more dialogue ... We take more responsibility in our lives and the way we live our lives ... There's more flexibility ... We're more involved in decision-making ... each person is heard ... and then it kind of goes through a process and then the decision ... is brought back to us ... Before that, the decision was made and that was it! Now there's more dialoguing and ... you begin to realize that we are mature women. (Sister Jeanette)

Sister Theresa experienced similar inclusivity as a result of the new consultative process in another congregation and she praised it highly: "The leadership team is forever encouraging, inviting us to participate, give our views on everything ... They just couldn't be more [inclusive]!"

While Sisters Noreen, Maureen, Jeanette, and Theresa appreciated the leadership team's efforts to reach out to the members, Sister Adele found the consultation process to be essential for herself as a member who brought forward ideas for consideration:

> Well ... there would be times when I wouldn't make a decision about [our social justice group] without talking with our leadership team and they might say, "We need to consult the whole community on this because it would affect us all" ... and maybe what we'd decide is we need to do some education for all of us so that when we speak, we really know what we're talking about.

Unlike in the past when obedience to the authorities' top-down decision-making was strictly enforced and non-negotiable, Sister Adele is no longer expected to seek permission from the leadership team for her social justice group's activities. Nevertheless, out of respect for her community's consultation process, she proactively communicates her proposed ideas to the team because she feels it is important that her peers be part of the collective decision-making over matters that reflect their shared community. As she also points out, the extended benefits of such a consultation often involve broader education on various social matters. These efforts result in deeper enrichment for which the sisters with whom I spoke are grateful because their awareness allows them to serve others more appropriately and effectively.

Although Sister Adele and her peers value the democratic process and the corresponding benefits, they do admit that there are limitations and acknowledge that their circular governance is constantly evolving as they attempt to improve it. Sister Adele's elaboration illustrates the ongoing evolution inherent within her community's concerted efforts away from authoritative governance (Ebaugh 1993, 72) and toward enlightened enhancement:

> [Now] it's more about sharing responsibility; it isn't about questioning authority ... it's just all of us have learned to live differently this community relationship ... I mean we are always shaping it. We have been for years ... and continue to shape and reshape [it] ... Like I'm on a committee leading up to our chapter in June and we're still saying, "We changed lots of things, but we still continue to need to change the way leadership functions in our community." So we're continually looking at "How are we all in this together?" There is a function for leadership and it's not on a pedestal ... it's a ministry and it's good hard work! [laughs] ... But how to go about that so it's not "we" and "them" and ... we've been growing in that ... for years! ... and we're still looking at how we go about choosing our leadership ... our whole process leading up to when we take the vote keeps changing all the time!

Whereas Sister Adele emphasized the ongoing need for reconsideration, Sister Loretta, a former general superior from another congregation, pointed to some of the limitations of the consultation process associated with her community's

circular governance model. Although she was frustrated by the obstacles including not only the commitment of time but also the practical impotence of the
superior (Wittberg 1994, 244), she conceded that the advantages made it all
worthwhile:

> Being in the leadership ... there's a lot of consultation and discussion ...
> it takes a lot more time to make decisions [laughs] ... one of the examples
> that I always have to laugh at is ... before Vatican II, in our earlier days,
> they [superiors] said you were going to go to [a location] ... in three days
> and this is what you were going to do, and in my time [as general supe-
> rior] ... I couldn't get a sister to move on this floor on this corner around
> to the other corner ... without a *lot* of discussion and even at that. But ...
> I wouldn't want to go back to what we had ... it's just a better way of
> living. It takes a lot longer to make decisions and ... it takes time to talk
> to people ... but it's worthwhile in the end 'cause people feel part of it ...
> A lot of listening.

As Sister Loretta attributed the consultation-based approach to feminine styles
of governance, just as most sisters have already, she qualified what she viewed
as a unique and determining dimension: "The femininity is relationships ...
and I think ... we've worked really hard ... at cultivating relationships ...
reconciliation and healing ... and that has to do with femininity a lot, I
believe." Whether they refer to them as feminist or feminine or both (Adichie
2014), the relational aspects that the sisters prioritize have enabled them to
confidently reclaim their own spaces and have fostered processes within them
that are productive on their own terms. In the following sections, I illustrate
other meaningful dimensions of that productivity.

   Solidarity and unity. While it is by no means their only source of unity,
the new governance structure has nevertheless fostered a deeper sense of solidarity among the sisters within their communities. As Sister Theresa revealed,
despite their differences of opinion, cohesion among the sisters occurs because
it remains a community priority:

> I've experienced solidarity very strongly in the community ... we have
> our differences, like there are conservatives ... right in this house espe-
> cially with the older sisters and with a couple of the younger ones too.
> But ... I certainly have experienced solidarity ... we [as a community]
> feel strongly about it.

As she reflected on the benefits of inclusive leadership involving both circles
and clusters, Sister Mabel echoed Sister Theresa's view on how solidarity prevails
despite the varying opinions in her own community as well. As she did so, she
emphasized the advantageous appeal of it:

> There's been a real opening up in our gatherings. There's such diversity and yet there's a reverence to listen to each person which I think is very beautiful … like I'll say to [a conservative-oriented sister], "I know your stand about the Church. You know mine. We're never going to meet. So let's agree to disagree." Well, I'll get another page or something [about one of her issues] on my desk. It's true! It's like on one level there is this deep unity and we can disagree up here about many things.

While Sisters Theresa and Mabel refer to how a sense of unity enables the sisters to manage their differences collegially among themselves, Sister Penelope illustrates how solidarity, and the corresponding support fostered within the smaller units of the decentralized framework, allow the women to resist requests more confidently: "You have the backing of our cluster, when we talk about it often that whole issue comes up … how comfortable are you in just saying no to some of these things that at times are being asked of us … we have the freedom to do so."

Solidarity was also manifested through a sense of responsibility to the wider collective that was made evident by Sister Agnes who is both enthusiastic and unapologetic about her feminist orientations and theatrical initiatives, yet who is simultaneously considerate of the differences of opinions and preferences of her peers within her community: "Well, we … have some sisters who … aren't that crazy about liturgical drama so I mean you use common sense, you know [not to impose your ideas]." Sister Agnes, along with other sisters who tend to initiate non-traditional activities more often than others, are mindful of the varied opinions within their community and are thus thoughtful in their efforts to consult with their leaders and members about the most appropriate ways to proceed with their innovative ideas. Such consultation does not seem to inhibit Sister Agnes' creativity; in fact, she feels well supported within her community's inclusive governance framework compared to the barriers she still encounters by the institutional Church: "The leadership says, 'Go ahead Agnes, develop your gifts.'" Such support of one and sensitivity to all are indicative of the ways in which personal empowerment is flourishing within the context of collective solidarity among women religious.

Collective empowerment and shared responsibility. Empowerment is considered by the sisters to be an important aspect of personal growth that has been engendered extensively by the new governance approach. Yet, in the context of the women's religious communities, it is also interwoven with a sense of mutual responsibility toward the common good and the collective mission, which was seen as an essential element of the changed conception of obedience (Ebaugh 1993, 73; Wittberg 1994, 243). Echoing another leadership team member's emphasis on "ownership" and from her perspective as a general superior, Sister

Mabel illustrates how the shared accountability has yielded a sense of pride of proprietorship among the members: "it makes everyone responsible, not just leadership ... the clusters are all for the whole congregation and I think that people feel more a sense that this is my congregation." The majority of the members shared the same view on accountability. For example, Sister Rita conveyed the complex layers of shared responsibility:

> It's wonderful because I feel more involved in community than ever before; I feel more accountable; I feel more responsible. I can't look at the leadership team and say, "Why aren't they doing this or that?" That's no longer ... If ... I'd like to see changes, I speak to somebody on the leadership team. You don't run around talking about that they aren't doing it ... I think they're doing great things and ... there's an inclusion that we have not felt before.

Sister Rita went on to explain how the new understanding of the leadership team has also led to a less fearful and more appreciative perception of the leaders governing her community:

> There's not that kind of fear there might have been in the past – "Oh, what would the leadership team think of this?" ... When I look back now, I haven't even heard this said in ages, we used to term [the city where the motherhouse is located], you'd be in [other towns or cities], wherever [and we would ask], "Oh, what would [city name of motherhouse location] think of this?" What you meant by "city name" was our central executive ... I don't hear that anymore. Like ... [Julia, Ava, Miriam, Sandra], these are four individual women; it's not "city" or "executive."

The extent to which the shared responsibility and the respectful appreciation of leadership, of which Sister Rita spoke, is now a prevailing practice among the sisters' congregations was made even more evident and in a particularly meaningful way among the women religious under Sister Mabel's leadership. Sister Mabel recalled that when her community was experiencing financial challenges and the leadership team was "feeling quite discouraged" and was very worried about the responsibility they carried, which at the time involved the potential sale of their motherhouse, the members reassured the leaders that "we're in this together ... the burden ... it's not for you people to carry this alone." Sister Mabel remembered how such a sense of reciprocal responsibility and mutual concern brought the leadership team considerable relief. The members' comment (alluded to by Sister Mabel) is a reflection of the sense of maturity and mutuality emerging from the collective empowerment that has been fostered and of the solidarity that has prevailed within the evolving context of inclusive governance, of which the renewed vow of obedience that is focused upon interdependence and collaboration is a considerable part (Ebaugh 1993, 73). As I elaborate in the subsequent section, a similar sense of mutuality on the part of women religious toward lay people and the community at large is manifested in the ways in which the sisters intentionally share the benefits of their support network.

External benefits

> *These changes brought about through our reflection on and adaptation to Vatican II gave us a broader vision of how we could serve the needs of others and the freedom to pursue new ways of doing so.* (Sister Shannon)

The sisters readily explained how their religious congregations' non-hierarchical governance processes have enabled them to pursue their feminist and social justice initiatives in more inclusive and effective ways. Sister Kelly took as a given that the new governance has empowered them to strive for greater gender equality: "Of course! Of course! Of course!" While the women confirmed that such processes facilitated their work on gender equality, they felt that they also sustained their efforts in other areas of concern including environmental justice and eliminating all forms of discrimination. Whereas many women religious, including Sisters Clara and Sophie, emphasized how the transformations in governance have led to an internal infrastructure that is conducive to supporting the sisters' individual and intersecting social, gender, racial, and environmental justice pursuits, others highlighted how they attempt to replicate their new models to the benefit of others.

Modelling inclusive governance and solidarity

> *I don't want people to call me sister. Whenever [they do], I just cringe … I'm Noreen … so … don't put me above you.* (Sister Noreen)

Just as sisters' strategies for resisting, or at least circumventing, unjustified clerical control serve as examples for other women (religious or secular) to emulate in other patriarchal settings (Mangion 2008, 234), so too can their models of governance, including their lessons learned from both their triumphs and tribulations, function as relevant and arguably exemplary templates for other organizations (feminist or otherwise) to replicate. The women religious themselves explain how the replication is already in progress.

For example, Sister Ella explained how she and her peers not only developed the inclusive governance model but also continue to apply it as they carry out their endeavours: "We have worked at a circular model within our own community and ... when we involve ourselves in things around justice and peace ... within our own [congregation], we ... use that model." In addition to having inspired other congregations of women religious to adopt non-hierarchical processes, the sisters also view their feminist models of collaboration as important examples for their lay staff (Sister Jeanette), associates[9] (Sister Maureen), and project recipients to carry forward and to reproduce in other locations. Sister Mabel referred to this exemplifying as "an opening out" and as "planting seeds." In this light, according to Sister Sarah, the circular model is seen to have external multiplying effects: "We've really tried to bring feminine structures to the kinds of social action groups that we're involved in." Sister Joelle shared a similar outlook: "We are advancing our own project and hopefully helping others to do that too." Yet, Sister Joelle further asserted that her community's modelling of inclusive governance in social justice activism enables her and her peers to work as equals in solidarity with all:

> I can see that it was influential in modelling but, perhaps in the sense that having adopted that model, when we work in social justice with others, we're much more comfortable being part of [it] whereas I think a lot of the clergy, for example, still feel that they are looked on as the experts and they feel they need to be in that role more.

Sister Joelle's intentional reference to the clergy as experts points to the contradistinction between the hierarchical approach commonly used by male priests – albeit not by all of them – and the sisters' contemporary promotion and implementation of a horizontal diffusion of leadership. Sister Joelle went onto to underscore how the concept and practice of solidarity is at the core of their modelling of inclusive governance within the context of their support of others: "Solidarity is a very ... primordial value for me ... so whatever we're doing, whether it's praying or teaching or health or direct social services, we are building solidarity among people. So it's very important."

Sisters' modelling of decentralized leadership and solidarity has certainly been noticed by people who have collaborated within and/or benefited from their inclusive approach. Sister Adele recalled both proudly and gratefully how her empowerment-generating leadership style was highlighted at an anniversary celebration for the spirituality and social justice group she co-leads: "At our dinner ... the fun song that ... [the hosts] wrote ... a line about me that I think that's the truth ... [starts to sing] 'leading not from the front but at the back' ... I've done a lot of that." As the sisters and others whom they serve have already experienced the benefits of their horizontal leadership, women religious are hopeful, however slightly, that their modelling may one day inspire those who are still maintaining the institutionalized structure of the Roman Catholic

Church. Sister Edna pointed out that in order for their internal modelling to be embraced externally, sisters had to first practise what they preached: "You cannot change that structure out there [Church] 'til you straighten your own and keep … sharing that." Now that their community has "straightened" things out, one of Sister Edna's peers, Sister Ella, offered advice on how the Church should do the same: "the structure has to be in the service of the people and that's what the Church has to somehow come to … again we're back to that circular model … that would work."

The sisters' modelling of their inclusive governance is relevant sociologically and societally in at least three ways. First, they remind us of how the transformations that women religious undertook in order to modernize their shared lived experiences were not only informed by feminism but the feminist, and therefore all-embracing dimensions of them, are now being replicated, or are at least available to be replicated, in other spheres in which the sisters are involved (Sullivan 2005, 3). Second, and relatedly, the sisters' modelling of their decentralized governance arrangements, particularly in secular spheres (e.g., social justice outreach projects), serves as an example of the ongoing interplay of faith-based groups and shifting organizational dynamics (Ebaugh 2003, vi), an interchange that points undeniably to the contemporary relevance of women religious' societal contributions.

Third, and in relation to both abovementioned points, the significance of sisters' modelling of their inclusive governance is timely, not in a coincidental way but rather in an imperative way. The urgency is based on an unfortunate, but undeniable, irony that both Wittberg (1988) and Ebaugh (1993, 156) pointed out over a quarter-century ago: as Catholic sisters modernized their governance arrangements, as well as their spiritual practices and advocacy priorities, the memberships in their religious orders declined simultaneously and in most cases drastically. Consequently, although the renewal has rendered their community life considerably more enriching than in the past, since their very survival is at stake, the extent to which they have been able, and are able, to enjoy the benefits of such a renewal are, and will be, relatively short-lived (Wittberg 1988). In this light, given both the relative temporariness of the gains, at least for the sisters themselves, and the imminent inevitability of their demise due to the sisters' advanced ages, if their exemplary governance models are to be replicated under the sisters' own leadership guidance and with a view to ensuring their effective sustainability over the long term, the time to do so is *now*, and as we have already seen, the sisters have indeed been proactively seizing the present moment.[10]

LIMITS OF NEW GOVERNANCE

There were some struggles along the way but I think they worked out. (Sister Edna)

Despite how the majority of women religious have enjoyed the progress resulting from decentralized governance practices, however temporary it is proving to be (Ebaugh 1993), it would be inaccurate to portray all other aspects of the advancements as solely linear and uniquely positive. In fact, as Sister Loretta reflected on the implementation of feminine circular governance, she candidly acknowledged the "trial and error" processes and outcomes: "We try … I mean we fail lots of times too." So too did Sister Adele:

> One of the questions that we asked when we were needing to make a decision [was] "What gives life and love?" So we've been moving more and more in that way … not that we did it perfectly. I mean we've made lots of mistakes when I was on the leadership team and others have made mistakes since and I have as a person. We have, all of us, but sort of as a movement forward, I think.

As David Steindl-Rast[11] has contended, such admissions by Sisters Edna, Loretta, and Adele are testaments to the humble and honest ways in which many women religious, compared to the Church's clerical hierarchy, are self-reflexive about their collective errors and uncertainties. Some of the other sincerely shared challenges are presented below.

While obstacles on both personal and collective levels were encountered at the outset, in some cases, they still exist today. In reminiscing about the initial post–Vatican II changes in governance, Sister Clara characterized them as "a struggle, just 'cause once you've been used to everything in a way; there's always a group that has a pain in [adjusting] to new things." In echoing the sentiment of struggle, Sister Noreen reflected simultaneously on the layered challenges experienced under the old regime and within the new model:

> In many ways, it was much easier to govern before because … once you start opening the doors and want people to participate, that's when you hear dissent and not everybody is able to dissent constructively … I can see the merit of the general superior when she spoke … but people got crushed. So this is much more healthy for sure and much more life-giving to be involved.

In a similar vein and lending further credence to how the constraints of the tightrope are experienced internally, Sister Agnes recalled a specific incident when she, as a councillor on her community's leadership team, encountered backlash from a group of sisters who resisted the leadership team's efforts to implement decentralized governance practices in local convents – a change that had been approved by the community's membership at a chapter meeting:

> It happened that I had to stay in that convent because I had to do something in [that city] and the other three [leadership councillors] went back. It was *very* unsuccessful and they were *mad* at the leadership team and I was the one that got it … So we didn't always succeed … But … I enjoyed the feistiness of those gals … I got a charge out of it. But they weren't ready yet for … more circular [governance] in their own convent … they didn't want it. So we went their way … for a while.

Sisters Noreen's and Agnes' accounts on how some women religious resisted change serve as important illustrations of the internal tightrope that they inevitably had to manoeuvre as their organizational innovations, like those in other societal spheres across time and location, underwent a period of transitional flux as they were being contested and adapted by a diverse membership from within (Ebaugh 1993; Wittberg 1988).

Sister Ella's testimony draws attention to additional challenges as she points to the partial ways in which some leadership "team" members embraced changes and thus occasionally did not share equally in the governance responsibilities and, by extension, left the most challenging work to the general superior who in this case was herself:

> Some of the councillors on that second council were so gung-ho on teamwork … but when there was some dirty work that had to get cleaned up, it came right back to good old [Ella] here, you know. I was very aware [that] … it's fine when it suits … when the rest of you don't want to have to face this conflictual issue … they wanted me to do it! [laughs]

While Sister Ella had to contend with the partial sharing of management tasks, Sister Mabel, in her capacity as general superior, dealt with elderly sisters who still had difficulty with decentralized governance – difficulties that she attributed to individualized factors: "it's totally … personality … psychological dependency on authority." Although she is sometimes tempted to revert to the hierarchical tactics of earlier times as she experiences frustration when the leadership that is "very engaging of the sisters" is not embraced or when it becomes too time consuming, Sister Mabel remains convinced of the merit of the new ways forward: "I used to sometimes say as general superior, it wouldn't be bad to go back to the old days when you could tell someone to do something [laughs] … [but] oh no that would ruin my health; I couldn't do that … sometimes you feel that, but not really."

The attitudes of the elderly women religious to which Sister Mabel referred are similar to those of Sister Nellie who, along with other senior sisters, struggles on practical levels with the decentralized governance that in some instances may not be implemented as fully or with as much clarity as was originally envisioned or as much as some sisters need or expect. Whereas in the first statement, Sister Nellie comments on the lack of cluster gatherings, in the second one, she points to an apparent lack of guidance within the residential context of the motherhouse in which tasks are shared horizontally and are thus supposed to be overseen and undertaken by life circles:

> We never meet ... the coordinator ... she never thinks of calling a meeting ... [but] the other members are the same ones ... we have in our circle so [I see them].
>
> The negative that I see here in the motherhouse is there is no one in charge ... in a community as big as ... here, I think you have to have somebody that you can go to ... I see some of the sisters are very frustrated with "Who do I go to?," you know. It's so much engrained in the older sisters that it's very hard.

Although from a different religious community, Sister Josephine expressed similar concern about what she perceived to be a lack of direction:

> Well, one thing that was brought in a while ago was ... in houses there was not a superior but a consensus ... consultation ... we're rarely told what to do ... Now sometimes ... I would like to know what they [leadership team] would like ... For instance ... we were talking about several houses; we might close them ... So a paper came out with "Would you be willing to live in this house?" And you say no and they go on from that. [But] they don't say why.

These examples suggest that some communities, while having already implemented a decentralized framework, are still struggling with growing pains, whereas other congregations are still in the midst of either imagining or developing their horizontally based governance. Such is the case for both Sister Edith's and Sister Corinne's respective orders and especially for the latter. Although some congregations like Sister Agnes' have been told by sisters from other religious orders that "you people are ahead of us," others like Sister Corinne's are comparatively late in considering a horizontal dispersal of decision-making: "with the present administration we are moving ahead but ... we are a little bit behind other congregations ... because ... some of our administrators at the top level were ... holding on to the old."

As Sister Edith illustrates, although her community has started to shift away from a hierarchical structure, their efforts are relatively nascent as they are still learning about shared leadership, and they are thus still living with, and seemingly accepting of, residual aspects of the pyramidal framework:

> I've been working on our constitutions these last couple of years and ... in some ways ... we're still hierarchical in a way ... it isn't that it's always bad ... 'cause ... some places have kind of done circle stuff and it may not necessarily be that ... efficient, you know. It's also important to bring people along so that there's kind of an ownership ... there's certainly much more focus ... on involving everybody as much as possible ... [but] it is a challenge.

Whereas some communities like Sister Edith's are "not quite there yet" in terms of fully implementing or experiencing decentralized leadership, others who have adopted the model wholeheartedly do encounter some challenges with efficiency and perhaps effectiveness but remain committed to sustaining their new arrangement because they consider that the gains far outweigh the limitations. As I elaborate upon below, such commitment was made evident by leaders' strategic communication with the Vatican.

Despite how far beyond the pyramidal configuration sisters have attempted to move, a complete implementation of their circular governance remains constrained "canonically" (Sister Adele). The Vatican, the overarching institution with which women's religious communities must still be officially registered, requires that hierarchically based authorities be formally identified. Sister Ella, a former general superior who initiated clusters within her community explains the institutional obligation: "There has to ... for Rome's sake, [be] a spokesperson, there has to be one named. Rome demands that ... if you get into something legal, you have to have *someone* who's going to speak for the group ... but we operate as a leadership team." Whereas Sister Ella simultaneously complied with the regulation on paper and sidestepped it in practise, Sister Mabel, a general superior at the time of her interview, fearlessly conveyed how she and her leadership team circumvented the same institutional expectation and how she was not at all concerned about paper-based evidence:

> Well we don't have superiors! Rome doesn't know that yet [laughs]! No we don't on paper either to them. Twelve to fifteen years ago, they formed clusters ... but they [Vatican officials] were intrigued. But I never mentioned the name "superior." There's a contact name.[12]

Sister Mabel's outwitting of the hierarchical regulation is indicative not only of sisters' determination to protect the changes in governance that they advanced both *by* and *for* themselves, as well as *among* those they serve but also of their deliberate employment of certain terms that most accurately reflect those changes.

BROADER SIGNIFICANCE OF THEIR ORGANIZATIONAL CHANGES

The sisters' persistence to uphold their renewed organizational arrangements is significant sociologically on multiple levels. First, the nuns' organizational structures and processes are unique but so is the sisters' relationship to their religious communities. They are not simply organizations through which they work for causes such as education, health care, and social justice. These organizations constitute the very substance of their material lives – the women have lived many years with these organizations and most will die within them. Thus, the ways in which their communal organizations operate must inevitably reflect their evolving values because they impact not only the effective management of their ministries but also the enrichment of their own individual and collective lives. The sisters have taken responsibility to strategically exercise their agency within their religious communities in order to make this happen, even if it has been a slow, complex, and sometimes painful process, amidst personality conflicts and diverse opinions internally and clerical interference externally (Holtmann 2011b). This is in stark contrast to the way that the Catholic hierarchy handles diversity within the Church. Censure, criminalization, and excommunication of feminist Catholics and other theological critics have led to increasing polarization and widespread disenchantment within the Church.

Second and relatedly, the sociological significance of the sisters' feminist organizational changes on both individual and collective levels within the structures of the Roman Catholic Church as an overbearing patriarchal religious institution cannot be overlooked. The constraints under which Catholic women religious have attempted to exercise innovative agency have indeed placed them on a tightrope and arguably on one of the tightest of all. Whereas the external constraints are obviously the Catholic clerical hierarchy including the Vatican, as this chapter has shown, the internal constrictions among the women themselves represent undeniably substantial obstacles.

The sisters' internal practices of circular governance in particular demonstrate that values of inclusivity imply collective effort among all the women in their organizations who come from a range of experiences and political perspectives (conservative to progressive). Not all of them embrace feminist values or engage in feminist-oriented change, or at least not fully. Consensus-based decision-making within a model of inclusivity is irrefutably frustrating and time-consuming for the sisters and their leadership teams. The women, especially the more progressive and feminist ones, clearly struggle with this process, yet they persist because of their religious values and spiritual principles that prioritize solidarity. This is particularly unique from a gender and religion perspective because the sisters are individuals with somewhat autonomous organizations embedded within a patriarchal institution. It is because of their firm belief in and dedication to working collectively that the sisters' individuality has been able to flourish (Holtmann 2011b).

Thus, the collective initiatives and processes of these primarily feminist Catholic women both parallel and extend sociological understandings of how women's gendered agency is both exercised and thwarted amidst the religious and organizational challenges faced by faith-based feminist women, including those within conservative and patriarchal religious traditions (Ammerman 2003; Beaman 2001; Ebaugh 1993; Griffith 1997; Holtmann 2015, 2011b; Jouili and Amir-Moazami 2008; Kaufman 1991; Mahmood 2006; Nason-Clark and Fisher-Townsend 2005; Neitz 2003; Wittberg 1994).

CONCLUSION

I think we've been really ... lucky in our community ... I never felt that held back ... since Vatican II ... and I don't think others have, and I think we've grown better and better ... We're far from being perfect and we're far from ... walking lockstep, and yet I really believe as community we have continued to move forward and pretty darn happily! [laughs] You know ... with ... always a growing respect for our individuality too, which ... wasn't the way it was before Vatican II in religious life ... it was like you were supposed to fade into the picture and ... just be one ... of the crowd, not stand out ... But we've really learned to allow individual expression and I think we've grown stronger as a community as we've done that. (Sister Adele)

Clearly the sisters have moved beyond the hyper-hierarchical and intensely institutional structure that once characterized their residential, spiritual, and charitable arrangements. The pivotal and gendered role that nuns themselves played in such major transitions cannot be overlooked given their wider feminist, sociological, and cultural significance (Ebaugh 1993; Sullivan 2005).

As Sister Adele has so fittingly summarized, while not without its challenges, and however temporarily it may be experienced by the women who remain (Ebaugh 1993), the new feminist-informed decentralized governance through which the women religious' communities now operate has fostered a greater sense of inclusivity which has translated into meaningful productivity on both individual and collective levels. In the next chapter, I demonstrate that productivity within the sisters' feminist activism.

CHAPTER 9

Engaging in feminist activism

Women religious are beginning to examine their own present actions in their attempts to refuse to participate in the perpetuation of an internally inconsistent system that preaches one definition of the equality of women but structures another. (Chittister 1995, 14)

The sisters and former sisters have aligned themselves in solidarity with the struggles of all women because they have "define[d] themselves in opposition to injustice toward women" and have thus devoted their efforts to overcoming systemic gender-based oppression "not only in the larger society, but in the Church as well" (Ruether 2003, 5; see also Chittister 1995). To this end, in this chapter, I first shed light on the origins of sisters' feminist orientations that have led to their activism. Then, I illustrate how sisters and former sisters have contested the Vatican's exclusion of girls and women from the Church's altars and sanctuaries. Third, I exemplify how, beyond their ongoing advocacy for girls' and women's education and employment, sisters' contemporary contributions have evolved into wider engagement and are sometimes at the forefront of feminist activism that promotes gender equality in various societal spheres, both locally and globally. Finally, I demonstrate the various ways in which women religious are engaged in a range of women's rights issues, including their complex and controversial association with abortion-related activism.

MISCONCEPTIONS ABOUT SISTERS' ACTIVISM IN EARLIER CENTURIES

In historical texts examining Church practices or religious communities in earlier centuries, women religious' charitable activities are either absent or critiqued by some historians as having been domestically oriented and passively carried out based on their obedience to the Church hierarchy and on their role as subservient assistants to male clerics (Mangion 2008, 111–12). Moreover, nuns' activism in past centuries is considered to have been ignored by academics due to its affiliation with religion (Smyth 2007), and to "its inattention to legislative reforms" (Mangion 2008, 112). However, while the patriarchal Church's control over sisters' endeavours is undeniable and while they may have been less confrontational[1] in their community engagement in the past, as other historians have uncovered, in many instances, convent leaders stood strongly against the male hierarchy in an effort to initiate and protect their involvement in non-domestic and non-Church spheres as well as in both Church and societal reforms – areas where women were commonly neither permitted nor welcomed (Gray 2007; Lux-Sterritt 2005; Magray 1998; Mangion 2008). In this light, I extend the nascent scholarly attention toward the activist and gendered dimensions of nuns' engagement by focusing on sisters' feminist activism from the mid-twentieth century to the early twenty-first century (Holtmann 2011b; Mangion 2008).

ORIGINS OF FEMINIST CONSCIOUSNESS AND ACTIVISM

Women religious themselves ... question their own role in the subjection of other women. (Chittister 1995, 14)

While women religious played an undeniably patriarchal and, thus, seemingly paradoxical role in the conditioning of generations of women into subservience, like many of their secular counterparts, women religious themselves "woke up" in the late 1960s and early 1970s to the feminist realizations of how problematic that subservience and their own conditioning of it were, and have since worked tirelessly to overcome it (Bonavoglia 2005, 7; Chittister 1995, 13–14; Magray 1998; Ruether 2003). Catholic sisters' own lives were unavoidably transformed by second-wave feminism (Schneiders 2013; Wittberg 1994) and, as a result, to varying degrees, women religious have become stewards of feminist principles as they work in solidarity with feminists (Chittister 1995, 154; Dumont 1995, 175). Sister Marian conveyed how such stewardship and solidarity are evident in her congregation, all the while echoing Chittister's claim that feminism "is alive and awake on the globe" (1995, 154): "Our congregation ... we've had women certainly [in] the last twenty years who ... are *very* aware of the issues and who are *very* aware that we've become educated to them and committed to them."

While such awareness and commitment enabled Sister Marian to freely express her feminist thoughts within her own congregation, the attentiveness and openness to feminist ideals was neither immediate nor absolute in many communities of women religious. For Darlene, such gradualism and partiality created profound tensions as she felt alone in her feminist pursuits early on: "I was the only acknowledged feminist in my community ... the only acknowledged ... feminist activist, publically ... I remember that." As Darlene shared about a transformative moment that led to her feminist activism, she shed light on how she initially felt at odds with her community as her feminist stance took root:

> The Montreal Massacre ... was another big shift for me because ... when the Massacre happened, I was part of the leadership team in my community. So there were five of us on the team and ... two of us were really, really shook up, and we went to the memorial that we had in [city] ... the day after it happened ... and with this one other sister, we became activists in the feminist community ... OXFAM and the women's centre and Status of Women. We became activists very publically after that. The other three that very same night went over to the Morgentaler clinic to be [anti-abortion] activists ... But that, in my head is very, very symbolic of how I was on the edge because my community would have affirmed them [those who went to the anti-abortion protest] and would have dismissed us, and so that was kind of a ... realization.[2]

Darlene's story elucidates the tension and complexity associated with advocating feminist values early on within her religious community and still today within the institutional Roman Catholic Church. In the wake of the Montreal Massacre, Darlene adopted a feminist identity in advocating against gender-based violence, even though her activist position was not originally supported in her community. She continued to feel conflicted as she attempted to reconcile how the other sisters who stood publically against abortion were backed by their community, but she did not feel supported given that her activist position at the time challenged patriarchal norms.

While Darlene's activism can be perceived as countering patriarchal rules, the other sisters' protest against abortion may be interpreted as helping to maintain patriarchal control over women's reproductive rights. Darlene's convoluted position must be situated within the context of the longstanding tension between anti-abortion activists who are presumed stereotypically to be antifeminists and pro-choice activists who are presumed stereotypically to be feminists. As I illustrate in more detail later in the sections on abortion by way of a clarification provided by bell hooks (2000), these seemingly diametrically opposed extremes are not necessarily mutually exclusive. In this light, Darlene's presence at the memorial for the Montreal Massacre in the immediate aftermath of that tragedy does not automatically imply that she is pro-choice simply because she chose to attend the memorial instead of the anti-abortion protest.

Then again, as Darlene faced other women-centred challenges mired in Roman Catholic Church contradictions, the lines between pro-life and pro-choice stances became even more blurred in both her mind and heart.

Consequently her feminist stance deepened and her feminist activism propelled further forward. The controversies regarding the treatment of women and their reproductive rights (or rather lack thereof) that both troubled and inspired her while she was still a nun were threefold:

> I also dealt with a man who had to choose to let his wife die and the baby to live, and he had six children at home, because of the [anti-abortion] pastoral advice [he was given by his parish priest] ... So I was very convoluted about this and while I will never say that I am pro-abortion, um, some part of me is pro-choice and to respect the ambiguity of it, you know.

> I got more activist in that [feminism] too when the Vatican ... used their status at the UN to get the morning-after pill taken out of the rape kits during the Bosnian War. I felt really, really upset about that.

> And then I heard about the sisters in Africa who were being raped [by Catholic priests] and who were given Vatican-approved abortions when they were pregnant. It was a policy, an under-the-carpet policy of the Vatican that in Catholic hospitals in Africa, they could have abortions.

The latter instance refers to the case of sexually abusive African priests impregnating schoolgirls, women, and nuns and forcing them to have abortions or sending them to other countries (to hide them) to give birth to the children they have fathered (Allen and Schaeffer 2001; Bonavoglia 2005, 34; Bouclin 2006, 33). While such convoluted cases enraged Darlene, they also led her to grieve tearfully – "I cried my eyes out" – because they represented "a very confusing and painful issue" that left her feeling profoundly conflicted, just as many other Catholic women do as they prioritize compassionate support for women over dogmatic principles in the context of reproductive health (Holtmann 2015). These emotionally taxing and confounding circumstances with undeniably grave consequences for women in various locations reveal the multiple subject positions from which and for which women religious like Darlene articulate and practise feminism (Shih 2010).

All three of Darlene's examples substantiate the persistent insensitivity and especially the hypocrisy on the part of Catholic Church officials (Gervais and Watson 2017). The Church's stance on abortion is doubly hypocritical in the context of its nuanced doctrine around killing life when it "is in the hands of men" – which permits killing by the state in self-defence as a sanction (Chittister in Bonavoglia 2005, 134) or arguably, as seen above, by male Church officials when the pregnancies for which they themselves are responsible inconvenience them (Allen and Schaeffer 2001). By contrast, when it comes to abortion, "When life is in the hands of a woman, it can never, ever, under any circumstances, for any reason whatsoever, be contravened" (Chittister in Bonavoglia 2005, 134).

Inevitably, such pain-filled inconsistencies and gendered injustices exacerbated the "feminist versus Catholic" conflict with which Darlene was already struggling. While the integration of the two identities and stances have certainly proven viable, albeit challenging (Gervais 2012; Schneiders 2004), at this point in Darlene's life they appeared too incompatible.

Thus, perhaps not surprisingly, as she herself explains, Darlene's growing radicalism and deepening feminist orientation eventually led her to leave her religious order: "So I became more radical and I became more secretive and I wasn't comfortable with that ... So I left my community." Darlene acknowledged both nostalgically and proudly, that after she left and joined an ecumenical worship community, her former religious sisters began to adopt a more women-centred approach to the charitable priorities they set and to the governance structures by which they continue to live. Yet, it is important to note that Darlene's former community is not alone in its gradual embracing and practising of feminist principles. Many other women religious recall the personal and communal tensions that surfaced in the 1960s and 1970s as they explored and eventually applied feminism both individually and collectively.

It has nevertheless become evident over the past several decades that feminism has "found a home within contemporary religious life" (Chittister 1995, 11), and that has certainly been the case within seven[3] of the eight communities represented by the women with whom I spoke. While sisters' involvement in the women's movement has had progressive implications for women within religious communities and in society, sisters' feminist awakenings have also led them to raise concerns about the value of women within the Roman Catholic Church (Chittister 1995, 13; Schneiders 2013). As a result, sisters' feminist orientations have enabled them not only to critically evaluate "their own role in the subjection of other women" both within and outside the Church (Chittister 1995, 14) but also to protest the widespread and long-lasting effects that the patriarchal structure of the Church has had on its female members (Chittister 1995, 13; Johnson 2002a,b; Manning 2006; Schneiders 2013; Wittberg 1994).

SISTERS' PROMOTION OF WOMEN'S RIGHTS IN THE CHURCH

They have allied themselves with the question of the spiritual wholeness of women in what is a male-controlled church. It is from within the institution itself ... that women religious have brought to the scrutiny of that institution in newly feminist ways their age-old predisposition toward women. (Chittister 1995, 12–13)

Women religious have indeed identified themselves with the struggles of women in the Church (Anthony 1997b; Chittister 1995, 12; Schneiders 2013; Wittberg 1994). In fact, most sisters I interviewed have been at the forefront of feminist activism as they have been attempting "to challenge unjust structures in society and in the Church" which for Sister Adele includes addressing "the treatment of women in our Church, the place of women in our Church." Current and former sisters have done so by both overtly and covertly contesting the Vatican's past refusal to include women in decision-making processes or to even meet with sisters, as well as its exclusion of females from both the priesthood and altar service in the Roman Catholic Church (Dumont 1995, 177; Roll 2015b; Schneiders 2013; Wittberg 1994).

When Sister Mabel referred to her 1970s involvement in public protests aimed directly against the Popes' and the Church's discriminatory stance on women as "fun" she recounted one instance where her activism did not have an immediate impact and a second one which did result in a momentous change:

> [In a city in the US] ... we've picketed the Holy Father coming ... all the religious getting out boycotting the event ... the nuns blocked the entrance ... with their placards "Go Home!" because he refused to meet with the religious sisters and they just wouldn't stand for it ... It didn't change anything. He didn't meet them.
>
> When the Holy Father came out, the girls could not serve on the altar ... I was in [a city in the US] and then the women got together and there were phone calls all over the place and we all picketed outside the cathedral ... They blocked the whole ... avenue and nobody could get to church ... Finally after an hour past Mass time, Cardinal [name of famous cardinal in the US] came out and he said, "I invite you all into the church and there will be girls serving on the altar" ... and they did and everybody put down their things [placards].

While Sister Mabel's second account illustrates how women's resistance both within and against the institutional Church is not always futile, it also points to the strategic spaces where Canadian women religious engage in activism. Sister Mabel and all the other sisters who recounted their public protests against the Church's discrimination against women all admitted that they did so in the United States, but not on Canadian soil. Sister Mabel underscored the improbability: "In Canada, never in a million years!" Then she offered the following reason: "But that was in [a US city], the [American] sisters ... they do a lot of that a lot more ... Oh! No [in Canada] we're much more ... conservative and much more placid and much more ... Canadian!"[4] While public demonstrations against the Roman Catholic Church's patriarchal constraints are indeed rare among Canadian women religious in part due to fear of consequences by "the local bishop" (Sister Joelle), they are nevertheless indicative of some sisters' willingness to express their intolerance openly despite potential repercussions.

Sister Mabel also added that even when they are not physically present within the United States, they still stand in solidarity with their progressive American counterparts: "The Leadership Conference of Women Religious [LCWR] in the States ... when there's some issue in the Church that they want us to sign a petition, they send that ... and it's usually signed." While some of those issues involve a range of social justice matters, they often pertain specifically to gender injustice within the Church. In fact, given the nature of its advocacy work, the LCWR is a testament to women religious' bonding together and collective refusal to accept institutionalized gender injustice by what is considered by some critics as "one of most oppressive of all religious superstructures [in other words, the Roman Catholic Church]" (Ruether 2003, 5). Unfortunately, however, the LCWR paid a high price for its outspokenness as it was scrutinized through a Vatican-based doctrinal assessment from 2008 to 2015. Yet, as difficult as that investigative process was for sisters who were both directly and indirectly affected, Sister Sarah viewed it somewhat optimistically as she considered the feminist activism under scrutiny as having been essential regardless of the repercussions: "To me it's like 'Oh! We're doing our job' in a sense when those kinds of things happen because I think that part of who we are is to make sure that ... that power is not abused ... there is a role I think for women religious to hold the hierarchy accountable."

As I explore next, Canadian sisters' campaign against Church-based gender discrimination is limited neither to American streets nor to collaboration with American sisters' initiatives. Canadian women religious are also engaging in well-founded, thoughtfully based, and inclusively oriented opposition strategies.

Sisters' collective opposition to Church-based gender discrimination

I sincerely hope that religious women, who have had many opportunities, will make some contribution toward correcting this false conception [of women's inferiority]. (Sister Shannon)

Sister Shannon's wish has been realized, at least partially, given that, as Dumont (1995, 184) has emphasized, there are enough signs to indicate that women religious are already redefining a new situation. Such is certainly the case with Sister Shannon's religious congregation, which sent an incisive message regarding gender discrimination in the Roman Catholic Church to the Canadian bishops via a Canadian Religious Conference survey in the mid-2010s.[5] Sister Sarah, a younger woman religious from one of three congregations whose sisters referred to this survey in their interviews, contextualized and rationalized the women's responses to the questionnaire: "it was really on the reality of how we experience the Church in Canada." Some of the many penetrating points that Sister Shannon's community raised included, but were not limited to:

Critiques.

We deplore that the Church continues its myopic and patriarchal obsession with celibate, male clergy only, giving that stance more importance than the right of God's people to regular Eucharistic Celebration.

We deplore the refusal by the Vatican even to be open to the question of a married clergy or the ordination of women.

We deplore the willingness of the Church in Canada and elsewhere to employ women as virtual pastors, especially in remote areas, while continuing to send out pointless directives about whether or not they can be in the sanctuary at ritual times, etc.

We deplore the real exclusion of women in the Church and the lack of a venue for true dialogue with the institutional Church.

Aspirations.

We hope for a venue for open dialogue with the Church where the experience of many women in the Church will be heard.

We hope that the hierarchy in the Church ... will allow for married, as well as celibate, male and female priests before this scandalous situation results in further division ...

We hope that the Church leaders will recognize the training and gifts of women, and their desire to serve God's people and that new opportunities will be created for women to exercise real authority in the Church restoring the full equality that Jesus envisioned ...

We long for the day ... when we women and our gifts will be truly valued and given an equal place in our Church, when a spirit of trust, open dialogue and the welcoming of questions will replace secretiveness and protectionism.

Such discerning statements reveal how, as Dumont (1995,184) predicted about a decade earlier, the patriarchal stronghold of the Roman Catholic Church has indeed triggered rigorous feminist opposition by the sisters. Similar to women's strategies in other conservative religious traditions who have sought to invert conventional hierarchies (Griffith 1997), they are also illustrative of women religious' capacities to develop feminist-based and soundly informed transformative strategies to effect change within the Roman Catholic Church. Sister Shannon's peer, Sister Theresa, underscored that such capacities entail the new circular governance model within their religious community that empowered and thus enabled their women's collective to generate such incisive critiques and to propose such insightful solutions.

The abovementioned declarations are further indicative of sisters' comprehensive attempts to counter their presumed religious identities that imply acquiescence (Ammerman 2003) and to then redraw the submissive roles that had been assigned to them as women and be prepared to face the consequences (Kaylin 2000, 12). Not surprisingly, there were repercussions to this rare openly pointed resistance against the Church hierarchy. According to Sisters Mabel and Edna, whose congregation[6] participated in the same process, "that created a stir" (Sister Edna) and "oh the bishops were wild with that, but no response" (Sister Mabel). The sisters were understandably frustrated by the male clerics' backlash and simultaneously disappointed with the Church hierarchy's lack of official consideration of their report into which they had invested much care and contemplation. Regardless of the outcome, this example illustrates how Sister Shannon's, Sister Mabel's, and Sister Edna's peers have joined the long line of strong-willed nuns who have courageously "contested the norms ... and [tried to] correct [...] them" (Chittister 1995, 12; Lux-Sterritt and Mangion 2011).

While Sister Joelle offered a pessimistic outlook ("Not in my lifetime, baby!") on the possibility of achieving gender equality within the current Church, some optimists feel that potential remains if women religious continue "stretching" the institution beyond its current restrictive form (Chittister 1995, 164–5). As such, women religious' feminist activism both within and against their own Church illustrates their shifting roles from "keepers" of tradition toward "changers" (Chittister 1995, 165), which also echoes Edwina Gateley's reference to women as "rebels" and "prophets"[7] as well as Sandra Schneiders' illustration of women religious as "prophets" who are the "prophetic lifeform in the Church" (Schneiders 2011, 71).

FEMINIST ADVOCACY, ACTION AND ACTIVISM BEYOND THE CHURCH

Some women religious have been feminist advocates and activists for as long as they can remember. Similar to Sister Irene Farmer (Anthony 1997b), Sister Clara claimed that her stance was shaped long before she entered religious life in 1955: "I was so strong before I ever entered on gender equality." Others recalled how they began to address women's rights in the 1960s amidst wider civil rights movements and the Second Vatican Council. Yet, as Dumont (1995, 170–1) has contended, concerns for women's conditions became even more central to Canadian congregations of women religious following International Women's Year in 1975 – the same year that the Women's Ordination Conference was founded and that the Leadership Conference of Women Religious prepared a study package entitled *Focus on Women*. Together, these initiatives led to the recognition of the role that religion had played in perpetuating gendered oppression and thus strengthened sisters' resolve to advocate for women's equality within the Roman Catholic Church (Ruether 2003, 5).

In this section, I explore how women religious' contemporary contributions have evolved into wider feminist advocacy, action, and activism that promote gender equality across a range of societal spheres. While there may be subtle differences among, as well as intertwining across advocacy, action, and activism, I distinguish them in order to illustrate the breadth of sisters' endeavours. While I concentrate on the feminist forms of all three levels of their initiatives, as Holtmann (2011b) clarifies, both their subtleties and intersections can also be understood within the modern Catholic approach to social action that many women's religious communities adopted based on the Second Vatican Council's primary document on Catholic social teachings, *Gaudium et spes*. Advocacy encompasses creating awareness about issues and/or speaking with/on behalf of marginalized people. Action refers primarily to the activities carried out to tangibly support marginalized people and to address their immediate needs; such social action most often takes on a charitable form (Holtmann 2011b). By contrast, activism involves concrete and potentially confrontational steps (e.g., protests, letter writing, etc.) to draw attention to issues and to effect social change (Mangion 2008, 112); it bears greater similarity to the second dimension of social action that focuses on first identifying the structural sources of inequalities and then engaging in efforts to change those "unjust structures" across political, economic, and even religious terrains (Holtmann 2011b, 141). As I shed light on the breadth and forms of their involvement, sisters' feminist endeavours prioritizing girls and women both locally and globally become apparent, as do their concurrent approaches of advocacy, action and activism-based social change (Holtmann 2011b).

Sisters' commitment to feminist advocacy

They [women religious] labored for the physical incorporation and the psychological worth of women in general ... they brought women to an educational plane where the impact and import of women was finally discussable on a grand scale. (Chittister 1995, 12)

Women religious have been raising awareness about women's rights in both personal and professional spaces for decades and arguably for centuries, although in earlier eras they did so simultaneously against a seemingly contradictory backdrop of training women toward gendered obedience (Chittister in Bonavoglia 2005; Magray 1998; Mangion 2008; Schneiders 2013). The following accounts shed light on a range of opinions and efforts by current and former sisters as they relate to how they advocate for women in contemporary contexts. For example, as one who claims to engage in feminist work both within and outside the Church, Naomi integrates feminist-based and pro-equality approaches in both her spiritual and personal endeavours by simultaneously moving beyond gender-based distinctions and drawing attention to gender inequity:

> Well for me, the gender question is not important. The question is like what needs to be done and who has the gifts to do it? And around [our church] ... I'm very insistent that women have a very collaborative role, and for example, and this is a non-clerical thing too, but we were working toward the creation of this healing centre ... so within those healing services, leadership is offered by the ordained, the unordained, men, and women. So I mean, I just, and in my personal life, I've always encouraged my students, and my nieces and nephews to not think gender lines. It's also to recognize that gender inequality is very entrenched, so it's real; it has to be addressed.

Similar to Naomi's encompassing stance, other sisters' pro-equality advocacy is informed by their growing awareness and appreciation of the notion of oneness. For example, Sister Clara insisted very emphatically that, "we are one family. It is one earth ... It's all connected, like human rights, gender rights ... women have a ... basic right to equality." Sister Noreen also promotes gender parity based on a non-hierarchical circular-based model of being:

> I advocate for it ... if ... there is some injustice going on, I will always speak about it okay; I will ... try to see what I can do about that, at least draw attention but I'm coming at it not as a woman; I'm coming at it as ... we are all one ... we're all equal in the eyes of God ... there's no more pyramid, just one big circle, so ... from that ... [I ask], "What are you doing putting this person down?"

While some may perceive Sister Noreen's view as not being reflective of feminist advocacy, it is important to note how many women religious and their congregations operate based not on a non-feminist model but rather on a post-feminist stance and/or often through eco-feminist approaches that encompass broader earth-centred and even universe-centred views that bring all relations into perspective (Chittister 1995). Sister Loretta proudly highlighted how she and her religious community engage in pro-equality advocacy:

> I do! I do! I think the congregation does quite a bit. But I do whenever I have the chance … I work a lot with sisters right now … but in doing that, I can help a lot of people too who are … out there … to encourage them or to be, you know, an advocate … for them. A lot of them that I work with have trouble with the Church! [laughs] And so we try to work around that.

While Sister Loretta's feminist advocacy may have been concentrated more recently among women religious, other sisters have advocated on behalf of other laywomen and, in some cases, women living in vulnerable contexts. For example, after hearing what she perceived to be a patriarchal message by a diocesan bishop in the mid-1990s, Sister Theresa came immediately to the defence of the Indigenous women whose choices he had criticized:

> [I] argued strongly with the Bishop about how like a lot of young people in that [First Nations] village were living together and not married. The Bishop went at them one day … I couldn't believe my ears when I heard him, in his last sermon before he left, talk about people living together who aren't married … When he came back to the trailer after, I said, "What got into you … that you went off on that angle in your last homily before you left here?" I was in tears … I was so upset with him and he knew it. He said, "Why do they do it?" and I said, "The women don't marry the men they're living with for the safety of their children." Well, I had to explain that to him … the women knew that if she married the guy, he owned her and he could do anything. He could be unfaithful to her and as long as she didn't marry him, he remained faithful and he didn't abuse the children and he wasn't drinking and running around … and until that woman really got to a point where she could trust him, she wouldn't marry him!

That Sister Theresa felt comfortable to criticize a bishop's homily is significant in and of itself, but to have challenged him on patriarchal grounds, and intensely so, is indicative of the risk that some sisters are willing to take in order to defend women's positions among Church authorities.

Echoing the integrity of women that Sister Theresa emphasized, Sister Jeanette explained how she seeks to advance gender equality by trying to affirm the other laywomen who work with her at her motherhouse and particularly those who have been in abusive relationships: "I try to help them see their value and their dignity as a person." She and numerous sisters, in their roles as spiritual directors, teachers, and relatives, have supported countless female victims of abuse, including women who endured decades of domestic violence as per their parish priests' instructions like the one Darlene assisted, as well as victims of clerical sexual abuse (Bouclin 2006). It is in these counselling contexts that sisters have respected women's accounts and have emphasized women's empowerment. Such examples are reflective of the multiplying effects generated when sisters integrate feminist orientations into various facets of their daily commitments.

In addition to their own individual moments where they have advocated on behalf of women, the sisters and especially their entire communities via their justice-oriented offices have also organized collective initiatives in which they create awareness about gendered vulnerabilities. Many congregations have organized awareness campaigns, hosted meetings, workshops, and conferences that have included prominent keynote speakers, developed specific pages on their websites, set up and maintained blogs, prepared and disseminated bulletins, brochures, and research reports, as well as produced countrywide theatrical presentations on issues affecting women including but not limited to homelessness, poverty, mental health, domestic violence, human trafficking, sexual exploitation, migration, addiction, parenting, Internet-based danger, and war. Regarding the latter, Darlene explained how she has addressed it in her retreats both within and outside sisters' spirituality centres: "I think war is patriarchal ... so I brought a feminist critique to that a long time ago." Such advocacy-based initiatives often feature dynamic and contemporary presentation methods, experiential accounts of women's lived experiences, and critical and intersectional feminist analyses that identify the wider structural, societal and global factors that render women more vulnerable to the stifling struggles mentioned above (Collins 2015; Shih 2010).

The justice-oriented offices that facilitate so many of the sisters' advocacy-oriented projects also reflect yet another wise organizational management strategy on their part. Many of the sisters' congregations have created and separately incorporated non-governmental organizations (NGOs) through which much of their feminist and social justice advocacy is carried out. Some of these NGOs have status at the federal government level and/or at the United Nations where the sisters can purposefully advocate for change. By establishing these separately incorporated entities, the sisters have strategically situated their advocacy work at arms-length from their religious communities, which constitutes a safeguarded position from where they can protect their fellow sisters from potential clerical scrutiny, antifeminist backlash, and financial liability.

Sisters' commitment to feminist action

> *Most of all, women's religious life has been significant in the education of other women. Feminism, the consciousness of the graced and gracing nature of women despite the subordinating role definitions to which they were subject, is one of the gifts of religious life across time.* (Chittister 1995, 12)

Sisters' and former sisters' "creative ways to help people" (Sister Ella) have consisted of engagement in many societal contexts. While Canadian women religious have been involved in the education and employment training of girls and women for centuries (Smyth 2007), they have widened their scope, particularly since the mid-twentieth century. Sisters are now founding and/ or financing women's shelters, women's drop-in programs, affordable housing projects for women, centres for victims of sexual violence, as well as school, home, and childcare support for young single mothers (Dumont 1995, 170–1).

It is significant to note that over the past few decades, the sisters' communities have been intentionally concentrating their efforts on initiating and sponsoring numerous local and international projects that specifically support girls' and women's safety, education, employment, and housing (Dumont 1995; Gervais and Turenne Sjolander 2015). Sister Joelle explained her community's distinct shift in support:

> We provide bursaries … a lot of congregations provide bursaries for women to study … When I was on the council … [in the] early '80s, we were elected and in our financial donations we were giving at that time a lot to the different men's orders … so we cut that out and … we prioritize women and children … I think that's pretty general with women's congregations now.

Seven of the eight congregations have established and supported housing projects for homeless women and sole support mothers within their communities. Mindful of appropriateness, the women's orders that have initiated the projects themselves have been thorough in their preparation including the completion of needs assessments. Others have made major financial contributions toward safe housing for women affected by domestic violence. In addition, all the congregations manage bursary programs that support girls' and women's education both in Canada and abroad. The global reach of the sisters' commitment to women's equality is considerable given how they support bursary, microcredit, housing, and human rights education projects for thousands of girls and women in eight African, Asian, and Latin American countries where they operate missions. Nevertheless, it is important to distinguish that their projects are often non-denominational and are therefore inclusive. Based on my own observations of Canadian women religious' projects in seven countries in the Americas, their contemporary mission work is less about evangelization than it is about promoting human rights, gender equality, social justice, education, health care, and environmental protection. For example, Naomi described her direct involvement with a pro-feminist project in a central African country in activist, not religious terms: "I was working with ... a project to support the women, the widows to become more ... self-reliant ... and self-sufficient ... I felt ... I was protesting what had happened by putting myself out to try and create another alternative."

Some sisters reflected on the multiplying effects of their equality-oriented priorities in the countries where they served as missionaries. For instance, Sister Corinne's favourite moment as a nun was related to the increasing gender equity resulting from the girls' education in which she was involved during her missionary work in Africa: "As I saw the girls being educated and moving on to ... professions and ... taking their place ... that was very fulfilling." Similarly, Sister Shannon felt proud of women's progress in a Latin American country where she served for decades:

> Women's attitude changed as young people received a basic education which enabled them to continue their studies and prepare themselves as professional teachers, lawyers, doctors, and nurses. They gained a sense of their worth and ability. Even simple courses given in the [countryside] on the dignity of the person and leadership skills changed their attitude as to the role they had not only in their family but also the impact they could have in their own communities. It was delightful to observe. Perhaps the progress of their children as they continued their studies gave them further reason to feel comfortable with themselves. Leaders for different activities came forth and they took their place with dignity and made very worthwhile contributions with their heretofore hidden gifts.

The accounts of Sisters Joelle, Corinne, and Shannon illustrate that women religious' involvement in pro-equality and pro-empowerment initiatives, resulting in concrete changes in women's lives in Canada and elsewhere, have been considerable and consequential. These accomplishments have undoubtedly been made possible by these Canadian sisters' relatively sound financial footing, secured primarily by their wise financial stewardship and often salaried professional positions, that has enabled them to carry out their feminist endeavours with greater financial ease.[8] Yet, it is essential to point out an interesting irony. While many, but certainly not all, congregations of women religious in

Canada may be more financially stable than their counterparts in the United States, and have thus been able to support multiple feminist and social justice projects, as Sister Mabel attests, they are comparatively less vocal and less publically "activist" about their feminist endeavours than their more open US colleagues who have tended to experience greater financial constraints (Ebaugh 1993, 170). Even so, regardless of how inconspicuous Canadian sisters' feminist engagement may be, it has certainly taken on activist forms in both Canada and abroad.

Sisters' commitment to feminist activism

> ... *engaging together in resistance to oppression and the creative praxis of liberation* ... (Johnson 2002a, 63)

These declaratory words by renowned feminist sister-scholar Elizabeth Johnson capture the essence of many women religious' activism which has long focused on countering and transforming the structural dimensions of gender inequality, among many other forms of injustice (Schneiders 2013; Wittberg 1994). While women religious have responded to girls' and women's immediate educational, employment, and safety needs for centuries, and still do, many of them have also dedicated considerable human and financial resources toward initiatives aimed at more fundamental, systematic, and sustainable changes in favour of gender equality (Dumont 1995; Schneiders 2013; Wittberg 1994). These structural approaches are further indicative of how, regardless of whether or not they self-identify as feminist of any strand, forward-thinking Catholic sisters are attentive to and engage in relatively critical and intersectional feminist projects (Ammerman 2003; Collins 2015; Shih 2010). While some religious communities are explicit in identifying gender injustice as one of their priority issues, others address it concretely by the specific societal issues (e.g., the abduction and trafficking of girls) upon which they concentrate their activist efforts.

The sisters' feminist activism has been undertaken in various forms and to varying degrees. Whether they are selected individually by sisters themselves or organized systematically by entire religious communities, the sisters have initiated and/or participated in campaigns, marches, vigils, petitions, letter writing,[9] and boycotts on issues pertaining to women's rights, including human trafficking, sexual exploitation, women's incarceration, missing Indigenous women, female refugees and migrants, violence against women, and women's victimization in conflict-affected areas, among many others.

Human trafficking has been a particularly significant issue upon which women religious have invested considerably, especially since the turn of the twenty-first century and apparently so much so that Sister Joelle contends that Canadian sisters have been at the "forefront" of advocacy efforts on this issue. All the congregations affiliated with the women religious I interviewed have dedicated significant attention, time, financial resources, web pages, and office space to activist efforts (e.g., events and projects) aimed at preventing and ending all forms of human trafficking, especially those affecting women and children. Beyond their congregational commitment to this issue via their own justice-oriented offices, some women religious, including Sisters Adele, Agnes, Corinne, and Sarah, have been involved in founding and leading secular non-governmental organizations committed to preventing human trafficking.

The sisters' rationales for engaging in activism related to all of these gendered issues reflect their profound concerns with and critiques of the multiple structural impediments as well as their persistent dedication to transformational and sustainable progress. Such reasons and actions are a testament to their willingness to adapt their attention and energy to evolving societal issues, as well as to their informed, incisive, and intersectional feminist and social justice lenses which, arguably, serve as expressions and examples of critical praxis (Collins 2015; hooks 2000; Shih 2010).

As Darlene reflected on her activist efforts over the years, the evolving nature of her engagement became apparent:

> I worked with a lot of women's groups, women in poverty groups. I worked ecumenically with Women's InterChurch Council of Canada. I was the social justice chair and I sat on the board for that for two terms. So it was about ten years of my life given to that group and that was a feminist group … one of the things that I introduced at that time that still happens is … the national prayer in December for the Montreal Massacre … The Aboriginal Lost Sisters, I was still working with them when that started; so we started to make connections with Aboriginal women. So … I'm very conscious of … African women, Afghan women, and … reaching out to women internationally. But I'm not so much activist … like I sign lots of things on the Internet and I'm a member of Avaaz and … lots of stuff like that but I do less [street-based] activism.[10]

Darlene may seem to be downplaying her feminist engagement as she is distinguishing between the various types of initiatives of which she has been, or still is, a part. Yet her own comparison is understandable given that in previous decades, Darlene was involved in a number of public protests, including an anti-war demonstration where she dumped garbage on the lawn of the American consulate while she was in full habit. She went on to explain how her feminist-oriented spiritual and activist contributions are intertwined at this stage in her life: "It comes out in other ways … absolutely. I'm doing a women's retreat … I'm going to do women's scripture stories; it's gonna be a part of that. You know what I'm saying? It's all integrated at this point. But I'm less activist about it." Darlene is implying here that as she conveys women's scrip-ture-based accounts, she draws attention to silenced women in the Christian biblical tradition and, as she does, she relates biblical women's experiences to both the subordination and the contributions of women in political, economic, cultural, and social contexts both historically and contemporarily. Similar to Sister Agnes' staging of the women-centred play, Darlene's work is part of a wider effort to contextualize and critique biblical texts and narratives through a feminist lens so as to draw attention to the problematic gendered aspects of their production, silences, and contradictions, as well as to advance transfor-mative meanings in contemporary contexts (Molesky-Poz 2003, 26; Schenk 2017). Thus, Darlene's retreat facilitation is infused with multiple strands of feminist advocacy and analyses simultaneously. For example, her analysis of gender inequality within the Bible, no matter how critical it may be, reflects a religious liberal feminist approach because it remains rooted in, and thereby does not constitute a rejection of, the Christian and Catholic religious tradi-tions (Shih 2010). Yet, some radical religious and intersectional feminist dimen-sions are also apparent as she draws attention to a multiplicity of structural impediments (Collins 2015; Shih 2010).[11]

Although Darlene may be involved in what she perceives to be moder-ated activism, the diversity and depth of her feminist engagement is further evidenced by her involvement with Avaaz, which should not be overlooked, given how that global Web-based organization's numerous activist initiatives, including petitions and marches, occur frequently, and many of the issues it addresses involve various forms of abuse against women. Furthermore, while some current and former sisters' activism may be less physically based and thus not involve street-level protests, given their advanced age, their letter-writing and petition-signing, often via the Internet, is a sign that sisters, even some of the most elderly ones, are still engaging in feminist activist efforts and arguably in partially fourth-wave feminist tactics through twenty-first-century Web-based technologies, which in some cases have rather effective outcomes.[12]

While Darlene may have been winding down her street-level activism, other sisters have been ramping theirs up in recent years despite their advanced age. When Sister Corinne returned to Canada to "retire" at the turn of the mil-lennium, she shifted her energies from the feminist-informed education of girls on another continent, which she had overseen for forty years, and toward street-side marches and vigils in Canada. She proudly explained that, "when I came to Canada in 2000 ... I started getting involved with groups." As part of a women-centred organization, Sister Corinne participated regularly in protest vigils in front of government buildings, often in extreme sub-zero temperatures – a testament to her dedication to feminist activism. She, along with many sisters from other congregations, also regularly attended feminist-oriented and uni-versity-based conferences on or around the eighth of March – International Women's Day. Her description of the protests and conferences as being "quite feminist ... quite ... strong" is illustrative of both her awareness and articu-lation of her feminist engagement. In the next section, I demonstrate how abortion represents an issue through which some women religious' activism is both "feminist" and "strong" yet also deeply convoluted.

Sisters' complex encounters with abortion-related activism

Contraception and abortion constitute controversial issues around which many nuns have manifested their feminist critique against the Roman Cath-olic Church's teachings and policies. In fact, 84 percent of the sisters and former sisters I interviewed reported their disagreement with the Church's stance on contraception and abortion.[13] While the women's opposition to Catholic Church doctrine on this subject may be trenchant, their attitudes and approaches toward the issues illustrate how their feminist orientations and faith-based traditions not only conflict but also coalesce – an actuality that further substantiates sisters' intersecting identities and practices across complex contexts, no matter how vexed the feminist and Catholic communities may perceive it to be (Ammerman 2003; Holtmann 2011a). The contention by hooks (2000, 6) – that a woman can choose not to have an abortion yet be pro-choice and still be an advocate of feminism – lends credence to the intersected standpoint through which a woman may be both personally "Catholic" and publically or politically "feminist."

As they negotiate their faith and feminist stance simultaneously in this regard, the women religious convey compassion, rather than judgment and rejection. While ethical tensions and emotional struggles linger, it is consid-eration, concern, and care – which are arguably both faith-filled and feminist principles – that prevail as they advocate for women's rights (Holtmann 2011a). In this light, I briefly illustrate the sisters' nuanced pro-life stance and their complex opinions of and encounters with pro-life protestors.[14] What is most revealing in these examples, perhaps because it seems unexpected of Catholic nuns, is their intentional non-participation in anti-abortion activism.

Sisters' nuanced pro-life stance and refusal to stand with pro-lifers. Stereo-types of religious institutions and their members may likely lead one to assume that when abortion-related demonstrations occur, all Catholic nuns would be found on the side of the street where the anti-abortion pickets are waved and pro-life slogans are chanted. While many of the women I interviewed did acknowledge that several of their conservative counterparts within their own religious communities have organized and/or attended pro-life protests, they themselves actually disagreed with a strict pro-life stance. Interestingly, some sisters disclosed less of the "expected" rigid religious outlooks and more of the "surprisingly" feminist stances they held:

> Well, I don't toe the party line. I find the pro-life movement one issue and quite anti-Christian in its approach. Oh, no I just get really turned off. (Sister Joelle)

> [It] is difficult … see what I do is not so much anti[-abortion] [laughs] as really advocating for the dignity of all people. (Sister Sarah)

Such critical and inclusive considerations form the backdrop of many sisters' unexpected abortion-related activism. While it would be rare to find a Canadian sister standing on the pro-choice side of a street-level demonstration, some, like Sisters Loretta and Adele, refuse to stand publically on the pro-life side of the street:

> I guess if there's any issue that gets to me it's the pro-life people. I mean I don't believe in abortion … But they are so self-righteous. Oh my! I just find them very judgmental and very self-righteous … we have them in the community and they're very, very hard to deal with … because … it's the one issue that clouds everything else … and … if I say, "I don't believe in abortion" [and] somebody says to me … "Well why aren't you out picketing?" [I respond], "Well I just don't feel like going out picketing right now." … It's not a one issue. There are many, many issues out there. (Sister Loretta)

> I want to be pro all of life … I don't believe abortion is a good thing and I want to be compassionate with anybody who's had one … and I guess I feel really sad that for the most part, pro-life is used in a very narrow sense … So I find I can't stand with a group that would call themselves pro-life because of the way they stand and maybe because of some of the other things they stand for that are not pro all of life … So for me the pro-life stance means that we include everyone. It means we protect the life of the unborn. It means we don't go to war [laughs] … It means we care for all as well as we can through all of life and now it even means caring for all of Creation; it's not just about humanity. It's about caring for this beautiful planet with all of the life on it. So I mean pro-life is so huge and I can say I'm pro-life if that's … the description. (Sister Adele)

Such nuancing of their pro-life stance and their refusal to picket publically against abortion speaks volumes about their more encompassing approach to the complexities of life. Such a broader vision also enabled Sister Adele to participate fully in a demonstration that advocated gender equality without feeling conflicted about being involved in the protest alongside pro-choice activists as the other laywomen who boycotted the march did:

> I remember the March for Women, the CWL [Catholic Women's League] withdrew because there were some groups that supported abortion who were part of the March for Women ... in ... something like 2003 ... it was connected with International Women's Day in one of those years ... we went out to join the March.

Sister Maureen took a position similar to that of Sister Adele as she critiqued a Church-based boycott against a Catholic aid organization:

> There's been some leak about Development and Peace money going toward abortion. The money [from collections in church] is not going there now ... [People are being told to] put it toward wherever you'd like ... and that is bothersome and I just think what's going to happen with Development and Peace and the excellent work that's been done?

Here, Sister Maureen is making reference to how in 2009 Church officials recommended that parishioners redirect their donations that are usually allocated toward Development and Peace during Lent because it was alleged[15] that the Catholic-based international development organization was supporting contraception and abortion in economically developing nations. Sister Maureen is clearly less concerned about the abortion aspect; rather, she recognizes and values the broader vision and benefit of the organization and thus perceives the Church's and parishioners' boycott tactics to be narrow-minded and limiting.

Taken together, Sisters Adele's and Maureen's reflections are illustrative of profound, yet somewhat unexpected positions among women religious. That Catholic nuns partook in a pro-women's demonstration and supported an international development organization that upheld women's reproductive rights, while Catholic lay people avoided them in order to underscore their anti-abortion stance, points to the all-embracing understandings through which sisters engage in feminist and social justice activism, as well as to "the different [and sometimes unexpected] practices through which women [religious] assert themselves as feminists" (Shih 2010, 222).

On the other side of anti-abortion protests. While the above-mentioned nuns' omission of anti-abortion activism may be difficult for some readers to comprehend, sisters' confrontations with pro-life protestors may be even harder to understand. Yet, one of the women I interviewed did experience such a troubling encounter.

While still a nun, Darlene recalled the ostracizing attacks by anti-abortion protestors:

> The whole right-to-life thing ... that's a very difficult and painful issue. But I had once gone to visit a student of mine who had had an abortion and the abortions were done in a wing, and so you could exit from the hospital from that wing and I came out and here were all these local "right-to-lifers" ... I was still in the habit in those days ... so they recognized me: "Sister, what are you doing in there?" and they started to push and shove me ... and I said, "Well you're not respecting my life right now, just get out of my way" ... They really were ... holding the rosary beads at me and ... they literally pushed me ...
>
> They were really very condemnatory of me. They were all Catholic; some of them I recognized from the [name] parish ... a couple of them were Catholic Women's League people and I had given them retreats ... they were just not nice to me and I said ... "You don't know what you're talking about; there's pain on both sides of this" ... But that's all I said because they just shouted me down ... So that wasn't a very good experience ... Besides I knew some stories of very sad cases ... and this case was one of them, where people had chosen the abortion route ... she was suicidal that day too ... and her story was just the worst kind of horror story you could imagine.

Darlene's valuing of her compassionate presence with the young woman over the Catholic Church's moral code, as well as her self-defence against anti-abortionists' scorn may seem uncharacteristic of Catholic nuns who are stereotypically associated with the pro-life movement. Yet, many other sisters shared the same outlook:

> You know, I worked with people who've had abortions and glory be to God! What they suffered ... But you don't judge them I mean. Oh! [sigh] (Sister Loretta)

> I'm anti-abortion but ... it's such a narrow ... they're fanatics almost; the Church is; it's all they ever get on is abortion! ... and I tell you ... the stuff I've seen over the years and the Church wasn't there for them, and their families weren't even there for them, you know! So there's all human dimensions in everything. (Sister Clara)

> I think ... we have ... [to] reach out and be compassionate too and we don't understand the reasons why ...We can't be judgmental. (Sister Jeanette)

Such empathetic attitudes undoubtedly influence women religious' motivation to engage less in anti-abortion activism. However, Church traditionalists and authorities perceive such non-attention to and non-engagement with anti-abortion crusades as problematic. In the case of women religious' congregations in the United States who were investigated between 2008 and 2015, the non-prioritization of pro-life efforts was actually considered a form of dissent and thus grounds for extended monitoring by the Vatican (Araujo-Hawkins 2016). By contrast and with a view to deepening understandings regarding coalescing and intersecting, rather than conflicting, religious and gendered identities and practices, I draw again on hooks (2000) to put forth a more encompassing interpretation of Catholic women religious' complex positions on abortion. By following hooks' (2000) aforementioned logic, one may also reason that just as a Catholic sister's personal choice not to have [or even agree with] an abortion should not make her any less feminist, at least when she is publically pro-choice (hooks 2000, 6), a Catholic sister's non-participation in anti-abortion protests should not make her any less Catholic.

Given the sisters' preference toward compassionate approaches in contradistinction to the appalling Church corruption and clerical control revealed earlier in Darlene's accounts (recall the plight of the sexually violated African sisters and Bosnian women), it can no longer be surprising that women religious have aligned themselves with many other Catholic women who have parted company with the Roman Catholic Church over the contentious issue of abortion (Bonavoglia 2005; Kalven 2003). In addition to the moral and emotional anguish that sisters may experience in this regard, their acknowledgement and analysis of the complications and contradictions therein are a testament to the structural level awareness and thus the intersectional depth that they bring to bear on all the gendered issues that they attempt to address within all of their feminist activism (Collins 2015).

CONCLUSION

By continuing to help women know their own dignity, I have hope that this attitude toward women will eventually change ... I do believe that women's rights are gradually being acknowledged. (Sister Shannon)

Women religious who are feminist activists are already contributing considerably to the imperative changes to which Sister Shannon refers, and they are doing so on multiple levels and in relatively intersectional ways (Collins 2015). Whether it is noticed or not by a wider public audience, women religious' feminist engagement must be considered significant for two important reasons. First, given that historically Catholic nuns did problematically indoctrinate gender inequality across multiple settings including schools, parishes, hospitals, prisons, workhouses, and foreign missions, their steadfast emphases on and efforts toward gender equality in the late twentieth and early twenty-first centuries constitute a fundamental shift in how they address gendered actualities. While some critics may view this shift as paradoxical, I contend that one must consider instead how it uncovers the complexity and duality of the roles that women religious have played as they too have negotiated gendered constraints from a relatively marginal position within the Roman Catholic Church and in society.

Second, while their prioritization of girls and women is exemplary in and of itself, their feminist advocacy and activism, that entail profoundly critical analyses and astute opposition against gendered oppression and its structural sources, as well as nuanced considerations of women's rights, demonstrate how many of them are both leading and modelling the penetrative efforts required to counteract systemic patriarchal domination in both their institutional Church and in society (Chittister 1995; Dumont 1995; Johnson 2002a, Ruether 2003; Schneiders 2013).

Nevertheless, as some sisters point out, there may understandably be fluctuating degrees of engagement going forward:

> Now there'll be varying levels of commitment because ... [softly] we're not too active anymore ... our average age is ... pretty high. (Sister Marian)

> A number of the sisters ... would not have agreed ... So congregations aren't uniform in this ... and there are a number of sisters ... who are quite happy with the hierarchal Church, the status quo and so on. (Sister Joelle)

Sister Joelle mentioned this constraint as she reflected on an instance when she wished that she had participated in a weekly protest advocating for women's ordination, but she refrained from doing so because she was the leader of her congregation at the time and was thus concerned about the public representation of her feminist stance when it was not shared by all members of her religious community. Despite these potential impediments, feminist activism among women religious does not yet appear to be over nor likely to end anytime soon, especially given their tenacity, their prophetic call, and their infrastructural might. First of all, their tenacity is indisputable – that women religious, many of whom are at very advanced stages of life including some who are well into their 80s and 90s, are still engaged in feminist endeavours at all is indicative of their enduring commitment to gender equality, and they do not appear to be relenting on this matter in the foreseeable future – neither individually nor collectively.

Furthermore, as Sister Joelle explained, both their prophetic and organizational positioning appears timely and compelling vis-à-vis their advancement of gender equality:

> I do think the call now for religious is to be prophetic … We have a network, we have supports, where often lay people don't … So I think it behooves us to assume that role more and more and I find myself willing to do so … To speak more and more freely.

As Sister Joelle and others like Sisters Shannon and Agnes contend, women religious can and should continue to play a pivotal role in helping to uphold women's rights. Their organizational and financial stewardship will undoubtedly facilitate their ongoing involvement and enduring impact. Thus, whether their endeavours remain clandestine for the sake of either strategy or modesty, or publically known for the sake of modelling and exemplifying, they should be regarded as noticeably significant, and sociologically so, given that women religious are one of the Roman Catholic Church's greatest threats to patriarchal power and thus also one of its most valuable resources, especially to the feminist cause (Chittister 1995; Reed 2004; Schneiders 2004). In this light, feminist nuns' potential as well as their proven capacities in societal spheres should not be discounted by secular activists.

Conclusion

Indeed we are not finished. The struggle for women is only just begun ... But it is precisely now we must not stop or we will stand to lose our hearts along the way. (Chittister 2004, 175)

In order to bring to the forefront Ontario-based Canadian sisters' resistance to their own and other women's sidelined status in the Roman Catholic Church, I have explored the patriarchal control they faced, the feminist critiques they generated, and the women-led spiritual and leadership contributions they advanced in the late twentieth and early twenty-first centuries beyond the Church altars dominated by male priests. By rendering both current and former sisters more visible through illustrations of their opinions, impediments, and accomplishments, I have shown how women religious who continue to be marginalized are at least no longer completely silenced because they have challenged gender injustice and have asserted gender equality, both subtly and overtly (Nason-Clark and Fisher-Townsend 2005). As such, their contemporary forms of individual and collective resistance, resilience, and resourcefulness have countered "outdated and belittling stereotypes" of nuns as passive, compliant, and subservient women (Coburn and Smith 1999; Kristof 2010; Mangion 2008; Sullivan 2005).

The women's accounts have also demonstrated how they have carefully mastered the tightrope of patriarchal constraint and obstructed originality. As I alluded to the tightrope in the introduction, I referred intentionally to "seemingly thwarted innovation." While the sisters' innovation may no longer appear thwarted in light of their all-encompassing endeavours, inevitably their freedom was, and still remains, hindered to varying degrees given that they have felt compelled to ingeniously render many of their practices clandestine in order to protect them and themselves from scrutiny and control by the Church's male clerical hierarchy. Nevertheless, like that of their counterparts across time and location, they have often risen above their stifled autonomy, and they have been innovative and productive in doing so (Gray 2007; Magray 1998; Mangion 2008). It is for this reason that the term "seemingly" was employed deliberately; it conveys a sense that while their innovation may appear to be thwarted, and is indeed, it is not absolutely so, as has been illustrated by their accomplishments in both open and underground spheres beyond the altar – spheres which also constitute, at least metaphorically but perhaps also literally, their own altars.

The image of the tightrope thus serves to understand the paradox of women religious' lives as they experience both restriction and liberation, both conflict and consensus (Mangion 2008), both rejection and involvement (Schneiders 2013), as well as power within constraint (Gray 2007). While on the one hand, the sisters' place on the tightrope remains a source of frustration due to the ongoing gendered restraints, on the other hand, and as I underscore next, it is the emancipation and innovation resulting from women religious' strategic mastering of the tightrope that are both illustrative and representative.

ILLUSTRATING GENDERED EMANCIPATION AND INNOVATION

The myriad examples throughout this book illustrate how women religious challenged patriarchal authority in an effort to both regain and maintain autonomy over their activities (Coburn and Smith 1999, 222). Their ability to move beyond patriarchal constraints, and their reasons for doing so, reveal a great deal about the ingenuity of the women religious featured herein. Rather than be stifled by power struggles (Magray 1998; Mangion 2008), the sisters often circumvented them by pursuing productive alternatives. As such, through their interweaving of and advancements in feminist spirituality, governance, and activism in the latter part of the twentieth century and in the earlier part of the twenty-first century, the Ontario-based women religious featured herein have been protagonists transforming consciousness and propelling change *by*, *with*, and *for* women toward indispensable spiritual, governmental, and societal renewal (Chittister 1995, 12; Gervais 2015; Schneiders 2004, 111).

The sisters' multipronged feminist engagement is an undeniable manifestation of their shifting religious identities, priorities, and practices. In this way, women religious have been contributing significantly and profoundly within gendered spheres and by extension they have been transcending gendered boundaries (Mangion 2008, 235). Just as women religious of earlier centuries hold an important place in the gender history of their particular eras (Mangion 2008, 238), contemporary women religious still play a significant role not only in showing us a "world that is gendered" (Neitz 2003, 293) and particularly their own "everyday world" (Ammerman 2003, 209) but also in actually shaping gendered dynamics and overcoming gendered oppression both within and outside of the institutional Roman Catholic Church.

Along parallel lines, while Canadian historians of women religious (e.g., Bruno-Jofré 2007; Gresko 2007; MacDonald 2007; McGahan 2007; and Smyth 2007) shed essential light on sisters' past contributions to the foundational infrastructure of Canada in the areas of education, health care, and social work, as well as toward post–Vatican II advancements, I have emphasized their more contemporary involvement in feminist leadership within spiritual, governmental, and activist endeavours including those in the twenty-first century. Similarly, while historians of women religious (e.g., Coburn and Smith 1999, Gray 2007, Magray 1998, Mangion 2008) often illustrate nuns' input toward the growth and reform of Catholicism, as well as Catholic education in past eras, I have called attention to their present-day innovations, many of which occur outside, and in some cases quite far beyond, the "Catholic" realm and its exclusionary altars.

This emphasis on "beyond" also applies to their transformative tactics involving counter-hegemonic governance and activism. Of central importance here is how the sisters' expressions and practices of faith have not only taken less institutional forms compared to the Church's male clerics, but they are also indicative of their resistance against the hierarchical pressure toward institutionalization (Wiesner 1993). It is through such a-institutional choices, including moving beyond both rule-bound religiosity and institutional preservation, that women religious are not only engendering autonomy that is beneficial to themselves but are simultaneously accomplishing a great deal for those whom they serve and with those whom they work (Lux-Sterritt and Mangion 2011, 2, 7; Sullivan 2005).

Representing gender equality, strategic spaces, and inclusive processes

Gender equality. As many women religious, including Naomi and Sister Sarah, have explained, they have intentionally modelled themselves as feminists and women leaders in order to exemplify strategies not only of resistance against patriarchal control but also of inclusive spirituality, non-hierarchical governance and feminist activism (Mangion 2008, 234; Reed 2004, 329). What is particularly significant about their modelling of strategies is not only what they have done in terms of gender equality but also where and how they have done so.

Strategic spaces: Readily "under the radar" and willingly "under the wire." While some women religious are known to have "emerg[ed] from the shadows" in order to assert their gender rights within the Roman Catholic Church (Kaylin 2000, 12), others, like the majority of women I interviewed, prefer to work strategically within the shadows in order to maximize their potential without clerical interference. As previously illustrated, yet worth repeating, such preferences were variously expressed by both current and former sisters. Rather than being deterred by patriarchal exclusion, recall how Sister Noreen readily flies "under the radar" in broader locations beyond the institutional Church. Similarly, it was Sister Sarah who underscored both the intentionality and necessity of working strategically and quietly in order to protect their endeavours: "It causes a lot of conflict because ... there's a lot of good that's done under the wire that in some ways we would be jeopardizing by becoming so public."

Gratefully "off the grid," fortunately "on the fringe," and eagerly "on the edge." Comparably, the women's preference toward the periphery was also articulated imaginatively. While the marginalized status of women religious within the institutional Church remains a serious source of contention, some women are actually more comfortable with both their conviction and their location. Recall how Naomi asserted that her people-based notion of church is just as valid as the institutional Church but that her version was "just not on the power grid." Likewise, recall Darlene's contentedness and confidence as she explained how she favoured operating "on the fringe" as she worked within a justice-oriented sisters' ministry that was "not part of the officialdom." By extension, Sister Ella illustrated that she eagerly works "on the edge" so that she can be away from the "centres of power" and thus more attentive to "the people's needs." It may be difficult for many observers to comprehend such preferences especially when fury and frustration would be understandable reactions in light of the ongoing marginalization that is still quite prevalent. Yet, such stances are illustrative of the sisters' conceptual and practical intentions. Conceptually, the sisters' attitudes reveal their awareness of what the "centre" of the Church represents, as well as why and how they avoid it as they concentrate on other priorities (Ammerman 2003). Practically, their approaches demonstrate how rather than being stifled by their dislocation or discouraged by the undeniable and sometimes overwhelming constraints they face on the periphery of the Church, many sisters and former sisters view this decentred position as ideal and capitalize on it especially for the benefit of others. Thus, it is in women religious' own recentring of both themselves and their work within decentred spheres that they serve as models of resilience and ingenuity, and by extension they also serve as models of women-centred productivity within their own spaces far beyond the Roman Catholic Church's patriarchal altars.

Modelling inclusive processes. Relatedly, it is within the preferred peripheral places where women religious' examples of inclusivity tend to emerge and to thrive. While some women religious have been quick to criticize the hierarchical structure of the Roman Catholic Church, they have also humbly acknowledged the pyramidal arrangement of their own religious congregations, and they have worked diligently for more than half a century to refine their inclusive approach. Thus, their modelling pertains not only to the nature and scope of their strategies but also, and perhaps more so, to the depth of their modesty and their discernment that served to engender those approaches.[1]

Their modelling of inclusivity is also significant insofar as it extends their non-hierarchical and a-institutional approaches toward the future. The majority of sisters whom I interviewed wish neither to retain nor to replicate the institutionalized form of their congregation. Recognizing that "the call to generativity is transformation" (Romey 2017), they are genuinely hoping that their communities will continue to evolve into more integrated and inclusive co-operatives. Thus, rather than seeking to maintain past forms of institutional control like the Church's male clerics (Schneiders 2013) and some contemporary conservative women's religious orders whose memberships have been curiously increasing[2] (Bradley Hagerty 2012; Ebaugh 1993), the sisters herein are accepting the inevitability of their demise, and they are thus planning their future accordingly – both gracefully and strategically. They are choosing this option because for them upholding their renewal and eventually coming to an end is far more important than ensuring their survival based on a return to the conservative ideals and hierarchical control methods of the past (Ebaugh 1993, 156; Wittberg 1988).

Sister Adele illustrates the discernment and intentions underlying their current and future a-institutional approaches:

> Once we're gone … I think the institution of religious life is something that's part of the history of the Church and … the whole Church keeps evolving and so this institution … was for a time … I don't see any institution as being forever. So maybe they evolve or maybe they die out and are replaced by something else. I think the institution of religious life is like so many institutions right now that were great for their time and as an institution, as a structure, it's had its day … As a community we've talked about this, and we've said … we have some wisdom because of who we are and what we've lived. We have some resources because of who we are and how we've lived and … it's our task now to really just support … initiate. We're still initiating and continuing to support for a while and we then let something go … Then we initiate something else, and then we let it go or else somebody else initiates something and we support it. … But … because we've been careful with our resources, we have been able to support some good initiatives too and then this [community-based building for low income outreach organizations and social justice groups] being one of them.

As Sister Adele implies, their longevity is not being measured by the number of recruits they acquire or maintain.[3] They are thinking and acting far beyond that expectation. Instead, many congregations of women religious are perceiving and planning their future with much consideration and selflessness as they envision a continuation of their societal contributions,[4] including feminist and social justice ones, beyond the institutional arrangements of religious life and even beyond the Catholic or Christian spheres. Their efforts to "move the grassroots up" (Sister Mabel) apply to both local and international contexts whereby they often lay the groundwork for community leaders and project beneficiaries to assume responsibility for the projects and institutions they have established or are developing. While such an approach may seem imperative given their declining population, and while that reality is indeed part of the backdrop of the required decision-making, their unique style is a testament to the specific choices that they are intentionally making toward inclusivity and longevity, as they accept the inevitability of their demise.

In this context, women religious view their role and involvement as one of leadership not ownership whereby they initiate a project not only "for" others but rather "with" others so that the beneficiaries and other community members, like their associates, become the leaders who own and carry it on. It is in this way that sisters are modelling innovation rather than stagnation as they seek to be inclusive and integrative of the collaborators and beneficiaries of their legacy. Regardless of the infrastructural challenges that will undoubtedly limit their enduring sustainability, their exemplary modelling of innovative projects and inclusive practices should not be overlooked because they serve as important reminders of what women religious have effectively achieved in spite of the complementarity-based exclusion of women from the priesthood and thereby from Roman Catholic Church altars (Case 2016, 7).

STILL CAUSE FOR CONCERN

> We're caught as women in the Church. We just have to keep inching toward balance where women have equal opportunity for decision-making. You wonder sometimes whether we're inching ahead or backwards. (Sister Ella)

However forward-looking and productive women religious' current and future projects may be, there is still considerable cause for concern and room for critique because, as Coco (2013, 222) reminds us, "[t]here is no evidence here that Catholic hegemonic masculinity is *really* moving toward equality among adults." It is profoundly disconcerting that women religious and other laywomen are still on unequal footing within the Roman Catholic Church and have thus still not yet achieved some of the most essential liberal and second-wave feminist goals within that religious institution. It is even more perplexing that women religious are still struggling against male clerics' ongoing efforts to delegitimize their women-centred initiatives (Chittister 2014; Schneiders 2013) and thus still feel compelled to be clandestine about their innovative endeavours. That women religious must still negotiate their place, both cautiously and creatively, in the twenty-first century is a testament to the extent to which the patriarchal power of the Roman Catholic Church's clerical hierarchy remains exceedingly entrenched and intolerably intractable.

Women religious' strategic negotiation within and around such patriarchal power remains vital not only as a matter of principle but also for very practical reasons given the assets and projects they seek to protect. Unlike the Catholic dioceses or male religious orders that have lost considerable sums of money due to financial mismanagement or lawsuits related to the male clergy's sexual abuse of minors, many Canadian women religious orders remain largely solvent due to their wise management of their properties and investments, which in some cases are extensive. Due to their sound financial administration, they are well positioned to simultaneously provide dignified care for their aging popu-lation and support their own and others' spiritual innovation and social justice engagement (Holtmann 2011b). Yet, these resources and endeavours represent crucial reasons why they are careful not to outright alienate members of the Church hierarchy. Censure can lead to a women's congregation being taken over by the diocesan bishop or by the Vatican and/or being officially deemed non-Catholic. Such control tactics could have dire repercussions for the finan-cial solvency and autonomy that the women's communities maintain. Thus, even in the twenty-first century when the right to free speech is upheld and gender parity is championed, as feminist women religious in the United States know all too well, and painfully so, there can still be real material consequences for Catholic sisters if they openly defy male religious authority. Therefore, the ongoing caution and strategic resistance exercised by the Ontario-based Canadian women religious herein remains not only warranted but actually imperative.

Furthermore, while there may appear to be signs of hope under Pope Francis' leadership compared to the reigns of Popes John Paul II and Benedict XVI, there is still cause for concern on two other levels. First, Pope Francis' mixed messages remain a source of confusion and frustration. While he has affirmed women religious (Fox 2015), he did not put an immediate end to the investigation of sisters in the United States and instead appointed an overseer to monitor their compliance. In fact, monitoring continued well into the fall of 2016 in which approximately fifteen religious orders from the United States were summoned to Rome over "some areas of concern" (Araujo-Hawkins 2016; McElwee 2016a,b; Stockman 2017). Another of Pope Francis' mixed messages was made evident when he authorized women's involvement in foot washing on Holy Thursday. While Pope Francis performed a counter action by example and thus allowed women to have their feet washed, they are still not allowed to be the foot washers (Gibson and Scammell 2016; Roll 2015b).

Moreover, while Pope Francis agreed to commission a study on whether or not women could become deacons, such an announcement was based on both questions and a proposal by representatives of the International Union of Superiors General at a meeting with the Pope on 12 May 2016 – a meeting at which Pope Francis had also reminded the audience of the harmful attitudes of both feminism and clericalism. Furthermore, on 13 May 2016, a Vatican spokesperson (Father Federico Lombardi) filtered the matter by stating that Pope Francis only agreed to the commission for the purpose of examining the question with greater clarity and that he had certainly not spoken about women's ordination to the priesthood (Vatican Radio 2016a,b). Only time will tell if the door to the diaconate will be opened at all and, if so, if it will be opened fully or left only slightly ajar. We also cannot possibly forget that while a commission on female deacons was indeed established in late 2016 (Vatican Radio 2016c), women's ordination remains criminalized under Canon Law in the meantime.

Relatedly, while Pope Francis is modelling and encouraging inclusiveness regarding a variety of social issues and among many marginalized populations, his refusal to open up to the question of women's ordination – including to decriminalize it or to integrate women more fully at decision-making levels – remains fundamentally problematic (Chittister 2014).[5] Thus, while some doors may have opened, albeit partially, others seem to remain firmly closed, and as a result, both women religious and other laywomen across all generations continue to hold second-class status not only within the Roman Catholic Church but also throughout the world (Chittister 2015; Dugan and Owens 2009).

Second, while Pope Francis may have established a more open and inclusive atmosphere generally (albeit relatively in some regards), there is very little to suggest that he represents a future trend in papal leadership in the Roman Catholic Church. Just as we have seen in earlier decades, the undercurrent of antifeminist conservativeness has resurfaced at various moments and often vehemently (Ruether 2003). The orchestration of such a recurrence by future popes is an undeniably real, serious, and therefore concerning possibility. Caution must still be exercised because the roots and resilience of patriarchy remain strong and persistent, and the conservative clout is inevitably lying just below, if not still at the surface, waiting to re-emerge and regain control in what is still a troubled Church (Chittister 2014; Gutierrez 2016; Johnson 2014; Schneiders 2014, 2013, 2011).

HOPE WITHIN THE SISTERS' INDOMITABILITY IN THE INTERIM

The best people in the church are the nuns! By far! I mean they're doing serious work. (Judith)

While the contested terrain between male clerics and women religious, variously manifested as patriarchal powers versus feminist orientations, is likely to persist for the foreseeable future and will thus warrant ongoing scholarly attention,[6] it is nevertheless a future that remains hope filled, particularly in the short term, due to the sisters' steadfastness. Although their advanced ages and declining numbers point to an inevitable demise of women's religious communities in their current form, that demise may neither be imminent nor absolute. Given that many women religious are still quite active as "third agers" in their retirement years (Schneiders 2011, 133), including some who are in their mid-nineties,[7] serving to advance spiritual renewal, as well as social, ecological, and gender justice, their interim impact is certainly worthy of observation as their spiritual and societal footprints will undoubtedly be evident, effective, and enduring. Moreover, as Sister Adele illustrated, similar to their counterparts in the United States who are also preparing for their demise (Ebaugh 1993, 157), the sisters' careful and creative entrustment of their charism and legacy onto others, including their associates and beneficiaries, will serve to extend the permanence of their presence and the effectiveness of their engagement over the long term.

The potential of that permanence and effectiveness is further propelled by the sense of hope inspired by the sisters as they point to other possibilities, and particularly inclusive ones, beyond the institutional Church:

> I trust that the Spirit will move us. It will take time, but I think there is a groundswell in the grassroots of the Church, in the underground church that is not going to be stemmed ... I do have hope for that. I believe that there is a movement. First of all within individuals ... and individuals come to consciousness ... before groups. So ... it will take a while but ... I believe that patriarchal hierarchical governance either in Church or in society, the problem's not going to be solved in them. It's going to be solved in the feminine in those of us who see otherwise, both ... men and women. (Sister Kelly)

Paralleling Judith's comment at the start of this section, when Cheryl Reed (2004) reminded us over a decade ago that women religious are the "Catholic Church's biggest – and littlest known – asset" she also contended that since sisters offer a sense of church outside the male-led hierarchy, then "if there is any hope in the Catholic Church for women, it is through the nuns" (Reed

2004, 328). Sister-scholars and authors Sandra Schneiders (2013, 2004), Elizabeth Johnson (2014, 2002a), and Joan Chittister (2014, 2004) echo such a contention, as well as Sister Kelly's proposed resolution "in the feminine," as they assert that the quest for gender equality can and should be led by women religious who are uniquely and institutionally placed both to experience the multiple frustrations that women feel within the Church most acutely and to be motivated to bring to bear feminist creativity and insight in order that their contributions might flourish despite the constraints of their institutional position (Gervais and Turenne Sjolander 2015). No matter how elderly the women religious featured in this book may be, as "midwives of new ways" (Sister Adele), there is undoubtedly still much to which we can look forward as their leadership is not only promising but actually already proven. The transformative potential of their interwoven women-led spirituality, governance, and activism remains propitious given that, as seventy-five-year-old Sister Edith reminds us, "the sisterhood is strong," and, as seventy-four-year-old Sister Ella proclaims, "we are just ... indomitable, really."

Epilogue

W hile this book has featured relatively unknown aspects of the current and former sisters' lives, it has not addressed the totality and complexity of the women's experiences. There are other significant dimensions of their historical and contemporary contexts that must also be brought to the fore. To this end, and with a view to continuing to take women religious' voices seriously, my future publications will explore the women's opinions and approaches regarding the twenty-first-century criminalization of women's ordination, the clerical sexual abuse scandal, women's reproductive rights, the inclusion of the LGBTQ community, their own broader social justice engagement including their resistance tactics in repressive contexts in international settings, as well as the future of both the Roman Catholic Church and their own congregations.

In the meantime, I leave you to ponder, over the next few pages, the current and former sisters' messages to women, their hope and scepticism of gender equality in the Roman Catholic Church, their pride over their active retirement, and their outlook on the future of women's religious life.

SISTERS' MESSAGES TO WOMEN

"If you believe something, stand up for it." (Sister Josephine)

"Speak out! Don't be intimidated." (Sister Mabel)

"Well, that would be ... my final word ... to achieve a bigger goal ... to see the women in the Church ... take their place." (Sister Corinne)

"In terms of the future of the Catholic Church, young women may be hesitant to commit to an organization which is blatantly sexist." (Sister Edith)

"Choose a lifestyle that will bring you joy, that will allow you to be who you feel and who you believe yourself to be, and then if you're not happy in that, then you should look to other alternatives ... A person is only going to be effective as they are ... happy with the life they've chosen." (Sister Penelope)

"I'd like ... to be really affirming of women more. I have been and I want to be all the time. But I'm going to work at it more ... and that's ... by talking about it, that's how that happens." (Sister Maureen)

"The Spirit of God works in the ordinary believer and that has to be honoured much more ... we need to remind ... whomever that this is God at work, it bubbles up from the ordinary community and we need to listen to that." (Sister Ella)

"If a person is called, and I believe there is a call ... follow it and you live it as best you can." (Sister Loretta)

"Live your baptismal call in whatever ... vocation you are." (Sister Edna)

"Come and see." (Sister Nellie)

HOPE FOR AND SCEPTICISM OF GENDER EQUALITY IN THE CHURCH

"Not in my lifetime, baby! [laughs] But it is inevitable." (Sister Joelle)

"I hope so. I hope it will be anyway. I think. But right now, you know, like with the power – they're so powerful, the men are so powerful, that it's pretty hard." (Sister Sophie)

"Oh it'll come someday, but it won't come in our time. I don't think." (Sister Clara)

"Probably, way down the line, I don't know when, [but] I don't see it as equal." (Sister Rita)

"No. Not right now. I hope it will be. I hope they open up their eyes, as I said, so they don't go on so long with this sin of sexism." (Sister Agnes)

SISTERS' PRIDE OVER THEIR ACTIVE "RETIREMENT": WOMEN RELIGIOUS AS ACTIVE "THIRD AGERS" (SCHNEIDERS 2011, 133)

"I'm not retired. Well, we don't retire, we recycle." (Sister Mabel)

"Each one serves where possible, depending on one's health and capacity." (Sister Shannon)

"You can always, always do something! ... You know who's the best to support [the social justice newsletter]? The infirmary! Ah, I tell you! They write! ... I find that totally inspiring!" (Sister Clara)

"That word retired is a question mark in our community because I don't know that we ever retire." (Sister Theresa)

"I never thought there was anything to retire from. Retirement is just not in my vocabulary. It's just my next ministry ... and that's what happens in our community. People just ... adjust ... I'm working ... very full time but not in a structured way that is pressured, most of the time. I mean some of the pressure is because we take on too much." (Sister Adele)

"As a sister ... we don't retire. We're a sister until we die so we continue in our ministry ... and ... I'm so glad ... we're free to look around and see what we want to do ... I have the health and I'm really happy to ... continue." (Sister Agnes)

SISTERS' OUTLOOK ON THE FUTURE OF WOMEN'S RELIGIOUS LIFE

"I think it will end. I don't doubt and I have no problem 'cause I think ... the world changes and God shows himself in many ways and there will be other ways." (Sister Clara)

"Well, I think it's not going to be like it is now. There's got to be a change and, uh, ooh, I guess you gotta look at what can I do by doing something?" (Sister Maureen)

"Well, I think her [foundress] spirit was like ... the spirit of Jesus which is the spirit of the way God's created everything. So I mean whether that's attached to [our foundress] I don't know if that matters either ... I think if we have made a contribution to that sense of all is one and the whole of our planet, if we have helped to move us humans toward being truly human, truly a community, an earth community. I guess that's what I hope replaces – well, not replaces, but evolves and that we've been part of its evolution is that there be an earth community that knows itself to be that." (Sister Adele)

"I think it's just to continue to be open to where the needs are ... you walk in your everyday walk and who is it that needs our help?" (Sister Rita)

"I wish I had ... a crystal ball, eh? There's no question we're ... in the diminishment stage ... this era of religious life is at an end. However ... I believe that there is a call ... I do believe that the religious life will subsist. I do think ... our model of sharing, of being in a relationship, of ... dialogue in terms of where God is leading us, if that interpretation of the vows ... if we can identify it for ourselves ... and accept our prophetic call ... of giving voice to the victimized ... then I do see a future." (Sister Joelle)

"Probably [our community] will not continue ... as, uh, we are and ... things should not be pushed that aren't meant to be ... So I think things will evolve and I don't think we know. But it could be ... married women still carrying out works like [our foundresses] and other people who are leaders in social justice and ... leading us to dignity of all people." (Sister Agnes)

"I still believe there'll be religious life but not the way we see it. It could be ... very different ... I don't see it as being institutional ... I feel like as we live it, as we make changes, like moving away from institutional living, I think that will continue." (Sister Jeanette)

"I don't know. I really don't know ... But actually the institution has disappeared. We don't have an institution anymore ... So people who are saying this style of life should die, it's already dead! ... Other than the motherhouse and ... our older sisters. But it's already gone ... I don't want to see it repeated either. But I would like to see us live on in some form." (Sister Loretta)

"I'm not a great advocate of spending too much time planning for the future. I'm a visionary. I like envisioning but ... I'm not overly concerned about ... like sustainability in the sense of sameness." (Sister Sarah)

"I think the charism will never die because it's at the heart of the universe. And the charism lives on in people that we don't even know. I hear stories ... from people of sisters who taught them and how they live love and they're trying to live that ... it's very difficult to measure but I think the whole associate movement is ... one way that ... faith communities ... can happen. I think ... it's a way of the future. I don't believe people are going to enter ... I wouldn't want them to; I wouldn't accept them to live the kind of monastic [life] ... that's engrained in so many sisters. But I think ... religious life is going to look very different in the future. I don't know if it's even going to be called that. But it will be people coming together for mission." (Sister Mabel)

"We shouldn't be around! You know, organizations don't normally stay around for 300 and ... some years. You know, we really should be gone ... and ... our charism ... is so resilient that it will always be needed. But it'll be in another form, a new form, and you don't put ... new wine in old skins so ... Most of us will die out as we know religious life. But ... the Spirit of God is up there. There are new groups forming and I think our role ... is to support them. To give them everything ... we can [and] value ourselves, like community living, like deep love for the Lord Jesus and spread that." (Sister Ella)

"I've been saying this for years ... institutions have to go! And that's one of the blessings of selling motherhouses. What I envision and I've envisioned this for years now is that persons would just stay where they are. Live where they are ... and come together, be together without being together, and could still live the ... vocation, the charism ... that's how I envision religious life in the future." (Sister Kelly)

"We are diminishing. We're going off the scene. So our role now is what is our legacy?" (Sister Marian)

Participants' profiles

(Details as of the Date of the Interviews or Questionnaires)

Table 1   Current women religious

Pseudonym	Age	Profile	Years as Sister	Interview Date
Adele	68	teacher, spiritual director, leadership team, pastoral associate	51	2009
Agnes	72	teacher, leadership team	51	2009
Benita	80	teacher, alternative education	62	2009
Carmen	84	teacher, principal, pastoral associate, counsellor	65	2009
Clara	72	teacher, principal, leadership team	53	2008
Corinne	74	teacher, librarian, provincial, council-lor, local superior, support staff	54	2009
Edith	76	teacher, professor	57	2009
Edna	73	teacher, religious education, pastoral services	55	2009
Ella	74	teacher, spiritual direction, leader-ship team, general superior	56	2009
Jeanette	63	chef, leadership team	44	2009
Joelle	67	teacher, editor, parish service, program coordination, formation, leadership, general superior	49	2010
Josephine	76	teacher, principal, spiritual direction	57	2009
Kelly	80	teacher, spiritual direction, therapist, leadership team	62	2009
Loretta	73	teacher, principal, leadership team, general superior, formation director	53	2009

Table 1   Current women religious (cont'd)

Pseudonym	Age	Profile	Years as Sister	Interview Date
Mabel	71	psychologist, public health, leadership team, councillor, general superior	55	2009
Marian	80	teacher, treasurer, health care administration	50	2009
Maureen	80	teacher, leader of associates program	46	2009
Mona	70	leadership team member	48	2009
Nellie	81	teacher, parish service	63	2009
Noreen	68	teacher, social worker, novice director, leadership team	48	2011
Penelope	62	teacher, formation, leadership team	44	2009
Rita	76	teacher, pastoral care, local leader, convent superior	52	2009
Sarah	49	pastoral work, leadership team	24	2009
Shannon	91	teacher, catechetics, adult education, superior of convent in mission	73	2009
Sophie	82	teacher, principal, pastoral care hospital, pastoral assistant	50	2009
Theresa	80	teacher, principal, leadership team	54	2009

Table 2   Former women religious

Pseudonym	Age	Profile	Years as Sister	Interview Date
Carol	62	teacher, principal, youth ministry	14	2009
Charlotte	75	teacher	26	2008
Darlene	68	teacher, spiritual direction	42	2011
Judith	76	teacher, women's rights program facilitator	20	2009
Mildred	73	teacher, psychotherapist	33	2011
Naomi	64	teacher, parish ministry, counselling, formation, holistic practitioner	28	2011

Notes

1 "Women religious" is the term scholars use to refer to vowed women in the Catholic tradition who are commonly known as "sisters" or "nuns" (Smyth 2007, 8). I use "women religious" and "sister" and "nun" interchangeably.

2 In Roman Catholic doctrine, purgatory is considered to be a place of suffering between "heaven" and "hell" where souls of sinners remain while they are expiating their sins.

3 The sacristy is the room where sacred objects are stored and where priests, readers, and servers prepare for Mass.

4 I also took comfort in recalling how the first priest who had asked us to be altar servers had defended our presence at an early 1980s diocesan centennial celebration that included a cardinal and scores of bishops and priests. Our parish priest submitted mine and my sister's names to attend the Mass as our parish's representatives and when the bishop's office called to inform him that we were not allowed to attend because we were "girls," he staunchly defended his choice and insisted that we accompany him due to our loyal weekly service. As the only two females present among dozens of male altar servers, we were certainly noticed and subject to the altar boys' sexist snickers and disapproving stares as we walked in the procession. However, as an eleven-year-old at the time, I was less aware of the broader structural constraints that were at play, and we stood proudly since we felt supported by our own priest, who had caringly reassured us of our right to be there.

INTRODUCTION

1 Canadian women religious' societal support parallels the impact that nuns had in the United States (Coburn and Smith 1999), all of which must be understood within the context of Catholic nuns' tending the sick, teaching the uneducated, and caring for the disadvantaged around the world for more than sixteen centuries (Ebaugh 1993, 1; Lux-Sterritt and Mangion 2011; Mangion 2008).

2 The capitalized terms "Roman Catholic Church," "Catholic Church," and "Church" are used interchangeably as they represent the official institutional Church and particularly its Romanized, and thus formalized, form. The term "church" in lower case refers to a church building as well as to wider conceptions and non-institutionalized forms of religious gatherings and practices (Chittister 2004; Johnson 2002b; Winter 2002; Wittberg 1994). My use of the capitalized version of Church is intended only for the purpose of clarifying the aforementioned distinctions; it does not imply that I think the institutional Church is

227

more important and thus warranting capitalization. For more on how these distinctions are manifested in religious practices among women religious, see Gervais and Turenne Sjolander (2015) and Johnson (2002b).

3 Other authors have referred to the "tightrope" to illustrate the constraints that sisters have long faced (see, e.g., Coco [2013, 176–85] on women's challenges with outward performances of gender justice and Coburn and Smith's [1999, 83] referral to Teresa of Avila having walked a tightrope of gender and religious orthodoxy in sixteenth-century Spain). That the tightrope remains a challenge more than five centuries later is of the utmost concern.

4 Not all women's religious congregations are forward-looking; see for example the traditionalist-based Council of Major Superiors of Women Religious (CMSWR) compared to the inclusively oriented Leadership Conference of Women Religious (LCWR) in the United States (Clark 2012). The recent rise of conservative orders that gained momentum under the previous two pontiffs is further testament to the maintenance of conventional religious traditions in the Roman Catholic Church.

5 I distinguish between "women religious" (or "vowed women") and "laywomen" (or "non-vowed women") in order to include all women within the Roman Catholic Church and all those affected by its patriarchal domination. As shown in chapter 8, it is understood that women religious have been defined as part of the laity of the Church since Vatican II. Although some of the sisters I interviewed referred to non-vowed women as laywomen, my use of the phrase "women religious and other laywomen" implies that both groupings are part of the laity.

6 For another example of the exclusion of women from the Church, see Lee (1996) and Roll (2003) on the churching or purification of mothers after childbirth.

7 In Roll (2015b) from *Actae Apostolicae Sedis* 41 (1949), English translation in T.L. Bouscaren, *Canon Law Digest 3* (Milwaukee, WI: Bruce Publishing, 1954), 335.

8 See paragraphs 100 and 101 of the 2002 "General Instruction" of the *Roman Missal*.

9 For more on the twenty-first-century prohibition and criminalization of women's ordination, see Cavanagh (2010); for how the women religious reacted to it, see Gervais (2015) and Gervais and Watson (2017); for more on the issue of women's ordination in earlier centuries and under various papacies, see Leonard (1995).

10 The LCWR is the association of the leaders of congregations of Catholic women religious in the United States. It is distinct from the more traditionalist Council of Major Superiors of Women Religious (CMSWR), which was not subject to the investigation carried out by the Vatican's Congregation for the Doctrine of the Faith (Clark 2012).

11 For more on how the Vatican's investigation framed the issues as matters of disobedience, thereby constructed feminist women religious as disobedient and even subversive, see Schneiders (2011, 112–13).

12 Initially, Pope Francis seemed an unlikely source, given his progressive stance on other social issues and structural inequalities. Yet, regarding women in the Church and women's ordination in particular, there appeared to be relatively little openness on his part until 12 May 2016 when he announced the creation of a commission to study the question of female deacons. Moreover, the very next day, a Vatican spokesperson (Father Federico Lombardi) clarified that the Pope's intention was to study the matter but not to introduce female deacons and certainly not to discuss women's ordination to the priesthood. For more on the original commentary and the subsequent clarifications and reactions, see Pope Francis (2016), Vatican Radio (2016a, 2016b), and McElwee (2016c).

13 In the case of the LCWR, multiple changes were expected in terms of the content featured in its publications and in its selection of speakers, programs, and award recipients, as well as in its spiritual celebrations (LCWR 2015a). In the case of the religious orders generally,

realignments are expected in their religious institutes' charism (foundational mandates), their efforts to promote religious vocations, their forms of prayer, their spiritual practices and ministry, their community life, and their financial stewardship (Braz de Aviz 2014). For more on the extended monitoring in 2016 and 2017, see Araujo-Hawkins (2016), McElwee (2016a,b), Stockman (2017).

14 See Bonavoglia (2005), Chittister (2004, 1998, 1995), Coco (2013), Daly (1968, 1973), Johnson (2002), Manning (2006, 1999), Schneiders (2013, 2004), Smyth (2007).

15 Joanna Manning, a former woman religious in England and now an Anglican priest in Canada, entitled her book *The Magdalene Moment* (2006) to illustrate the magnitude of the shift that was initiated in 1945 with the discovery of Gnostic Christian texts in Egypt. The completion of their translation in the mid-1970s led to a major reconsideration of the role of women in early Christian history and of Mary of Magdala in particular as a central Christian figure, as well as to the rediscovery of the sacred feminine and its potential for deeper spiritual meaning, modern social justice, and for the reestablishment of women's prophetic leadership (Manning 2015, 2006, 26–7; Schaberg 2002; Schenk 2004). As Sandra Schneiders (2004, xvi) notes, Mary Magdalene has been claimed ever more enthusiastically in recent years as the patron of feminists in the Church since her androcentrically constructed biblical role as a "prostitute" was called into question when evidence of her role as one of Jesus' disciples surfaced. While the disciple–prostitute conflation, and particularly the prostitute label therein, remains the subject of debate in popular culture (Hornsby 2006, 76; Schaberg 2002; Schenk 2004), the gendered gains associated with the claims of Mary of Magdala having been a disciple are undeniably consequential.

16 Sue Monk Kidd is the author of *The Dance of the Dissident Daughter* (1996).

17 Dan Brown is the author of the popular, yet theologically flawed, fictional book *The Da Vinci Code* (2003), which features the central role of Mary Madgalene in the Christian tradition, albeit problematically so (Schenk 2004).

18 While Dumont (1995) has explored the feminist influences and outcomes among francophone women religious in Quebec, a similar study has not been conducted extensively among English-speaking women religious especially in Ontario. For other studies on francophone women religious in Canada, see for example, D'Allaire (1983), Danylewycz (1987, 1981), Gray (2007), Laurin, Juteau, and Duchesne (1991), among others. For an experiential account of how an elderly French-speaking Canadian woman religious (Sr Mariette Milot) struggles with the prohibition of women's ordination, see the Pauline Voisard film *Je vous salue Mariette* that was produced by Vidéo Femmes in 2010.

19 Exceptions to this partial void include the works of theologian Ellen Leonard (2007) and sociologist Cathy Holtmann (2011b), as well as Sister Geraldine Anthony's (1997b) book, in which the author frames Canadian Sr Irene Farmer's biography through Farmer's own feminist orientation that dates back to the early 1900s and thus sheds light on her early twentieth-century and long-standing critique of gender inequality in the Roman Catholic Church. However, despite Anthony's emphasis on Farmer's feminist leanings, critics have pointed to the book's significant shortcomings, including the serious flaws in its analysis.

20 Thirty-one participants were interviewed; one sister completed the original questionnaire. Of the original thirty-two participants, twenty-one completed a questionnaire or interview that specifically explored the 2010 controversy over women's ordination.

21 One participant was in her 90s, eight were in their 80s, fifteen were in their 70s, seven were in their 60s, none were in their 50s, and one was in her late 40s.

22 The experiences of current and former sisters may not be entirely comparable, since their trajectories are different given former sisters' departure from religious life. Nevertheless, they do share experiences in common, especially those pertaining to early convent life, Vatican II, earlier influences of feminism, and patriarchal constraints. To varying degrees, they all

remain in touch with their previous religious community and former peers, and some also participate regularly in special events held by their respective congregations. Thus, given the commonalities, the former sisters' experiences remain thematically relevant.

23 "New Age" refers to a broad range of alternative spiritual beliefs (e.g., cosmology) and healing practices (e.g., yoga, Reiki, meditation) that have been popularized since the 1970s. Despite their controversial appeal and their unconventional status, New Age practices are documented herein as they reflect women religious' evolving societal and spiritual encounters. More specific examples of the sisters' New Age practices are detailed in chapter 5.

24 I recruited participants among ten Ontario-based religious communities that were members of the Canadian Religious Conference (CRC), which is a governing body that supports the leaders of 200 religious communities of women and men in Canada. Within its combined approach of advocacy and service, the CRC's current emphasis is on a "prophetic witness to justice and peace within society and the church" (Canadian Religious Conference 2017). For more on the history of the CRC, its feminist-oriented advocacy, and how Canadian women religious repositioned themselves strategically within it, see MacDonald (2017).

25 I exercised caution in order to maintain anonymity and confidentiality. My presence in the communal residences or spirituality centres at the time of the interviews did not seem to be a concern since none of the convents were closed. Since I meet with sisters in these spaces occasionally on matters relating to social justice and international development, my presence would not have necessarily been assumed by others to be associated with this study.

26 All interviews were conducted during the day or evening; I did not remain in their convent or residential settings overnight or for extended stays.

27 To my knowledge, after the interviews were conducted and participant observation was completed, three participants have passed away; approximately five others are experiencing symptoms of dementia or Alzheimer's; thus their ability to follow up with the publication phase of the study is limited.

28 I was not informed of any issues regarding who was included or excluded from the sample. Given the voluntary-basis of the participation, exclusion from the sample was based on non-participants' choices.

29 This androcentric dimension is both theological and operational whereby the male is the norm and female is constructed as the other.

30 My study differs from historical analyses of women religious that are based primarily on archival data. While written congregational records have revealed the complex ways in which women religious have negotiated the patriarchal power of the Church's clerical authority (Gray 2007; Lux-Sterritt 2005; Magray 1998; Mangion 2008), they do not (and understandably cannot) always provide the women whose texts are under study with the opportunity to contextualize, clarify, or critique the conditions and relations being analyzed. Thus the qualitative interviews that I conducted serve to complement others' analyses of historical texts because they allow women themselves, who are well positioned to shed direct and clearer light on the nuances, as well as to both describe and analyze their own circumstances, rather than have them interpreted retrospectively by others.

31 I was once questioned about sisters' vulnerability by a male audience member after a conference presentation. He contended that sisters have enjoyed a rather privileged position given their educational, institutional, and financial opportunities. While this may seem relatively true now, not all congregations are in stable financial shape, and his critique did not consider how sisters sacrificed tremendously in the past and worked diligently over the years to steward their funds responsibly. His critique also does not acknowledge that despite the opportunities they created for themselves through their mutual support and innovation, they still suffered gender-based discrimination and in some cases gender-based violence by the male-dominated Church hierarchy.

32   While they were all invited to contribute, not all the participants chose to be involved in all phases of the research process. The interview guide was co-prepared with a smaller group of women comprised of both leaders and members (former and current) of four religious congregations.

33   While Mander (2010) is referring to people in very difficult, impoverished, and/or life threatening situations in the context of human rights violations – and while this is not reflective of the plight of women religious in Canada – there are degrees of vulnerability and risk pertinent to the women's stories for which I needed to exercise extreme caution. Thus his inclusive approach is relevant to my ethical commitment to the women I interviewed.

34   Within the last week of the final preparation of this manuscript, Sister Agnes very enthusiastically shared such a book with which I was not yet familiar, and it was integrated into the analysis.

35   Due to space limitations, a chapter on past hierarchical and disciplinary contexts in convents was not included in this book, but these issues have been covered elsewhere (see Gervais and Watson 2014).

CHAPTER 1

1   Howard Ecklund (2003) encountered similar reactions by scholars regarding a study on feminist Catholic laywomen. Dumont (1995) posed the question "Are sisters feminists?" rhetorically in her book title to reveal not only the existence of feminist women religious but also their societal contributions, especially pertaining to gender equality (Dumont's title is translated here from the original French version: Les religieuses sont-elles des féministes?). The perception of the contradiction is relevant because nuns have been viewed as having been involved in the conditioning of gendered obedience, compliance, and subservience among generations of women (Bonavoglia 2005, 7; Magray 1998). Nevertheless, when they were enlightened in the 1960s and 1970s by feminist consciousness, women religious themselves, including renowned sister-author Joan Chittister, recognized that problematic role and have worked hard to both amend it and make amends over it ever since (Bonavoglia 2005, 7).

2   For an understanding of all-encompassing and incisive explanations of feminism by sister-scholars, see Chittister (1995), Johnson (2002a); and Schneiders (2013).

3   While some sisters did not agree with Manning's confrontational style, others felt that her incisive tone was essential: "Sometimes I find it a little bit jarring, you know, but ... we need people who aren't afraid to say it just as it is" (Sister Sophie).

4   Although the wave-based periodization of feminism is problematized (Gillis et al. 2004; Hewitt 2010), it still carries meaning. Second-wave feminism is considered to have addressed gender equality in the domestic, employment, health, and legal spheres from the early 1960s to the early 1990s.

5   Some sisters articulated a definite detachment from a feminist identity. Nevertheless, the majority of the women who agreed to be interviewed did have feminist leanings and/or were strongly in favour of gender equality. While some participants remarked that some other sisters may not feel comfortable participating in the study due to the gender-oriented content, non-participants never expressed that concern to me. Those who declined the invitation cited lack of time, ill health, and discomfort with interviews as the reason for their non-participation. Nevertheless, given the diversity of women's perspectives, it will be important that the voices of non-feminist women religious be represented in future studies (Griffith 1997).

6   Notwithstanding the importance of the pluralized form of feminisms, I employ the singular version of "feminism" in part for ease of reference given its common use in both popular and academic discourse, and as Neitz (2003, 278) contends, "feminism, much changed,

with and without modifiers, persists as the most useful word to identify a way of thinking that begins with questions about the status and experiences of particular groups of women."

7   With the intention of being open to their own interpretations, I did not predefine feminism nor were the women asked to define or distinguish feminist perspectives; their understandings seemed apparent in their explanations and comparisons; this omission may have contributed to the ambiguous use of the singular term "feminism."

8   For an understanding of how similar outlooks are interpreted as non-liberal feminism, see Mahmood (2006), who analyzes agency among religious Muslim women within the broader context of what she views as the vexed relationship between feminism and religion.

9   For more on how Catholic women reject feminism altogether, see Manning (1999) and Howard Ecklund (2003).

10   Germaine Greer is a self-identified "anarchist communist" who became mired in controversy around her publication *The Female Eunuch* (1970), in which she criticized the nuclear family and Western attitudes toward sexuality. While Sister Benita's distancing from Greer's style of feminism may be related to Greer's anarchist style, she gives the impression that she supports women's rights in some sense yet denies the necessity of a feminist movement.

11   As I illustrate in the next chapter by way of a clarification offered by Adichie (2014), femininity and feminism are not necessarily mutually exclusive, and Sister Kelly does not believe so either.

12   While neither the author nor the interviewees defined "radical" per se, their explanations and examples served as illustrations of their interpretations. The lack of specific definitions for the term "feminism" or any of its qualifiers (e.g., liberal, radical) is acknowledged as an oversight.

13   The differential treatment of women religious by diocesan priests versus congregation-based priests was not discussed during the interviews. Thus, I cannot analyze the impact of communal experience or lack thereof on the treatment of sisters by either diocesan or congregation-based priests. Future studies should explore this potentially relevant context.

14   CNWE is the Catholic Network for Women's Equality, which advocates for gender equality in all aspects of church and society. Catholics of Vision sought church renewal in the late twentieth century. The Coalition of Concerned Canadian Catholics is a national group seeking structural reform within the Roman Catholic Church. The Church International Movement is a worldwide network endeavouring to promote the Catholic faith "without hierarchy."

15   Although many feminist theorists no longer consider the wave metaphor to be an adequate representation of the diverse women's rights and feminist movements (Gillis et al. 2004; Hewitt 2010), a distinction is provided here for the sake of clarification. Whereas third-wave feminism accentuates diversity and intersectionality and is thought to have originated in the early 1990s, fourth-wave feminism is considered to have emerged in the latter part of the first decade of the twenty-first century and extends the debates on intersectionality, particularly via online or social media avenues (Gillis et al. 2004; Hewitt 2010; Munro 2013). Sullivan contends that compared to their liberation-oriented awakening during second-wave feminism, sisters "stand as caricatures of repression against the liberated woman" within the context of third-wave feminism (Sullivan 2005, 223). While Sullivan's contention may be true for some rather conservative or liberal feminist nuns, it is not reflective of those who engage in profoundly critical interventions that address structural sources of marginalization.

16   For a comprehensive examination of feminist philosophy and its reflections in Christianity and the pursuit of human dignity, see Chittister's (1995), Schneiders' (2013, 2004), and Johnson's (2002a, 2002b) foundational works; see also the contributions of feminist theologian Kochurani Abraham in Mathew (2017).

CHAPTER 2

1   While Judith had already left her religious community almost a decade earlier, she cited this image, as well as the Church's exclusion of marginalized populations including members of the LGBTQ community, as having contributed to her eventual departure from the Roman Catholic Church itself.

2   After I posed the aforementioned question on the Church as patriarchal, I then asked the participants if they thought that the Church was also misogynous. The latter question was suggested by some of the women religious themselves who had provided feedback on the original interview guide and who recommended that the dimension of misogyny be added.

3   Notwithstanding the actuality of Sister Sarah's explanation of women religious' sibling status, "Mother" is a term that was commonly used within sisters' religious communities not only in reference to the "Mother Superior" but also in some orders for women who had taken their final vows, whereby choir sisters were also called "mother."

4   Sister Sarah does acknowledge the official way in which "the Church is [considered] the Mother. It's Mother Church." Such a construction is in itself gendered and the implications of control of the *female* Church by the male hierarchy cannot be overstated.

5   On the context in the United States, see Bonavoglia (2005), Coburn and Smith (1999), Ebaugh (1993), Schneiders (2013), and Wittberg (1994); in Europe, see Magray (1998) and Mangion (2008); in Africa, see Eze et al. (2015).

6   The remaining 25 percent did not experience discrimination personally, but they had all observed it happening to other women religious; many of them were very confident women whose strong personalities may have shielded them from direct disrespect. Some openly stated that they would not allow themselves to be dominated or bullied.

7   The term "chapter" refers to a meeting that is held among all the members of the religious congregation.

8   Many sisters do in fact facilitate chapters and lead spiritual retreats including Ignatian thirty-day retreats.

9   Rectories are known as priests' residences and are usually located beside a parish church.

10 While I have emphasized sisters' marginalized position, others may interpret their approach as a compassionate one. However, it is difficult to comment on their intentions since not all sisters within congregations are aware of priests' perpetration of sexual abuse until after they are charged by law enforcement officials. Due to the shortage of priests, sisters may have limited choices if they want Masses held in their retirement homes.

11 In commenting on the plight of women in the Roman Catholic Church in the late 1960s, renowned American Sister Margaret Traxler perceived the gravity of the situation as worse than second-class status: "If women in society have second-class citizenship, then women in the church have third-class." (As quoted in an article entitled "Battling for Nuns' Rights" in *Newsweek* on 8 September 1969, p. 81 in Sullivan 2005, 202.)

12 While some people may view "fatherly" as patronizing, comparatively for Sister Corinne it seemed to be an improvement over being inquisitorial.

13 It was under the leadership of Sister Madeleva Wolff that theological studies began for lay people – both women and men – at St. Mary's University, School of Sacred Theology in Notre Dame, Indiana, in 1943 (Fox 2016). When the study of theology was open to lay people at this time, women religious were the first to enrol.

14 While I do not elaborate here upon Carol's experience as a lesbian in the Roman Catholic Church, I plan to do so in future publications in which I will explore current and former sisters' inclusive approaches with members of the LGBTQ community.

15 Some may prefer "gendered performance" or "gender essentialism" because they reflect advanced and contemporary considerations more accurately. However, the construction of gender is also contested (Nason-Clark and Fisher-Townsend 2005).

16   While not elaborated upon in this book, the current and former sisters viewed the 2010 criminalization of women's ordination as the example par excellence of the intensification of the Church's patriarchal domination in the twenty-first century (see Gervais 2015; Gervais and Watson 2017). Others, in post-interview conversations, also considered the last round of modifications to the Roman Missal in 2011 as evidence of the further entrenchment of male domination due to the generic remasculinization of the Mass text (Roll 2015a, 2011).

17   The *New Revised Standard Version* of the Bible is referenced because of its emphasis on accessibility and inclusivity; the online source is found here: http://www.biblestudytools .com/nrs/luke/13.html. According to Luke's Gospel (13:10–17), Jesus' healing of the bent woman on the Sabbath angered the synagogue officials because he violated the rules of the day of rest; however, Jesus is said to have countered their restrictions with a message that emphasized compassion over regulation.

18   While permission has been granted by Sister Kelly to include her drawings of the bent woman, they are omitted here to protect her identity.

CHAPTER 3

1   While I emphasize how former women religious have left the Roman Catholic Church itself, it is important to note that other former sisters left their religious communities for a variety of reasons including what they perceived to be bullying by their female superiors and/or peers. Thus, the male clerical hierarchy was not the only source of oppression that contributed to women leaving their religious congregations and/or the Church.

2   After Mary Daly's original questioning in the late 1960s and early 1970s, it is a recurring question among scholars, writers and activists (see, e.g., Bonavoglia 2006; Coco 2013; Couture 2008, 61; Dillon 1999; Kaylin 2000; Leonard 2008, 25; Molesky-Poz 2003; Schneiders 2011; Winter et al. 1994).

3   Sister Benita divulged that she struggled with a sense of alienation from her community as a result of differences of opinion and approaches.

4   Future studies should explore the extent of the spiritual, psychological, and practical tensions that women religious encounter within the Church's constraining patriarchal contexts, as well as the complex interplay among them.

5   Here Carol is referencing a message from *Women Who Run with the Wolves* by Clarissa Pinkola Estés.

6   Sister Carmen's reference to "*de facto* rather than *de jure*" means that although she was not legally authorized to be the pastor, in reality, she fulfilled many aspects of the role and did so without much recognition. Such an actuality was commonly experienced by sisters who worked tirelessly in parishes, yet the priest would maintain the control and receive the credit (Coburn and Smith 1999).

7   While women's religious congregations may include lay people in their initiatives, ultimately, non-members cannot fully access the broader benefits, including infrastructural independence that congregational members can, and such a limitation remains a serious concern among women religious.

CHAPTER 4

1   According to the pre–Vatican II conception and control of obedience among women religious, the sisters' critiques would be viewed as highly disobedient. However, as I illustrate in chapter 8, they clearly felt emboldened by a post-1960s sense of autonomy generated by updated interpretations of the vow of obedience and by decentralized governance arrangements (Ebaugh 1993; Wittberg 1994).

2   See Zenit Staff (2009) for the article to which Sister Theresa refers.

3   At the time of the interviews, the Vatican was ruled by Pope Benedict XVI. The Creed, commonly known as the Apostles' Creed refers to the statement of belief principally in God the *Father*, Jesus the son, and the Holy Spirit.

4   Holy Week is the week preceding Easter Sunday starting with Palm Sunday and includes the Triduum of Holy Thursday, Good Friday, Holy Saturday (Easter Vigil). A diocese is a predetermined geographic area composed of faithful members of the Church and is overseen by a bishop who is an ordained minister, appointed by the Pope to govern the Church in a diocese. A cathedral is the official church of a diocesan bishop; given that it is the principal church in a diocese, it is usually a larger edifice than parish churches. A basilica is a larger church with architectural prominence and is usually associated with some special privilege or saint.

5   In the Roman Catholic tradition, there are seven sacraments including baptism, Eucharist, confirmation, reconciliation (of which confession is a part), anointing of the sick, marriage, and holy orders. Confession involves first an individual confessing or admitting to a priest that they have "sinned" or done wrong; after the individual confesses their sins, the priest assigns a minor penance, such as the reciting of additional prayers, usually ones of contrition. Then the priest, acting through the ministry of the Church, grants the individual pardon or forgiveness (Cornwell 2014).

6   Traditionally, most often located on the sides of the nave within a church, a confessional is a booth-like enclosure in which, from their respective compartments, the priest listens to the penitent confess their sins and say their prayer of contrition, and then grants them absolution, otherwise known as forgiveness (Cornwell 2014).

7   While confession consists of the act of confessing one's sins to a confessor, reconciliation is considered to be the last component of the sacrament of confession whereby the individual who has confessed is reconciled with, or forgiven by, God; however, in popular Catholic discourse among lay people confession and reconciliation are often used interchangeably.

8   By contrast, as Coburn and Smith (1999) have shown, some communities of women religious have strategically used the at-a-distance papal governance of their religious communities to repel control by diocesan bishops. As Coburn and Smith (1999, 61) specifically stated: "many Catholic sisterhoods felt that the submission to male authority in Rome, thousands of miles away, was far preferable to subjugation to a local bishop who could closely monitor and control every aspect of community life." Similar examples of women religious circumventing Vatican-based control are found in studies conducted by, or referred to by Gray (2007), Magray (1998), Mangion (2008), Schneiders (2013), and Wittberg (1994).

9   Including Mary Ward who resisted clerical expectations of traditional enclosure for the Institute of the Blessed Virgin Mary that she founded in England in 1609 (Lux-Sterritt 2005, 37; Mangion 2008, 218). Similarly, Catherine of Siena was a fourteenth-century mystic and tertiary of the Dominican Order in Italy who defied papal prohibitions and refused to live in traditional monastic convents (Coburn and Smith 1999, 14). Mechthild of Magdeburg was a thirteenth-century mystic from Germany who was also a Beguine and tertiary of the Dominican Order who withstood condemnation by male clerics for her claim of Mary being a Goddess (Armstrong et al. 1990). Hildegard of Bingen was a twelfth-century German Benedictine foundress and abbess and Christian mystic who engaged in preaching, teaching, and writing and who proposed the feminization of the divine (Mazzonis 2011); she is also renowned for having refused male clerics' demands to remove the body of an excommunicated man from a Church-affiliated cemetery; she became a saint and a doctor of the Church in 2012. While the entitlement of doctor to Hildegard of Bingen has been met with widespread approval, some feminist critics (e.g., Case 2016, 4) view it somewhat sceptically given that the mystic is alleged to have promoted sex complementary, and they

are thus not surprised that Pope Benedict XVI whose antifeminist stance was unequivocal, canonized, and granted the status of doctor to a woman who appeared to share his view of complementarity. Yet, other scholars (e.g., Mazzonis 2011) contend that while Hildegard of Bingen may have adopted the notion of "weak woman" which is implied within the complementarity argument, she did so ingeniously in order to justify her preaching, teaching, and writing as a woman within the confines of the Church's twelfth-century patriarchal control. For more on her outspokenness, feminist stance, theological insights, and environmental contributions, see Fox (2012).

CHAPTER 5

1   While "Native spirituality" is commonly used in popular and religious discourses, and it was employed in the interviews with the women religious, in order to emphasize the importance of inclusivity and diversity, I employ "Indigenous peoples' spiritual traditions" or "Indigenous spiritualities" since they are more encompassing. Furthermore, while this section draws attention to positive aspects of women religious' spiritual development in light of "Native spirituality," it is essential to acknowledge how some sisters in past centuries contributed to the destruction of Indigenous peoples' spiritual traditions through residential schools and other Christian/Catholic evangelizing and colonization tactics.

2   Sister Jeanette used the term "Native" as she explained her mixed ethnic background of French, Native, and German origins.

3   A set of workshops offered at Sister Theresa's community's spirituality centre included "Native Sharing Circles," the "Seven Grandfather Teachings," and the use of traditional medicine plants.

4   Both influenced by Pierre Teilhard de Chardin, Thomas Berry (eco-theologian, cosmologist, geologian, author, Catholic priest) and Brian Swimme (professor, evolutionary cosmologist) are renowned and well-published proponents of ecology-centredness and universe-oriented understandings of humanity and the earth community.

5   The Golden Rule refers to an ethic of reciprocity ("Do unto others as you would have them do unto you") held by numerous religious traditions. Its relative universalism has been conveyed in the form of a poster that features the ethic as articulated by the following religions: Buddhism, Confucianism, Taoism, Sikhism, Christianity, Unitarianism, Native spirituality, Zoroastrianism, Jainism, Judaism, Islam, Baha'i Faith, Hinduism (see for example: http://www.scarboromissions.ca/golden-rule). The Green Rule refers to a similar ethic, but it draws on ecological wisdom and applies to a respect of the earth ("Do unto the Earth as you would have it do unto you"). The Green Rule poster includes statements from the same faith traditions as are featured on the Golden Rule poster and it also features one from Shintoism (see Vansittart 2006).

6   Despite their distinct observances, Christianity, Judaism, and Islam are all Abrahamic faiths and thus share the same patriarchal origins and structures (Shih 2010). Hence, feminist critiques against all three traditions share common concerns regarding gender inequality, and women across all three traditions experience tensions as they negotiate their feminist orientations with these religious traditions (Beaman 2001; Jouili and Amir-Moazami 2008; Kaufman 1991; Schwartz 1991).

7   In the Catholic tradition, the "Mass," including ones for weddings and funerals, must be celebrated inside official churches and chapels. According to rule 108 set out by the Vatican's Congregation for Divine Worship and the Discipline of the Sacrament (chapter V, n.d.), exceptions can be made only by diocesan bishops if "necessity requires otherwise," yet "the celebration must be in a decent place" as per *Code of Canon Law,* can. 932. Exceptions are granted, especially for special celebrations involving large gatherings of people, including those with the Pope.

8   The identity of the group and the details of the spiritual and educational activities are withheld to protect the sister and her religious community.

9   For more on the new cosmology, see Cannato (2006); Fox (1991); O'Murchu (2008; 1997); and Swimme and Berry (1992).

10   Sister Loretta referred very enthusiastically to key texts such as O'Murchu's (2008) *Ancestral Grace* and Cannato's (2006) *Radical Amazement.*

11   Not every sister was as enthusiastic or in "awe" of the new cosmology. Similar to the context of Sister Mabel's childhood memory, eighty-four-year-old Sister Carmen insisted that the "new" ways of enriching spirituality that are influenced by cosmology are not that different from longstanding relationships between spirituality and land previously understood particularly in rural areas. She contended that these new spiritual practices may only be new in the sense that they are connecting urban churches to ecosystems that are not as immediately felt in their built environments: "I can't get as excited about the environment and cosmology and all this as people who've lived in cities all their lives. I've had it! My brother [and I], my dad would drive us in the country. "Look at the cows. What are the cows? Who made the cows? Therefore God is good!" That's my teaching being brought up ... Oh nature ... you're sitting on the wharfs at night watching the sun go down and the moon come up."

12   The clerical field refers to clerics who are officials (priests) who preside over the Eucharist and Mass; in the Roman Catholic Church, only males are priests.

13   Dream therapy is presented here as an alternative to the Catholic tradition out of recognition for the criticisms that Sister Kelly has faced from a diocesan priest who condemned her work with dreams.

14   This list of "radicals" includes ordained and practising priests such as Hans Küng, a renowned Swiss Catholic priest, theologian, prolific author, and a theological advisor at the Second Vatican Council with a reputation as a voice for reform. He is openly critical of various dimensions of the Roman Catholic Church, especially papal infallibility. John S. Spong is a retired American bishop of the Episcopal Church and liberal progressive theologian whose views are considered controversial and heretical by some critics, particularly his outspoken advocacy of inclusivity toward members of the LGBTQ community and of the ordination of women priests and bishops. All other "radicals" listed here have been explained in other notes.

15   Such leanings toward complementary spiritualities among Canadian women religious are similar to the inclusive practices of American women religious (Kaylin 2000; Reed 2004, 299).

16   Sister Adele's spirituality and social justice centre has included not only the Scarboro Missions poster series on outstanding witnesses to the dignity of all creation (see https://www.scarboromissions.ca/product/witnesses-posters) but also the Buddhist-based poster series emphasizing empowerment and reflection toward earth justice (see Soka Gakkai International Buddhism in Action for Peace: http://www.sgi.org/in-focus/2010/seeds-of-hope.html).

17   Regarding baptism or confession, the sisters were not performing the sacraments secretively; rather, official permission was granted as exceptions to the institutional Church rules were made in order to fulfill the sacramental obligations within parish life where the presence of the priest was irregular or almost non-existent. While traditionalists may criticize the sisters' contributions to baptisms and not recognize them as valid because they were performed by women, others may, and arguably should, critique the bishops' and priests' selective permission to "allow" women religious to carry out sacraments because such approval was granted not out of interest for gender inclusivity but rather out of necessity and convenience in the absence of male priests. In this sense, sisters' greater involvement is only considered acceptable by the hierarchical Church as a "last resort."

18　Sister Agnes' parish is somewhat less constrained because it is owned and operated by a religious order, and it is thus less controlled by the diocesan bishop despite the latter's attempts to scrutinize the parish's activities.

CHAPTER 6

1　While women-secretaries and collection counters may predate Vatican II in some parishes, the inclusion of women in such roles at that time was not universal; the presence of women in the sanctuary either at or near the altar as active participants and on higher level administration committees are more recent phenomena.

2　For an experiential account of the sacred feminine, see Sue Monk Kidd's (1996) *The Dance of the Dissident Daughter*.

3　Historically, a convent, especially one that housed both the main residence and the central administration offices, including those of the mother superior, were referred to as a "motherhouse."

4　Teresa of Avila is a sixteenth-century Spanish mystic, theologian, author, reformer of religious orders, and innovator of prayers.

5　Joyce Rupp is a sister of the Servants of Mary (Servites) and a renowned author and speaker; her writings and retreats emphasize feminine spirituality including Sophia as Holy Wisdom. For more information, consult: http://www.joycerupp.com/.

6　Macrina Wiederkehr is a Benedictine sister, as well as a feminist-oriented author and retreat director on spirituality. For more information, consult: http://www.macrinawiederkehr .com/.

7　While O'Murchu is a male ordained priest, he was referenced by the sisters because of his inclusive and counter-institutional orientations, which have inspired many women and men religious. For more information, consult: http://www.diarmuid13.com/.

8　With permission, the exact source is not identified here so as to protect the identity of the sisters and the religious communities.

9　As shown in Gervais (2012), based on Schneiders'(2004) conceptual analysis, feminist Catholic, with feminist as the modifier, refers to practices that are grounded in Catholic ritual with some appended feminist elements; as such, male leaders could still curtail feminist efforts.

10　The male-only tradition has been called into question by scholars like Sister Christine Schenk (2017), who have brought to light the existence of women preachers in earlier centuries.

11　While not explicitly prohibited by Canon Law, liturgical dance is not an approved practice; the National Conference of Catholic Bishops commented on the matter and it was published by the then Congregation for the Sacraments and Divine Worship, *Notitiae*, 11 (1975) 202–5. The article was later republished with permission in the April/May 1982 newsletter of the Bishops Committee on the Liturgy of the National Conference of Catholic Bishops, which declared that dancing was not permitted during liturgical celebrations.

12　The intentional absence of priests may seem exclusionary and may thus appear to contradict the sisters' own current emphasis on inclusivity. Yet, their tactics should be understood within the context of the centuries of gendered exclusion that they have endured; thus their pre-emptive plans should be recognized for enabling the sisters to avoid the patriarchal controls that have historically constrained, and sometimes cancelled, their spiritual practices. Nevertheless, it should be noted that sisters' exclusion of priests tends to be selective rather than absolute; they do collaborate with them on various occasions.

13　This term is drawn from the "Feministing Christianity" presentation by Woligrosky et al. (2011) at the Women's Worlds Conference.

14　These forms of underground gatherings parallel the historical origins of Christian traditions; yet ironically, women have been and continue to be persecuted by their own Church for organizing or participating in such rituals beyond church walls (Armstrong et al. 1990; Stone 1976).

15 Sister Adele leads such a group but in the spirit of inclusivity, she insists that pro-feminist men be welcomed to partake in the gatherings.

16 Michael Morwood is a progressive Christian author, speaker, and facilitator. Some of his publications have been condemned by the Vatican's rule-enforcer: The Congregation for the Doctrine of the Faith.

17 See Schenk (2015) for a similar account of a girl's contention that God is female.

18 Inclusive images and names of God, all rooted in feminine imagery, comprise Sophia, Shekinah, and Shaddai (Winter 2002). Sophia is a Greek term that refers to the biblical depiction of Wisdom, which is consistently female (Johnson 2002a, 87) and often associated with the Holy Spirit; for a popular depiction of Sophia as "Wisdom" see The Shack (Young 2007) in which both God and the Holy Spirit are presented as feminine characters. Shekinah is a Hebrew word that means "dwelling"; Shekinah signifies a divine feminine presence – God's Spirit, otherwise referring to God as She-Who-Dwells-Within (Johnson 2002a, 85-86). El Shaddai has Hebrew roots and refers to God as the Almighty but with feminine imagery related to nourishment, fertility, and comfort (Biale 1982).

19 The name of the play is withheld to protect the sisters' identity and that of their congregation.

20 Charism refers to the unique spirit that inspires a religious community. It is part of the essence and heritage of the community that guides its mandate, rituals, regulations, missions, etc.

21 The name is withheld to protect the religious community's identity.

CHAPTER 7

1 An apostolic delegate is a representative of the pope.

2 Edwina Gateley is a world-renowned feminist theologian, counsellor, educator, and speaker.

3 While her book promoted feminist spirituality, it actually endorsed mutuality that encourages a balanced spirituality that recognizes the gifts of both masculinity and femininity. As part of her courageous efforts to disseminate knowledge on inclusivity and gender equality, Sister Kelly intentionally sent her book to the Vatican, but she has not yet "heard anything" back.

4 While I did not interview Sister Hilda, Sister Mabel made reference to this example. A pseudonym was assigned to protect her identity.

5 The Polish ethnocultural identity of the priest is considered significant as it relates to how Sister Theresa's experience was not unique within that particular diocese. Many Canadian dioceses recruited parish priests from Poland and found themselves with young inexperienced clergy who were educated in seminaries that were structured and oriented theologically and practically to pre–Vatican II tenets.

6 Here Sister Agnes alludes to Saint Augustine as a proponent of "anti-body" (see Gudorf 1994).

7 Joanna Manning is perceived as a controversial author and activist, given her confrontational style.

8 Reiki is a therapeutic technique of Japanese origin in which the therapist channels healing energy to the patient by way of hands-on touch. Reiki was banned by clerical Church officials because it is considered to be incompatible with the Christian faith. For more on the ban and the implications for women religious, see Enlightened Catholicism (2009) and Filteau (2009).

9 The exception is Sister Corinne, who does not feel as much support from her religious community because she does not consider it to be as progressive as she would like or as

advanced as the communities of other sisters with whom she engages in feminist and social justice initiatives.

10   While Sister Jeanette is more timid and thus less outspoken than Sister Mabel, she also defended Sister Kelly's book; in light of other sisters' concerns about the controversial attention that Sister Kelly's book brought to their religious community, Sister Jeanette thought that the book should be viewed more optimistically and productively as "a wake-up call" about what she viewed as the undeniable reality of gender inequality in the institutional Church.

11   Judith's experience is not unique, because the inclusion of former members has become a common practice across congregations in recent decades. However, depending on the reasons and circumstances surrounding their departure, not all former sisters (e.g., Mildred) remain in touch with their former congregations.

12   Like Judith, Carol left the Roman Catholic Church altogether due to experiences with discrimination related to her sexual orientation; thus, she is no longer involved in Church choirs – a contribution that she was praised and appreciated for as a talented singer and musician; while Carol's departure was disappointing for the parishioners who enjoyed her music, the exclusion was profoundly painful for her. Naomi still contributes to a Catholic parish because of its progressive and inclusive orientation.

CHAPTER 8

1   Since obedience was channelled through the formal authoritative structure, obedience evolved as governance arrangements were transformed (Wittberg 1994, 125, 241).

2   Renowned sister-scholar Sandra Schneiders also referred to the "military" model of obedience (2013, 459).

3   For more on the abuse of children in orphanages and workhouses (laundries) in Ireland, see the advocacy work of Christine Buckley and in Canada, see 16x9onglobal (2012). For more on residential schools in Canada, see Finkel (2006), and on Canada's Truth and Reconciliation Commission, consult www.trc.ca.

4   Compared to the progress made by women's religious communities in this area, the extent to which the institutional Church has transformed into a democratic organization has been the subject of endless debate and of feminist critique given the retrenchment of patriarchal power under Pope John Paul II and Pope Benedict XVI.

5   At this tumultuous time in the Church's history, many nuns left their religious orders in the aftermath of Vatican II (Ebaugh, 1993; Wittberg, 1994). This book does not explore that exodus among the former sisters I interviewed because many of them left much later in the twentieth and early twenty-first centuries and in most cases for reasons not related to Vatican II–based uncertainties.

6   An expression shared by Sister Kelly.

7   Clusters are neither new nor unique to the sisters featured in this book. Ebaugh (1993, 75) documented the cluster system developed by women's religious communities in the United States in the 1970s. This book's illustration is distinct insofar as it presents how Canadian sisters articulate the processes, challenges, and benefits related to the clusters that they developed.

8   One of the two communities that do not officially have life circles has a decentralized governance arrangement via round tables. The six orders that have life circles also have clusters. Thus, only one community represented in this study had not, at the time of the interviews, formally implemented circular groups.

9   Associates are lay people who commit to a religious orders' charism and who participate in many of the community's spiritual and charitable activities.

10   Sister Corinne's religious order is the outlier because, in her view, it has not established inclusive governance like the seven other communities. It is also less urgent for Sister Sarah's community because its international membership is comparatively young; thus its renewed governance practices will remain ongoing organically.

11   See Steindl-Rast's marketing endorsement on the jacket of Sister Joan Chittister's 2004 book *Called to Question.*

12   While it may seem that Sister Mabel is referring to the superiors of local residences, whereas Sister Ella is referring to the superior of the entire religious congregation, both examples are relevant and related because the Vatican has expected both levels of authority to be documented.

CHAPTER 9

1   Activism is widely understood as having confrontational dimensions (Mangion 2008, 112).

2   The Montreal Massacre was an antifeminist attack perpetrated by Marc Lépine on 6 December 1989 at L'École Polytechnique, in which fourteen young female students were killed and fourteen others were wounded.

3   Sister Corinne claims that her religious order is less progressive in its feminist orientations and practices.

4   Sister Mabel's use of the term "conservative" refers more to the sisters' cautious demeanours than to their political or ideological views; nevertheless, the latter is certainly applicable to some sisters' religious views.

5   The list of statements is included here verbatim and the page numbers are identified; however, with permission from the religious congregation, the title and full reference of the booklet has been intentionally omitted in order to protect the identities of the women religious involved, as well as their religious communities.

6   Sister Mabel's congregation participated in the same process, but copies of their document were not obtained despite her intention and willingness to do so.

7   As emphasized by Edwina Gateley in her world-renowned retreats including the one hosted by the Catholic Network for Women's Equality in June 2011 in New Brunswick (McCloskey 2011; see also http://www.edwinagateley.com/retreats-workshops/).

8   Given that historically Canadian sisters' societal contributions have been predominantly charitable, individual women religious have not always been paid for their labour in the health care, social work, and educational fields. Contrary to popular belief, as teachers in Ontario, many sisters did not receive full salaries, especially in high-school settings, until full funding came into effect for Catholic separate schools in 1984. Thus, many sister-teachers in Ontario as well as many sister-nurses and sister-social workers "employed" in their orders' own hospitals, services, and/or in parish schools did not receive a state-based income for many decades in the twentieth-century – a circumstance that renders their financial stewardship all the more remarkable.

9   While the sisters' letters focus on a wide range of issues and are addressed to politicians and institutional leaders on local, regional, provincial, national, and international levels, some of the congregations' letters focused particular attention on concerns related to the trafficking of women in the lead-up to the 2010 Olympics in Vancouver.

10   Avaaz is a global online activist network.

11   For a complex critique against feminist biblical scholarship, see Hornsby (2006).

12   It is understood that current or former sisters' general use of email or the Internet does not necessarily constitute fourth-wave feminist activities; however, their use of social media and other Internet-based communications that disseminate feminist critiques and contributions could be considered fourth-wave feminist methods.

13   For some current and former sisters, their disagreement was exemplified through their admiration for and solidarity with their counterparts in the United States, including, as Judith mentioned, Sister Agnes Mary Mansour, who were sympathetic to "choice" regarding abortion and who had signed in 1984 "the *New York Times* ad" (otherwise entitled "A Diversity of Opinions Regarding Abortion Exists among Committed Catholics").

14   While in this book I briefly highlight examples related to sisters' activism associated with abortion, I plan to explore their complex opinions on the topic in greater detail in future publications.

15   The allegations against Development and Peace were investigated by the Canadian Conference of Catholic Bishops (CCCB) and deemed unfounded. See: http://www.theinterim .com/issues/catholic-bishops-respond-to-lifesite-dp-report/.

CONCLUSION

1   While not explored in detail in this book, women religious' social and environmental justice endeavours are undoubtedly forward-thinking and leading edge (e.g., in the form of green buildings, street-based activism, and awareness workshops within which they are modelling inclusive processes among others).

2   Given that the memberships of some traditionalist conservative women's religious orders, especially in the United States, have been increasing or at least stabilizing rather than declining it may appear tempting for some congregations to return to past practices in order to recruit among younger populations to whom conventional values are of interest. However, none of the congregations represented herein, with perhaps the exception of Sister Corinne's community, albeit only partially, would be remotely interested in pursuing this path.

3   One notable exception to this actuality is Sister Sarah's internationally based congregation in which recruitment is ongoing, and thus the membership remains relatively stable worldwide. However, it is by no means a traditionalist conservative order.

4   When I was finalizing this manuscript, I was invited to attend the closing ritual of Sister Adele's social justice spirituality centre. While the ceremony signified the end of the sisters' official involvement, in both the written and spoken words shared, the ritual emphasized the intention of going forward and of being open to the future, and plans to that effect were already under way. Despite the two founding sisters' withdrawal from the coordination tasks, some group members had already been planning to assume the leadership of some of the organization's work. Thus, the women religious, who led the group for almost twenty-years, were pleased to soon assume their new roles as participants.

5   The same critique can be raised regarding the Vatican's position on women's reproductive rights, which represents a major public health issue facing millions of Catholic women around the globe (Holtmann 2015). Despite Pope Francis' sympathetic regard for women's reproductive health and his forgiving tone toward those who have had abortions that he expressed during the 2015–16 Year of Mercy, women religious were still being reprimanded by the Vatican in 2016 for their approach to the abortion issue (Araujo-Hawkins 2016).

6   Future research should explore the views and experiences of women religious as they negotiate the Church's entrenched patriarchal structures (Schneiders 2013), changing societal dynamics (Griffith 1997), and the reshaping of gendered identities and relations within the context of institutionalized religion (Nason-Clark and Townsend 2005) and grassroots spirituality over both the short and long term.

7   Many of the current and former women religious interviewed are still quite active in their retirement years. As I completed the book's final edits in the spring of 2018, Sister Kelly, who is now more than eighty-five years old, is still working as a spiritual director; Sister Agnes, who is now more than eighty years old, is still directing children's pageants in her parish and serving on committees for refugees and human trafficking; Sister Ella, who is also more

than eighty years old, is still operating a retreat centre full time; and Sister Shannon, who is almost one hundred years old, is still sending handwritten thank-you cards on behalf of her congregation to the donors of their foreign missions.

References

16x9onglobal. 2012. "16x9 – Slave Labour: Magdalene Laundries disgraced Irish Catholic Women." Toronto: Global News. https://www.youtube.com/watch?v=hD9uffgeg7w.

Acker, Joan. 1990. "Hierarchies, Jobs, Bodies: A Theory of Gendered Organizations." *Gender and Society* 2(1): 139–58.

Adichie, Chimamanda Ngozi. 2014. *We Should All Be Feminists.* New York: Anchors Books.

Ahmed, Sara. 2014. *Willful Subjects.* London: Duke University Press.

Akers, Louise. 2013. "Speaking from her own silencing experience." *The Seed Keepers.* Toronto: Catholic Network for Women's Equality 25(3): 3–4.

Allen, John L., and Pamela Schaeffer. 2001. "Reports of Abuse: AIDS Exacerbates Sexual Exploitation of Nuns." *National Catholic Reporter*, 16 March. http://natcath.org/NCR_Online/archives2/2001a/031601/031601a.htm.

Ammerman, Nancy. T. 2003. "Religious identities and religious institutions." In *Handbook of the Sociology of Religion,* edited by Michelle Dillon, 207–24. Cambridge, UK: Cambridge University Press.

Anthony, Geraldine. 1997a. *A Vision of Service: Celebrating the Federation of Sisters and Daughters of Charity.* Kansas City: Sheed & Ward.

———. 1997b. *Rebel, Reformer, Religious Extraordinaire: The Life of Sister Irene Farmer.* Calgary: University of Calgary Press.

Araujo-Hawkins, Dawn. 2016. "Sisters of Mercy also being asked to come to Rome for conversation." *Global Sisters Report*, 5 July. http://globalsistersreport.org/news/trends/sisters-mercy-also-being-asked-come-rome-conversation-40771.

Armstrong, Karen. 2004. "The Eve of Destruction" *The Guardian.* 15 January. http://www.theguardian.com/world/2004/jan/15/gender.religion.

Armstrong, Karen. 1981. *Through the Narrow Gate.* New York: St. Martin's Press.

Armstrong, M., M. Pettigrew, S. Johansson (producers), Read, D. (director). 1990. *The Burning Times.* Montreal: National Film Board of Canada.

Badran, Margot. 2008. "Engaging Islamic Feminism." In *Islamic Feminism: Current Perspectives*, edited by Anitta Kynsilehto, 25–36. Tampere, Finland: Tampere Peace Research Institute.

Barr Ebest, Sally. 2003. "Evolving Feminisms." In *Reconciling Catholicism and Feminism? Personal Reflections on Tradition and Change*, edited by Sally Barr Ebest and Ron Ebest, 263–79. Notre Dame, IN: University of Notre Dame Press.

Baum, Gregory. 2005. *Amazing Church: A Catholic Theologian Remembers a Half-Century of Change.* Ottawa: Novalis.

Beaman, Lori G. 2001. "Molly Mormons, Mormon Feminists and Moderates: Religious Diversity and the Latter Day Saints Church." *Sociology of Religion* 62(1): 65–86.

Beavis, Mary Ann, Elaine Guillemin, and Barbara Pell, eds. 2008. *Feminist Theology with a Canadian Accent: Canadian Perspectives on Contextual Feminist Theology.* Toronto: Novalis Publishing.

Berg, Bruce L. 2007. *Qualitative Research Methods for the Social Sciences.* Boston: Allyn and Bacon.

Bessey, Sarah. 2013. *Jesus Feminist: An Invitation to Revisit the Bible's View of Women: Exploring God's Radical Notion That Women Are People, Too.* New York: Howard Books.

Biale, David. 1982. "The God with Breasts: El Shaddai in the Bible." *History of Religions* 21(3): 240–56.

Bloch, Jon P. 1997. "Countercultural Spiritualists' Perceptions of the Goddess." *Sociology of Religion* 58(2): 181–90.

Bonavoglia, Angela. 2006. *Good Catholic Girls: How Women Are Leading the Fight to Change the Church.* New York: Regan Books. HarperCollins.

Bouclin, Marie. 2006. *Seeking Wholeness: Women Dealing with Abuse of Power in the Catholic Church.* Collegeville: Liturgical Press.

Bradley Hagerty, Barbara. 2012. "Sisters and Vatican II: A Generational Tug of War." *National Public Radio.* 10 October. http://www.npr.org/2012/10/10/162650803/sisters-and-vatican-ii-a-generational-tug-of-war.

Braz de Aviz, João. 2014. *Final Report on the Apostolic Visitation of Institutes of Women Religious in the United States of America.* Rome: Congregation for Institutes of Consecrated Life and Societies of Apostolic Life. Bulletin 0963. 16 December. https://lcwr.org/sites/default/files/media/files/final_report_of_apostolic_visitation.pdf.

Briggs, Kenneth A. 2006. *Double Crossed: Uncovering the Catholic Church's Betrayal of American Nuns.* New York: Doubleday.

Brown, Dan. 2003. *The Da Vinci Code.* New York: Anchor Books.

Brown, Sylvia. 2007. *Women, Gender and Radical Religion in Early Modern Europe.* Leiden, The Netherlands: Brill.

Bruce, Tricia C. 2011. *Faithful Revolution: How Voice of the Faithful Is Changing the Church.* New York: Oxford University Press.

Bruno-Jofré, Rosa. 2007. "The Process of Renewal of the Missionary Oblate Sisters, 1963–1989." In *Changing Habits: Women's Religious Orders in Canada,* edited by Elizabeth M. Smyth, 247–73. Ottawa: Novalis.

Canadian Religious Conference. 2017. "Who We Are." Accessed 25 October 2016. http://www.crc-canada.org/en.

Cannato, Judy. 2006. *Radical Amazement: Contemplative Lessons from Black Holes, Supernovas and Other Wonders of the Universe.* Notre Dame: Sorin Books.

Carter, Lewis F., ed. 1996. *The Issue of Authenticity in the Study of Religions* 6, Religion and The Social Order (Series edited by David G. Bromley). Greenwich, CT: JAI Press.

Case, Mary Anne. 2016. "The Role of the Popes in the Invention of Complementarity and the Vatican's Anathemization of Gender." *Religion and Gender* 6(2): 155–72. DOI: http://doi.org/10.18352/rg.10124.

Cavanagh, Catherine. 2010. *Women Priests: Answering the Call.* Brockville: Butternut Publishing.

Charlton, Joy. 2015. "Revisiting Gender and Religion." *Review of Religious Research* 57(3): 331–9.

Chittister, Joan. 2015. "A letter to Pope Francis." *Benetvision*. 19 September. http://www
.joanchittister.org/word-from-joan/9-19-2015/letter-pope-francis.

———. 2014. "The ending should have been the beginning." *Global Sisters Report*,
17 December. http://globalsistersreport.org/column/where-i-stand/ending-should
-have-been-beginning-16791.

———. 2013a. "'Tainted by radical feminism'? More like 'living the Gospel'." *National
Catholic Reporter*, 24 April. http://ncronline.org/node/50416/%C2%A0.

———. 2013b. "We are at a crossroads for women in the church." *National Catholic
Reporter*, 11 December. http://ncronline.org/blogs/where-i-stand/we-are-crossroads
-women-church.

———. 2004. *Called to Question: A Spiritual Memoir*. Oxford: Sheed & Ward.

———. 1998. *Heart of Flesh: A Feminist Spirituality for Women and Men*. Ottawa: Novalis.

———. 1995. *The Fire in These Ashes: A Spirituality for Contemporary Religious*. Kansas City,
MO: Sheed & Ward.

———. 1990. *Womanstrength: Modern Church, Modern Women*. Kansas City, MO: Sheed
& Ward.

———. 1986. *Winds of Change: Women Challenge Church*. Kansas City, MO: Sheed &
Ward.

———. 1983. *Women, Ministry and the Church*. Ramsey, NJ: Paulist Press.

Christ, Carol P., and Judith Plaskow, eds. 1979. *Womanspirit Rising: A Feminist Reader in
Religion*. San Francisco: Harper and Row.

Chowning, Margaret. 2006. *Rebellious Nuns: The Troubled History of a Mexican Convent,
1752–1863*. New York: Oxford University Press.

Clark, Monica. 2012. "Two groups, two paths for US women religious." *National
Catholic Reporter*, 26 May. https://www.ncronline.org/news/women-religious/
two-groups-two-paths-us-women-religious.

Coburn, Carol K., and Martha Smith. 1999. *Spirited Lives: How Nuns Shaped Catholic Culture and American Life, 1836–1920*. Chapel Hill: University of North Carolina Press.

Coco, Angela. 2013. *Catholics, Conflicts and Choices: An Exploration of Power Relations in
the Catholic Church*. Durham, UK: Acumen.

Code of Canon Law. 1983. Accessed 5 June 2017. http://www.vatican.va/archive/ENG1104/
_INDEX.HTM.

Cohen, Stanley. 1985. *Visions of Social Control*. Cambridge: Polity Press.

Collins, Patricia Hill. 2015. "Intersectionality's Definitional Dilemmas." *Annual
Review of Sociology* 41: 1–20. http://www.annualreviews.org/doi/pdf/10.1146/
annurev-soc-073014-112142.

Congregation for Divine Worship. 1994. Vatican Communication on Female Altar Servers.
15 March. https://www.ewtn.com/library/curia/cdwcomm.htm.

Congregation for Divine Worship and the Discipline of the Sacraments. 2004. Instruction – *Redemptionis Sacramentum. On certain matters to be observed or to be avoided
regarding the Most Holy Eucharist. Chapter V: Certain Other Matters Concerning the
Eucharist*. http://www.vatican.va/roman_curia/congregations/ccdds/documents/
rc_con_ccdds_doc_20040423_redemptionis-sacramentum_en.html.

Congregation for the Doctrine of the Faith. 2012. *Doctrinal Assessment of the Leadership Conference of Women Religious*. 18 April. http://www.vatican.va/roman_curia/congregations/
cfaith/documents/rc_con_cfaith_doc_20120418_assessment-lcwr_en.html.

Congregation for the Sacraments and Divine Worship. 1975. "Dance in the Liturgy." *Notitiae* 11: 202–5.

Connell, Raewyn. 2006. "Glass Ceiling or Gendered Institution?" *Public Administrative Review* 66(6): 837–49.

Cornwell, John. 2014. *The Dark Box: The Secret History of Confession*. New York: Basic Books.

Couture, Denise. 2008. "Feminist Theologies in Quebec: Interspirituality and the Feminine Divine." In *Feminist Theology with a Canadian Accent: Canadian Perspectives on Contextual Feminist Theology*, edited by Mary Ann Beavis, Elaine Guillemin, and Barbara Pell, 58–77. Toronto: Novalis Publishing.

Daly, Mary. 1991. "The Spiritual Dimension of Women's Liberation" In *A Reader in Feminist Knowledge*, edited by Sneja Gunew, 335–41. London: Routledge.

———. 1973. *Beyond God the Father: Toward a Philosophy of Women's Liberation*. Boston: Beacon Press.

———. 1968. *The Church and the Second Sex*. New York: Harper and Row.

D'Allaire, Micheline. 1997a. *Les communautés religieuses de Montréal: Tome I. Les communautés religieuses et l'assistance sociale à Montréal 1659–1900*. Montréal: Editions du Méridien.

———. 1997b. "L'obéissance religieuse: discours romain, attitudes canadiennes." *Études d'histoire religieuse* 63: 97–111.

———. 1983. *Vingt ans de crise chez les religieuses du Québec 1960–1980*. Montréal: Éditions Bergeron.

Danylewycz, Marta. 1987. *Taking the Veil: An Alternative to Marriage, Motherhood, and Spinsterhood in Québec, 1840–1920*. Toronto: McClelland and Stewart.

———. 1981. "Changing Relationships: Nuns and Feminists in Montréal, 1890–1925." *Histoire sociale/Social History* 14(28): 413–34.

Dillon, Michele. 1999. *Catholic Identity: Balancing Reason, Faith, and Power*. Cambridge, UK: Cambridge University Press.

Dillon, Michele, ed. 2003. *Handbook of the Sociology of Religion*. Cambridge, UK: Cambridge University Press.

Dionne, E.J., Jr. 2013. "The Best Choice for Pope? A Nun." *Washington Post*. 15 February. http://articles.washingtonpost.com/2013-02-15/opinions/37114895_1_american-nun-catholic-church-priests.

Dugan, Kate, and Jennifer Owens, eds. 2009. *From the Pews in the Back: Young Women and Catholicism*. Collegeville, MN: Liturgical Press.

Dumont, Micheline. 1995. *Les religieuses sont-elles féministes?* Québec: Bellarmin.

Eagan, Margery. 2014. "Joan Chittister: You can lose everything, but win in the end by simply going on." *Crux*. 17 November. http://www.cruxnow.com/faith/2014/11/17/joan-chittister-you-can-lose-everything-but-win-in-the-end-by-simply-going-on/.

Ebaugh, Helen R.F. 1993. *Women in the Vanishing Cloister: Organizational Decline in Catholic Religious Orders in the United States*. New Brunswick, NJ: Rutgers University Press.

———. 1977. *Out of the Cloister: A Study of Organizational Dilemmas*. Austin: University of Texas Press.

Echols, Alice. 1989. *Daring to Be Bad: Radical Feminism in America, 1967–1975*. Minneapolis: University of Minnesota Press.

Enlightened Catholicism. 2009. *The Reiki Ban and the LCWR Investigation Go Hand in Hand*. 16 April. http://enlightenedcatholicism-colkoch.blogspot.ca/2009/04/reiki-ban-and-lcwr-investigation-go.html.

Eze, Chika, Graham C. Lindegger, and Susan Rakoczy. 2015. "Catholic Religious Sisters' Identity Dilemmas as Committed and Subjugated Workers: A Narrative Approach." *Review of Religious Research* 57(3): 397–417.

Filipovic, Jill. 2008. "Offensive Feminism: The Conservative Gender Norms That Perpetuate Rape Culture and How Feminists Can Fight Back." In *Yes Means Yes!: Visions of Female Sexual Empowerment and a World Without Rape*, edited by Jaclyn Friedman and Jessica Valenti, 13–28. Berkeley, CA: Seal Press.

———. 2013. "Rape Is about Power, Not Sex." *Guardian*, 9 August. http://www.theguardian.com/commentisfree/2013/aug/29/rape-about-power-not-sex.

Filteau, Jerry. 2009. "Reiki: good health, spirituality – or only superstition?" *National Catholic Reporter*, 16 April. http://ncronline.org/news/spirituality/reiki-good-health-spirituality-or-only-superstition.

Finkel, Alvin. 2006. *Social Policy and Practice in Canada: A History.* Waterloo, ON: Wilfrid Laurier University Press.

Fischer, Kathleen. 1988. *Women at the Well: Feminist Perspectives on Spiritual Direction.* Mahwah, NJ: Paulist Press.

Fox, Diana J. 2009. "The Anthropological Collaborator: Feminist Scholarship and Activism in Africa." In *Power, Gender and Social Change in Africa*, edited by Muna Ndulo and Margaret Grieco, 112–41. Newcastle, UK: Cambridge Scholars Publishing.

Fox, Matthew. 2012. *Hildegard of Bingen – A Saint for Our Times: Unleashing Her Power in the 21st Century.* Vancouver: Namaste Publishing.

———. 1991. *Creation Spirituality: Liberating Gifts for the Peoples of the Earth.* New York: HarperCollins.

Fox, Thomas C. 2016. "Sr Madeleva Wolff forever changed the face of Catholic theology." *Global Sisters Report*, 7 January. http://globalsistersreport.org/news/trends/sr-madeleva-wolff-forever-changed-face-catholic-theology-36166.

———. 2015. "Pope Francis affirms US women religious." *Global Sisters Report*, 24 September. http://globalsistersreport.org/blog/gsr-today/pope-francis-affirms-us-women-religious-31666.

Friedman, Jaclyn, and Jessica Valenti. 2008. *Yes Means Yes!: Visions of Female Sexual Empowerment and a World Without Rape.* Berkeley: Seal Press.

Ganley, Elizabeth. 2007. "Strengthened for an Uncertain Future" *The Seed Keepers.* Toronto: Catholic Network for Women's Equality 19(1): 1–2.

Gebara, Ivone. 2002. *Out of the Depths: Women's Experience of Evil and Salvation.* Minneapolis: Augsburg Fortress.

———. 1999. *Longing for Running Water: Ecofeminism and Liberation.* Minneapolis: Augsburg Fortress.

Gervais, Christine. 2012. "Canadian Women Religious' Negotiation of Feminism and Catholicism." *Sociology of Religion* 73(4): 384–410.

———. 2015. "Alternative Altars: Beyond Patriarchy and Priesthood and Towards Inclusive Spirituality, Governance and Activism among Catholic Women Religious in Ontario." In *Canadian Woman Studies: An Introductory Reader*, 3rd ed., edited by B. Cranney and S. Molloy, 54–64. Toronto: Inanna Publications.

Gervais, Christine, and Amanda Watson. 2017. "Countering Renewed Patriarchal Commitments in the Institutional Catholic Church: Feminist Perspectives among Women Religious in Canada." In *Global Currents in Gender and Feminisms: Canadian and International Perspectives*, edited by Glenda Bonifacio, pp. 49–63. Bingley, UK: Emerald Press.

Gervais, Christine, and Claire Turenne Sjolander. 2015. "Interrogating and Constructing the 'Authentic' Roman Catholic Church: Feminist Perspectives among Canadian Women Religious." *Review of Religious Research* 57(3): 365–96.

Gervais, Christine, and Amanda Watson. 2014. "Discipline, Resistance, Solace and the Body: Catholic Women Religious' Convent Experiences from the Late 1930s to the Late 1960s." *Religions* 5(1): 277–303.

Gibson, David, and Rosie Scammell. 2016. "Pope Francis opens foot-washing rite to women in gesture of inclusion." *Religion News Service,* 21 January. http://www.womensordination.org/2016/01/26/rns-pope-francis-opens-foot-washing-rite-to-women-in-gesture-of-inclusion/.

Gillis, Stacy, Gillian Howie, and Rebecca Munford, eds. 2004. *Third Wave Feminism: A Critical Exploration,* London: Palgrave Macmillan.

Gray, Colleen. 2007. *The Congrégation de Notre-Dame, Superiors, and the Paradox of Power,* 1693–1796. Montreal & Kingston: McGill-Queen's University Press.

Greer, Germaine. 1970. *The Female Eunuch.* London: MacGibbon & Kee.

Gresko, Jacqueline. 2007. "Gender and Mission: The Sisters of Saint Ann in British Columbia." In *Changing Habits: Women's Religious Orders in Canada,* edited by Elizabeth M. Smyth, 274–95. Ottawa: Novalis.

Griffith, R. Marie. 1997. *God's Daughters: Evangelical Women and the Power of Submission.* Berkeley, CA: University of California Press.

Gudorf, Christine E. 1994. *Body, Sex, and Pleasure: Reconstructing Christian Sexual Ethics.* Cleveland, OH: Pilgrim.

Gutierrez, Luis T. 2016. "Fostering Gender Balance in Religion." *Mother Pelican: A Journal of Solidarity and Sustainability* 12(6). http://www.pelicanweb.org/solisustv12n06supp6.html.

Harding, Sandra. 1991. *Whose Science? Whose Knowledge?* Ithaca: Cornell University Press.

Helman, Ivy A. 2012. *Women and the Vatican.* Maryknoll: Orbis Books.

Hewitt, Nancy. 2010. *No Permanent Waves: Recasting Histories of US Feminism.* New Brunswick, NJ: Rutgers University Press.

Hirschman, Albert O. 1970. *Exit, Voice, and Loyalty: Responses to Decline in Firms, Organizations, and States.* Cambridge: Harvard University Press.

Hochschild, Arlie. 1989. *The Second Shift.* New York: Penguin.

Hoffman, Elizabeth. 1991. *The Liturgy Documents: A Parish Resource,* Vol I. Chicago: Liturgy Training Publications.

Holtmann, Catherine. 2015. "Women, Sex, and the Catholic Church: The Implications of Domestic Violence for Reproductive Choice." In *Religion and Sexuality: Diversity and the Limits of Tolerance,* edited by Pam Dickey Young, Heather Shipley, and Tracy J. Trothen, 141–64. Vancouver: University of British Columbia Press.

Holtmann, Cathy. 2011a. "The Vexed Question of Catholic Women, Abortion and Public Policy – Workshop Report." *The Seed Keepers.* Toronto: Catholic Network for Women's Equality 23(1): 14–15.

———. 2011b. "Workers in the Vineyard: Catholic Women and Social Action." In *Religion, Spirituality and Everyday Practice,* edited by Giuseppe Giordan and William H. Swatos, 141–52. New York: Springer.

———. 2010. "Exploring the Role and Influence of Catholic Feminism on the Liberal Arts Campus." Workshop presented at the *International Conference on the Liberal Arts.* St. Thomas University, Fredericton, NB.

———. 2008. "Resistance Is Beautiful: The Growth of the Catholic Network for Women's Equality in New Brunswick." In *Feminist Theology with a Canadian Accent,* edited by Mary Ann Beavis, Elaine Guillemin, and Barbara Pell, 200–19. Ottawa: Novalis.

hooks, bell. 2007. *Soul Sister: Women, Friendship, and Fulfillment.* Cambridge: South End Press.

———. 2000. *Feminism Is for Everybody: Passionate Politics.* Cambridge: South End Press.

Hornsby, Teresa J. 2006. "The Annoying Woman: Biblical Scholarship after Judith Butler." In *Bodily Citations: Religion and Judith Butler,* edited by Ellen T. Armour and Susan M. St. Ville, 71–89. New York: Columbia University Press.

Howard Ecklund, Elaine. 2003. "Catholic Women Negotiate Feminism: A Research Note." *Sociology of Religion* 64(4): 515–24.

Hunt, Mary. 2009a. "American Nuns Under the Vatican Microscope." *Religion Dispatches.* 17 August. http://www.religiondispatches.org/archive/religionandtheology/1766/american_nuns_under_the_vatican_microscope.

———. 2009b. "Women-Church: Feminist Concept, Religious Commitment, Women's Movement." *Journal of Feminist Studies in Religion* 25: 85–98.

Jackowski, Karol. 2004. *The Silence We Keep: A Nun's View of the Catholic Priest Scandal.* New York: Harmony Books.

Johnson, Elizabeth A. 2014. "Remarks for Leadership Award Dinner." Leadership Conference of Women Religious. 15 August. https://lcwr.org/sites/default/files/calendar/attachments/elizabeth_johnson_csj_response_-_8-15-14.pdf.

———. 2003. *Truly Our Sister: A Theology of Mary in the Communion of Saints.* New York: Continuum International Publishing Group.

———. 2002a. *She Who Is: The Mystery of God in Feminist Theological Discourse.* New York: Crossroad.

Johnson, Elizabeth A., ed. 2002b. *The Church Women Want: Catholic Women in Dialogue.* New York: Crossroad.

Johnson, Elizabeth A. 1993. *Women, Earth, and Creator Spirit.* Mahwah, NJ: Paulist Press.

Johnson, Penelope D. 1991. *Equal in Monastic Profession.* Chicago: University of Chicago Press.

Jouili, Jeanette S., and Schirin Amir-Moazami. 2008. "Knowledge, Empowerment and Religious Authority among Pious Muslim Women in France and Germany." In *Islamic Feminism: Current Perspectives,* edited by Anitta Kynsilehto, 57–90. Tampere, Finland: Tampere Peace Research Institute.

Kalven, Janet. 2003. "Feminism and Catholicism." In *Reconciling Catholicism and Feminism? Personal Reflections on Tradition and Change,* edited by Sally Barr Ebest and Ron Ebest, 32–46. Notre Dame: University of Notre Dame Press.

Kaufman, Debra R. 1991. *Rachel's Daughters: Newly Orthodox Jewish Women.* New Brunswick, NJ: Rutgers University Press.

Kaylin, Lucy. 2000. *For the Love of God: The Faith and Future of the American Nun.* New York: Perennial.

Kristof, Nicholas D. 2012. "We Are All Nuns." *New York Times.* 28 April. http://www.nytimes.com/2012/04/29/opinion/sunday/kristof-we-are-all-nuns.html?_r=0.

———. 2010. "A Church Mary Can Love." *New York Times.* 17 April. http://www.nytimes.com/2010/04/18/opinion/18kristof.html.

Lachapelle, Lucie. 1999. "Femmes et religieuses: Femmes de Dieu, et Ouvrières de Dieu." Montréal: Office National du Film du Canada. https://www.onf.ca/film/femmes_et_religieuses_ouvrieres_de_dieu.

Lahav, Rina. 2011. "Marguerite Porete and the Predicament of Her Preaching in Fourteenth-Century France." In *Gender, Catholicism and Spirituality,* edited by Laurence Lux-Sterritt and Carmen M. Mangion, 38–50. Basingstoke: Palgrave Macmillan.

Laurin, Nicole, Danielle Juteau, and Lorraine Duchesne. 1991. *À la recherche d'un monde oublié. Les communautés religieuses de femmes au Québec de 1900 à 1970.* Montréal: Les Éditions du Jour.

Leadership Conference of Women Religious [LCWR]. 2015a. "Congregation for the Doctrine of the Faith Concludes Mandate Regarding LCWR." 13 April. https://lcwr.org/media/news/congregation-doctrine-faith-concludes-mandate-regarding-lcwr.

———. 2015b. "Statement of the LCWR Officers on the CDF Doctrinal Assessment and Conclusion of the Mandate." https://lcwr.org/media/statement-lcwr -officers-cdf-doctrinal-assessment-and-conclusion-mandate.

Leddy, Mary Jo. 1990. *Reweaving Religious Life: Beyond the Liberal Model.* New London, CT: Twenty-Third Publications.

Lee, Becky R. 1996. "The Purification of Women after Childbirth: A Window onto Medieval Perceptions of Women." *Florilegium* 14: 43–55.

Lei, Christine. 2007. "The Educational Work of the Loretto Sisters in Ontario, 1847–1983." In *Changing Habits: Women's Religious Orders in Canada*, edited by Elizabeth M. Smyth, 172–90. Ottawa: Novalis.

Leming, Laura M. 2007. "Sociological Explorations: What Is Religious Agency?" *Sociological Quarterly* 48(1): 73–92.

Leonard, Ellen. 2012. "Vatican II … The Role of Women Religious." *Scarboro Missions Magazine.* January/February. http://www.scarboromissions.ca/Scarboro_missions_magazine/ Issues/2012/Jan_Feb/women.php.

———. 2008. "The Emergence of Canadian Contextual Feminist Ideologies." In *Feminist Theology with a Canadian Accent: Canadian Perspectives on Contextual Feminist Theology*, edited by Mary Ann Beavis, Elaine Guillemin, and Barbara Pell, 23–38. Toronto: Novalis Publishing.

———. 2007. "The Process of Transformation: Women Religious and the Study of Theology, 1955–1980." In *Changing Habits: Women's Religious Orders in Canada*, edited by Elizabeth M. Smyth, 230–46. Ottawa: Novalis.

Leonard, Richard. 1995. *Beloved Daughters: 100 Years of Papal Teaching on Women.* Ottawa: Novalis.

Létourneau, Diane. 1978. *Les servantes du bon Dieu.* Montréal: Productions Prisma.

Lorde, Audre. 1984. *Sister Outsider: Essays and Speeches.* Berkeley: Crossing Press.

Lux-Sterritt, Laurence. 2005. *Redefining Religious Life: French Ursulines and English Ladies in Seventeenth-Century Catholicism.* Aldershot: Ashgate.

Lux-Sterritt, Laurence and Carmen M. Mangion. 2011. *Gender, Catholicism and Spirituality.* Basingstoke: Palgrave Macmillan.

Lyons, Kathleen. 2005. *Repairers of the Breach: Masculine-Feminine Reconciliation and Future Church.* Pembroke: Labine Printers.

MacDonald, Heidi. 2017. "Smaller Numbers, Stronger Voices: Women Religious Reposition Themselves through the Canadian Religious Conference, 1960s–80s." In *Vatican II and Beyond: The Changing Mission and Identity of Canadian Women Religious*, edited by Rosa Bruno-Jofré, Heidi MacDonald, and Elizabeth Smyth, 17–54. Montreal & Kingston: McGill-Queen's University Press.

———. 2007. "Entering the Convent as Coming of Age in the 1930s." In *Changing Habits: Women's Religious Orders in Canada*, edited by Elizabeth M. Smyth, 86–102. Ottawa: Novalis.

———. 2003. Review of *Spirited Lives: How Nuns Shaped Catholic Culture and American Life, 1836–1920* by Carol K. Coburn and Martha Smith. H-Catholic, 23 August.

http://h-net.msu.edu/cgi-bin/logbrowse.pl?trx=vx&list=H-Catholic&month=0308& week=d&msg=dD18q/Tv7q7YflJhQ1fsWg&user=&pw=.

Mahmood, Sara. 2006. "Agency, Performativity, and the Feminist Subject." In *Bodily Citations: Religion and Judith Butler*, edited by Ellen T. Armour and Susan M. St. Ville, 177–221. New York: Columbia University Press.

Mander, Harsh. 2010. "'Words from the Heart': Researching People's Stories." *Journal of Human Rights Practice* 2(2): 252–70.

———. 2001. *Unheard Voices: Stories of Forgotten Lives*. New Delhi: Penguin Books.

Mangion, Carmen. 2008. *Contested Identities: Catholic Women Religious in Nineteenth-Century England and Wales*. Manchester: Manchester University Press.

Manning, Joanna. 2015. "Why a Magdalene Moment?" Magdalene Moments: Reflections by Joanna Manning. 5 January. http://www.magdalenemoments.com/why-a -magdalene-moment-2/.

———. 2006. *The Magdalene Moment*. Vancouver: Raincoast Books.

———. 1999. *Is the Pope Catholic? A Woman Confronts Her Church*. New York: Crossroad.

Magray, Mary. 1998. *The Transforming Power of the Nuns: Women, Religion, and Cultural Change in Ireland, 1750–1900*. New York: Oxford University Press.

Mathew, Philip. 2017. "Q & A with Kochurani Abraham, examining new forms of religious life in an hour of need." *Global Sisters Report*, 26 April. http://globalsistersreport.org/column/q/ equality/q-kochurani-abraham-examining-new-forms-religious-life-hour-need-45921.

Mazzonis, Querciolo. 2011. "The Impact of Renaissance Gender-Related Notions on the Female Experience of the Sacred: The Case of Angela Merici's Ursulines." In *Gender, Catholicism and Spirituality*, edited by Laurence Lux-Sterritt and Carmen M. Mangion, 51–67. Basingstoke: Palgrave Macmillan.

McCloskey, Eleanor. 2011. "Women – Mystics, Rebels and Prophets: Reflections on the CNWE National Conference." *The Seed Keepers*. Newsletter. Toronto: Catholic Network for Women's Equality 23(1): 8–9.

McGahan, Elizabeth. 2007. "Charity in the East: Sectarianism, Ethnicity and Gender in Saint John, New Brunswick Schools." In *Changing Habits: Women's Religious Orders in Canada*, edited by Elizabeth M. Smyth, 38–68. Ottawa: Novalis.

McElwee, Joshua. 2016a. "Vatican contacting about 15 orders of US sisters for 'serene' dialogue." *National Catholic Reporter*, 14 June. https://www.ncronline.org/news/vatican/ vatican-religious-congregation-contacting-15-orders-us-sisters-serene-dialogue.

———. 2016b. "Loretto sisters summoned to Rome, raising questions on closure of apostolic visitation." *Global Sisters Report*, 9 June. http://globalsistersreport.org/news/trends/ loretto-sisters-summoned-rome-raising-questions-closure-apostolic-visitation-40306.

———. 2016c. "Francis to create commission to study female deacons in Catholic church." *National Catholic Reporter*, 12 May. http://ncronline.org/news/vatican/ francis-create-commission-study-female-deacons-catholic-church.

———. 2013a. "Pope Francis' LCWR reaffirmation leads sisters to hard questions." *National Catholic Reporter*, 17 April. http://ncronline.org/news/sisters-stories/ pope-francis-lcwr-reaffirmation-leads-sisters-hard-questions.

———. 2013b. "Pope Francis reaffirms critique of LCWR, plan for reform." *National Catholic Reporter*, 15 April. http://ncronline.org/news/vatican/pope-francis-reaffirms -critique-lcwr-plan-reform.

McGuire, Meredith B. 2008. *Religion: The Social Context*. Long Grove, IL: Waveland Press.

McLaughlin, Mary M. 1989. "Creating and Recreating Communities of Women: The Case of Corpus Domini, Ferrara, 1406–1452." *Signs: Journal of Women in Culture and Society* 14(2): 293–320.

Milestone, Katie, and Anneke Meyer. 2011. *Gender and Popular Culture*. Cambridge, UK: Polity.

Molesky-Poz, Jean. 2003. "The Form Didn't Fit: Charting New Maps, Illuminating New Spaces." In *Reconciling Catholicism and Feminism? Personal Reflections on Tradition and Change*, edited by Sally Barr Ebest and Ron Ebest, 13–31. Notre Dame: University of Notre Dame Press.

Monk Kidd, Sue. 1996. *The Dance of the Dissident Daughter: A Woman's Journey from Christian Tradition to the Sacred Feminine*. San Francisco: Harper.

Morgan, Joëlle. 2017. "Our Legacy as Settler Christians: Facing the Colonial Wound. Towards a Praxis of Just Relations in Canadian Contact Zones." Catholic Network for Women's Equality National Conference. Ottawa: St. Paul University, 27 May.

Morrill, Bruce T., and Susan K. Roll. 2007. "The Duties and Ministries in the Mass." In *A Commentary on the General Instruction on the Roman Missal*, edited by Edward Foley, Nathan D. Mitchell, and Joanne M. Pierce, 199–223. Collegeville: Liturgical Press.

Munro, Ealasaid. 2013. "Feminism: A Fourth Wave?" *Political Insight* 14(2): 22–5. https://www.psa.ac.uk/insight-plus/feminism-fourth-wave.

Murdoch, Cassie. 2012. "Settle Down Sisters: American Nuns Busted for Being a Crazy Bunch of Radical Feminists." *Jezebel*, 19 April.

Nason-Clark, Nancy. 1997. *The Battered Wife: How Christians Confront Family Violence*. Louisville, KY: Westminster/John Knox Press.

Nason-Clark, Nancy, and Barbara Fisher-Townsend. 2005. "Gender." In *Handbook of Religion and Social Institutions*, edited by Helen R. Ebaugh, 207–23. New York: Springer.

New Revised Standard Version of the Bible. 1989. Division of Christian Education of the National Council of the Churches of Christ in the United States of America.

Neitz, Mary Jo. 2003. "Dis/location: Engaging Feminist Inquiry in the Sociology of Religion." In *Handbook of the Sociology of Religion*, edited by Michele Dillon, 276–93. New York: Cambridge University Press.

O'Murchu's Diarmud. 2008. *Ancestral Grace: Meeting God in Our Humanity*. Maryknoll, New York: Orbis Books.

———. 1997. *Quantum Theology: Spiritual Implications of the New Physics*. New York: Crossroad.

Parrish, Rebecca. 2015. *Radical Grace*. Chicago: Interchange Productions and Kindling Group.

Peddigrew, Brenda. 2008. *Original Fire: The Hidden Heart of Religious Women*. Indianapolis: BookSurge.

Pittaway, Eileen, Linda Bartolomei, and Richard Hugman. 2010. "'Stop Stealing Our Stories': The Ethics of Research with Vulnerable Groups." *Journal of Human Rights Practice* 2(2): 229–51.

Pope Francis. 2015. General Audience. The Family – 10. Male and Female (I), Vatican Online Archive, Wednesday, 15 April. https://w2.vatican.va/content/francesco/en/audiences/2015/documents/papa-francesco_20150415_udienza-generale.html.

———. 2016. Address of His Holiness Pope Francis to the International Union of Superiors General (UISG) at Paul VI Audience Hall Vatican. Thursday, 12 May. http://w2.vatican.va/content/francesco/en/speeches/2016/may/documents/papa-francesco_20160512_uisg.html.

Pope John Paul II. 1988. *Mulieris Dignitatem*. Apostolic Letter of the Supreme Pontiff John Paul II on the Dignity and Vocation of Women on the Occasion of the Marian Year.

15 August. http://w2.vatican.va/content/john-paul-ii/en/apost_letters/1988/documents/hf_jp-ii_apl_19880815_mulieris-dignitatem.html.

———. 1994. *Ordinatio Sacerdotalis*. Apostolic Letter of John Paul II to the Bishops of the Catholic Church on Reserving Priestly Ordination to Men Alone. 22 May. http://w2.vatican.va/content/john-paul-ii/en/apost_letters/1994/documents/hf_jp-ii_apl_19940522_ordinatio-sacerdotalis.html.

Pope Paul VI. 1965. *Perfectae Caritatis*. Decree on the Adaption and Renewal of Religious Life. 28 October. http://www.vatican.va/archive/hist_councils/ii_vatican_council/documents/vat-ii_decree_19651028_perfectae-caritatis_en.html.

Reed, Cheryl L. 2004. *Unveiled: The Hidden Lives of Nuns*. New York: Berkley Books.

Rink, Deborah. 2000. *Spirited Women: A History of Catholic Sisters in British Columbia*. Vancouver: Sisters' Association Archdiocese of Vancouver.

Rogers, Carole G. 1996. *Poverty, Chastity and Change: Lives of Contemporary American Nuns*. New York: Twayne Publishers.

Roll, Susan K. 2015a. "Mystery without Mystique: The Question of Sacred Language, Post Roman Missal 2011." In *Mediating Mysteries, Understanding Liturgies*, edited by Joris Geldhof, 67–82. Leuven: Peeters.

———. 2015b. "(Un)Completed Touch: The Presence and Touch of Women in The Roman Catholic Liturgy Today." In *Noli me tangere in Interdisciplinary Perspective. Textual, Iconographic and Contemporary Interpretations*, edited by Reimund Bieringer, Barbara Baert, and Karlijn Demasure, 457–74. Bibliotheca Ephemeridum Theologicarum Lovaniensium, Leuven: Peeters.

———. 2011. "The New Roman Missal – What Happened to Inclusivity?" *The Seed Keepers*. Newsletter. Toronto: Catholic Network for Women's Equality 23(1): 6–7.

———. 2003. "The Old Rite of the Churching of Women after Childbirth." In *Wholly Woman Holy Blood. A Feminist Critique of Purity and Impurity*, edited by Kristin De Troyer, Judith A. Herbert, Judith Ann Johnson, and Anne-Marie Korte, 117–41. Harrisburg, PA: Trinity Press International.

Romey, Linda. 2017. "On Generativity." *Global Sisters Report*, 30 May. http://globalsistersreport.org/column/spirituality-trends/generativity-46976.

Ruether, Rosemary Radford. 2003. "American Catholic Feminism: A History." In *Reconciling Catholicism and Feminism? Personal Reflections on Tradition and Change*, edited by Sally Barr Ebest and Ron Ebest, 3–12. Notre Dame: University of Notre Dame Press.

———. 1983. *Sexism and God-Talk. Toward a Feminist Theology*. Boston: Beacon Press.

Schaberg, Jane. 2002. *The Resurrection of Mary Magdalene*. New York: Continuum.

Schenk, Christine. 2017. *Crispina and Her Sisters: Women and Authority in Early Christianity*. Minneapolis, MN: Fortress Press.

———. 2015. "Olive's vision of God." *Global Sisters Report*, 3 September. http://globalsistersreport.org/column/simply-spirit/spirituality/olives-vision-god-30486.

———. 2014. "The apostolic visitation report was laudatory, but sisters remain caught in ambiguity." *National Catholic Report*, 18 December. http://ncronline.org/blogs/simply-spirit/apostolic-visitation-report-was-laudatory-sisters-remain-caught-ambiguity.

———. 2004. "Mary of Magdala: Witness, Leader, Friend & Apostle of the Apostles." Lakewood, OH: Future Church. Educational Resource.

Schneiders, Sandra M. 2014. "Engage the future: Reflections on the apostolic visitation report." *Global Sisters Report*, 18 December. http://globalsistersreport.org/column/trends/engage-future-reflections-apostolic-visitation-report-17046.

———. 2013. *Buying the Field: Catholic Religious Life in Mission to the World.* Mahwah, NJ: Paulist Press.

———. 2011. *Prophets in Their Own Country: Women Religious Bearing Witness to the Gospel in a Troubled Church.* Maryknoll: Orbis.

———. 2004. *Beyond Patching: Faith and Feminism in the Catholic Church.* Mahwah, NJ: Paulist Press.

Schüssler Fiorenza, Elisabeth. 1976. "Interpreting Patriarchal Traditions of the Bible." In *The Liberating Word*, edited by L. Russell, 39–61. Philadelphia: Westminster.

Schwartz, Sharon. 1999. "Women and Depression: A Durkheimian Perspective." *Social Science and Medicine* 32(2): 127–40.

Shih, Fang-Long. 2010. "Women, Religions and Feminisms." In *The New Blackwell Companion to the Sociology of Religion*, edited by Bryan S. Turner, 221–43. Oxford: Wiley-Blackwell.

Smith, Dorothy E. 1990. *The Conceptual Practices of Power: A Feminist Sociology of Knowledge.* Toronto: University of Toronto Press.

———. 1987. *The Everyday World as Problematic: A Feminist Sociology.* Boston: Northeastern University Press.

Smyth, Elizabeth M., ed. 2007. *Changing Habits: Women's Religious Orders in Canada.* Ottawa: Novalis.

Smyth, Elizabeth M. 2000. "Preserving Habits: Memory Within Communities of English Canadian Women Religious." In *Century Stronger – Women's History in Canada 1900–2000*, edited by Sharon A. Cook, Lorna McLean, and Kathryn O'Rourke, 22–26. Montreal & Kingston: McGill-Queen's University Press.

Stockman, Dan. 2017. "Apostolic visitation brought dialogue with Rome, new unity of women religious with laity." *Global Sisters Report*, 14 February. http://global sistersreport.org/news/trends/apostolic-visitation-brought-dialogue-rome-new-unity -women-religious-laity-44941?utm_source=GSR%20digest%202-15-17 &utm_campaign=GSR%20digest%202-7-17&utm_medium=email.

Stone, Merlin. 1976. *When God Was a Woman.* New York: Harcourt Brace & Company.

Sullivan, Rebecca. 2005. *Visual Habits: Nuns, Feminism, and American Postwar Popular Culture.* Toronto: University of Toronto Press.

Swidler, Leonard. 2007. *Jesus Was a Feminist: What the Gospels Reveal about His Revolutionary Perspective.* Lanham, MD: Sheed & Ward.

Swimme, Brian, and Thomas Berry. 1992. *The Universe Story.* New York: HarperCollins.

Trimble-Alliaume, Karen. 2006. "Disturbingly Catholic: Thinking the Inordinate Body." In *Bodily Citations: Religion and Judith Butler*, edited by Ellen T. Armour and Susan M. St. Ville, 93–119. New York: Columbia University Press.

Uebbing, David. 2013. "Pope Backs Reform of Leadership Conference of Women Religious. The Congregation for the Doctrine of the Faith issued a doctrinal assessment of the LCWR a year ago." *National Catholic Register*, 15 April. http://www.ncregister.com/ daily-news/pope-backs-reform-of-leadership-conference-of-women-religious.

Vansittart, Katherine. 2006. "The Green Rule Poster: A collection of texts from the world's great religions … all have a concern for the integrity of creation." *Scarboro Missions Magazine.* http://www.scarboromissions.ca/Scarboro_missions_magazine/Issues/2006/ April/green_rule.php.

Vatican Radio. 2016a. "Fr Lombardi on Pope's remarks about female deacons." 13 May. http://en.radiovaticana.va/news/2016/05/13/fr_lombardi_on_pope%E2%80%99s _remarks_about_female_deacons/1229620.

———. 2016b. "UISG president issues statement on meeting with Pope Francis." 13 May. http://en.radiovaticana.va/news/2016/05/13/uisg_president_issues_statement_on_meeting_with_pope_francis/1229597.

———. 2016c. "Vatican commission on female diaconate holds first meeting." 25 November. http://en.radiovaticana.va/news/2016/11/25/vatican_commission_on_female_diaconate_holds_first_meeting/1274887.

Weaver, Mary Jo. 1985. *New Catholic Women: A Contemporary Challenge to Traditional Religious Authority.* San Francisco: Harper & Row Publishers.

Wiesner, Merry E. 1993. *Women and Gender in Early Modern Europe.* Cambridge: Cambridge University Press.

Wills, Gary. 2012. "Bullying the Nuns." *New York Review of Books (NYR Daily)*, 24 April.

Winter, Miriam Therese. 2002. "Feminist Women's Spirituality: Breaking New Ground in the Church." In *The Church Women Want: Catholic Women in Dialogue,* edited by Elizabeth Johnson, 23–31. New York: Crossroad.

Winter, Miriam Therese, Adair Lummis, and Allison Stokes. 1994. *Defecting in Place: Women Taking Responsibility for Their Own Spiritual Lives.* New York: Crossroad.

Wise, Tim. 1999. "The Threat of a Good Example." *Social Justice* 26(2): 182–94.

Wittberg, Patricia. 2012a. "A Lost Generation?" *America Magazine: The National Catholic Review,* 20 February. http://americamagazine.org/issue/5129/article/lost-generation.

———. 2012b. *Building Strong Church Communities: A Sociological Overview.* New York: Paulist Press.

———. 2006. *From Piety to Professionalism – and Back? Transformations of Organized Religious Virtuosity.* New York: Lexington Books.

———. 1996. "'Real' Religious Communities: A Study of Authentication in New Roman Catholic Religious Orders." In *The Issue of Authenticity in the Study of Religions,* edited by Lewis F. Carter, 149–74. Greenwich, CT: JAI Press.

———. 1994. *The Rise and Decline of Catholic Religious Orders: A Social Movement Perspective.* Albany: State University of New York Press.

———. 1991. *Creating a Future for Religious Life: A Sociological Perspective.* New York: Paulist Press.

———. 1989a. "Nonordained Workers in the Catholic Church: Power and Mobility among American Nuns." *Journal for the Scientific Study of Religion* 28(2): 148–61.

———. 1989b. "The Dual Labor Market in the Catholic Church: Expanding a Speculative Inquiry." *Review of Religious Research* 30(3): 287–90.

———. 1988. "Outward Orientation in Declining Organizations." In *Claiming Our Truth: Reflections and Identity by United States Women Religious,* edited by Nadine Foley. Washington, DC: Leadership Conference of Women Religious.

Woligrosky, Bre, Caitlin Reilley Beck, Gabriella Richichi-Fried, and Joëlle Morgan. 2011. "Feministing Christianity." *Women's Worlds Conference.* Ottawa: University of Ottawa.

Young, William Paul. 2007. *The Shack.* Newbury Park, CA: Windblown Media.

Zagano, Phyllis. 2011. *Women & Catholicism: Gender, Communion, and Authority.* New York: Palgrave Macmillan.

Zeni, Jane. 2003. "Journey from/to Catholicism." In *Reconciling Catholicism and Feminism? Personal Reflections on Tradition and Change,* edited by Sally Barr Ebest and Ron Ebest, 190–201. Notre Dame: University of Notre Dame Press.

Zenit Staff. 2009. "Pontiff Says Contemplatives Give Breath to World." Zenit: The World Seen from Rome. 10 March. https://zenit.org/articles/pontiff-says-contemplatives-give-breath-to-world/.

Index